THE
TAROT
HANDBOOK

Practical Applications Of
Ancient Visual Symbols

ALSO BY ANGELES ARRIEN

The Four-Fold Way: Walking the Paths of the
Warrior, Teacher, Healer, and Visionary

Signs of Life: The Five Universal Shapes
and How to Use Them

THE
TAROT
HANDBOOK
Practical Applications Of
Ancient Visual Symbols

ANGELES ARRIEN

JEREMY P. TARCHER/PUTNAM
a member of Penguin Putnam Inc.
New York

Most Tarcher/Putnam books are available at special quantity discounts for bulk purchases for sales promotions, premiums, fund-raising, and educational needs. Special books or book excerpts also can be created to fit specific needs. For details, write or telephone Putnam Special Markets, 200 Madison Avenue, New York, NY 10016; (212) 951-8891.

Jeremy P. Tarcher/Putnam
a member of
Penguin Putnam Inc.
200 Madison Avenue
New York, NY 10016
http://www.putnam.com

First Jeremy P. Tarcher/Putnam Edition 1997
Originally published by Arcus Publishing Company, Sonoma, California
Copyright © 1987 by Angeles Arrien
Introduction copyright © 1997 by Angeles Arrien
All rights reserved. This book, or parts thereof, may not be
reproduced in any form without permission.
Published simultaneously in Canada

Library of Congress Cataloging-in-Publication Data

Arrien, Angeles, date.
The tarot handbook : practical applications of ancient visual
symbols / Angeles Arrien.—1st J. P. Tarcher/Putnam ed.
p.   cm.
Originally published: Sonoma, CA : Arcus Pub. Co., 1987.
Includes bibliographical references and index.
ISBN 0-87477-895-6 (alk. paper)
1. Tarot.   I. Title.
BF1879.T2A77   1997   97-22386 CIP
133.3'2424—dc21

Cover design by Isabella Fasciano
Book design, original artwork, and cover illustration © 1987 by Peggy MacKenzie
Photograph of the author by Twain Hart Hill

Printed in the United States of America

5   7   9   10   8   6

This book is printed on acid-free paper. ∞

For my sister

JOANNE ARRIEN

who over the years has given me constant
support and love during all my triumphs
and failures, and who continues to be my
greatest friend and teacher.

TABLE OF CONTENTS

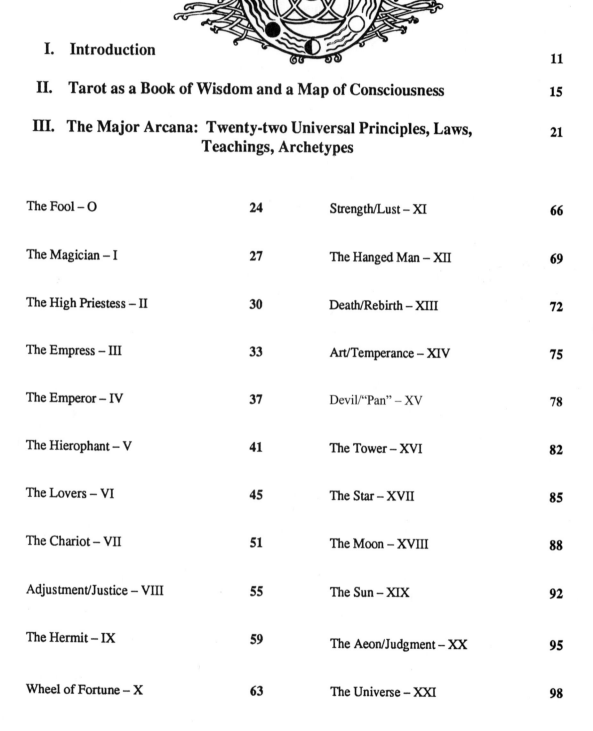

How to Use This Book:

1. The easiest way would be to refer to Section VII (Methodology) to find your Life-time symbols and current Growth Symbol and Cycle. Section III gives you an in-depth description of the Major Arcana symbols which function as your Life-time symbols. Section VI (The Constellations) gives you an over-view of all the cards associated with your life-time cards and growth card.

2. For use of spreads, use Section VIII. The Daily Spread is highly recommended for daily use and a way of beginning to learn about the cards. Sections VI and V give detailed information about the Royalty Cards and the Ace through Ten of each suit. Section III discusses in depth the trump cards or Major Arcana cards.

3. The Glossary on p. 278-281 will assist you in understanding the astrological signs and planets as they are represented on the cards.

SECTION I
INTRODUCTION

INTRODUCTION

Creative ideas, in my opinion, show their value in that, like keys, they help to "unlock" hitherto unintelligible connections of facts and thus enable man to penetrate deeper into the mystery of life.

> – M. L. von Franz
> Conclusion: Man and His Symbols, by C. G. Jung

It occurred to me twenty-five years ago when I read the above quote by M. L. von Franz that symbols may well be the creative ideas that function as a universal language in that area where an individual's internal and external worlds intersect and attempt to dialogue with one another. In any kind of inner work, whether it be in dreams, meditation, contemplation, guided imagery, or creative visualizations, symbols appear to us as signposts or keys and they function as containers, revealers, or concealers of meaning to enable us "to penetrate deeper into the mystery of life."

The Tarot is a symbolic map of consciousness and an ancient book of wisdom that reveals to us visually and symbolically the creative ideas and states of consciousness that appear in multiple existence in all cultures. The seventy-eight symbols are portraitures and archetypes of inner and outer experiences that are prevalent within human experience. In looking through the Tarot literature, I was dismayed to find that no comprehensive work addressed the mythological, psychological, or cross-cultural themes prevalent in the Tarot. Much of the literature was extremely esoteric or filled with personal and non-consistent interpretations of the symbols. At the time, I was deeply influenced by Carl Jung's book *Man and His Symbols,* and began to see the mythological and psychological themes represented in the Tarot, and later I deeply appreciated the work of Sallie Nichols in the 1980s when her book, *Jung and Tarot,* appeared. It was then that I began to see what an important self-help tool this could be for people to use personally, rather than to have it remain misunderstood and misused within only a fortune-telling context. It was Frances Vaughan's book *Awakening Intuition* that inspired me to look at Tarot as a tool that could acknowledge and awaken an individual's intuitive processes. From there I saw that Tarot could well be the Western equivalent to the Oriental Book of Changes, the *I-Ching.* Both Tarot and the *I-Ching* are reflective books of wisdom which address human experience and humankind's relationship to change and transformation. Both are used for guidance and validation of an individual's current experience; and both are oracular and synchronistic mirrors of inner and outer changes.

I wondered whether Jung was correct when he stated that "the psychological mechanism for transforming energy is the symbol." Between 1972 and 1987, I worked with Tarot personally and did over six thousand readings in order to see how symbols mirror one's processes. Over and over I saw the synchronicity of symbols accurately mirroring people's current issues. More importantly, I witnessed how the visual symbols themselves evoked memories, associations, inspiration, clarification, and validation for an individual's current issues, goals, and choices. I found that Jung was correct: symbols *are* the "psychological mechanism for transforming energy" and additionally, they function as audio-visual suggestology tools which set up a matrix for self-fulfilling prophecy, thereby enhancing an individual's trust in his or her own intuition and inner guidance.

I was most drawn, of all the decks available at the time, to the Thoth deck which was designed by Aleister Crowley and painted by Lady Frieda Harris. Visually, it captured my attention because of its artistic execution and cross-cultural symbolism. It was the only deck at the time which contained Egyptian, Grecian, Eastern, Medieval, and Christian symbols. Additionally, it was the only deck which incorporated numerology, astrology, alchemy, and the Cabala within it. It was cross-cultural in its symbolism as well as multi-disciplinary.

I read Crowley's book that went with this deck and decided that its esotericism in meaning hindered rather than enhanced the use of the visual portraitures that Lady Frieda Harris had executed. I instantly felt that a humanistic and universal explanation of these symbols was needed so that the value of Tarot could be used in modern times as a reflective mirror of internal guidance which could be externally applied. In reading about Lady Frieda Harris, the illustrator of this deck, I was inspired to write this book to honor her execution of these universal symbols. The following quote about her perception of the Tarot's value particularly touched me:

> *The Tarot could be described as God's Picture Book, or it could be likened to a celestial game of chess, the Trumps being the pieces to be moved according to the law of their own order over a checkered board of the four elements.*

> – Lady Frieda Harris
> Instructions for Aleister Crowley's Thoth Tarot Deck

Somehow I feel that the visual design of this deck holds to her perception of Tarot as being a tool for inner guidance or as being a validation, rather than a substitute, for one's own intuitive processes. I feel these visual symbols stand by themselves because of the artist's integrity and commitment to their being representative of something greater, "God's Picture Book." It is Crowley's interpretation of these symbols, regardless of his reputation, with which I have issue; and it was this issue which led me to interpret these symbols from a cross-cultural and universal view, honoring their visual execution.

Within this book, you will find a general history and use of Tarot, followed by the Major Arcana section, which explores in depth the major universal principles or archetypes that all humankind experiences at different times in life. The next section deals with the levels of mastery that we achieve in life and are symbolized by the Royalty cards. Following that, we have the Ace through Ten of each suit, the Minor Arcana, which function as mirrors of our challenges and inherent talents: mentally, emotionally, physically, and spiritually. The methodology, which follows, was developed by me twenty-five years ago and has been tested with over six thousand people to find out whether their life-time symbols based on birthdays and the growth cycles were relevant when applied to people's experience. The results, positive and more than statistically significant, further validated that symbols function as dynamic energy in tangible ways, that they convey meaning to the psyche, and that they point beyond themselves to the reality that they represent.

The works of Marie Louise von Franz, Joseph Campbell, Ralph Metzner, Mircea Eliade, Stan Grof, and Robert Bly sparked my curiosity to see if there were symbolic clusters or mythic constellations within the Tarot, which led to a three-week, ecstatic experience for me during which I uncovered the nine basic constellations in Tarot and was inspired to design the daily spread, the self-esteem spread, the relationship spread, the summary spread, and the permutation on the traditional Celtic cross spread. In those weeks, I experienced what Lady Frieda Harris described as "a celestial game of chess, the Trumps being the pieces to be moved according to the law of their own order over a checkered board . . ."

As you work with the Thoth deck, please use the symbols as keys or creative ideas that can "help to 'unlock' hitherto unintelligible connections of facts and thus enable [you] to penetrate deeper into the mystery of life."

Since 1987, *The Tarot Handbook* has gone through nine printings and has been distributed nationally and internationally. This book has been translated into German, Dutch, and Hebrew, and people of all ages and professions have been drawn to its ancient wisdom and study of symbols. *The Tarot Handbook* is considered a classic because it restores the Tarot as the tool for practicing self-reflection and gaining wisdom that it originally was. It includes practical how-to methods and tools, which many professionals have applied in the fields of business, psychology, literary and performing arts, science, and government. These professional uses of the Tarot are well documented in the first Tarot anthology, *The Wheel of Tarot: A New Revolution* (Carmel, CA: Merrill-West Publishing, 1992), edited by James Wanless and myself.

In the last ten years, many people have made outstanding contributions to the field of Tarot. I would especially like to acknowledge the creative and scholarly work of Mary Greer, and the innovative and practical applications of Tarot by Jim Wanless with his Voyager deck.

What is changing in the field of Tarot symbols is the realization that we need to look beyond our cultural viewpoint or bias when we approach the Tarot, and to rely instead on these more important universal principles, thereby deepening the quality and accuracy of our interpretations and expanding our awareness of the human psyche.

Angeles Arrien
Sausalito, CA
1997

SECTION II

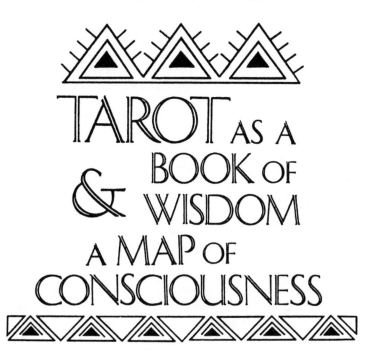

TAROT AS A BOOK OF WISDOM & A MAP OF CONSCIOUSNESS

The History of Tarot

The best descriptions of the origins and use of Tarot have been offered by Alfred Douglas. On the next two pages is a synthesis of some of his key points. (Douglas, 1972)

Historians have turned to the word, *Tarot*, to attempt to solve its origin. Some have suggested that *Tarot* comes from the ancient Egyptian word, *Ta-rosh*, meaning *the royal way*; others have asserted that it is an anagram of the Latin word, *rota*, meaning *a wheel* – the cards then symbolizing the circle of life from birth to death. Still others have felt the Hebrew word, *Torah*, which means *the law* may link the cards with the mystical system of the *Cabalah*, forgetting that the Cabalah originated in Spain, a country which has never known the Tarot major trumps.

Some have seen in it a corruption of the name *Thoth*, the ancient Egyptian god of magic or wisdom; an attempt to reaffirm the legend that the cards were created in the initiation temples of the mysterious East. It may, perhaps, be derived from the Hungarian Gypsy word, *tar*, meaning *a deck of cards*, which in turn derives from Sanskrit, *taru*. The word *gypsy*, itself, is old English abbreviation of *Egyptian*. Today the Crypt of the Church of Les Saintes Maries de la Mer in the Camargue area of Southern France is reserved exclusively for Gypsies; it contains the shrine of Saint Sara of Egypt, supposedly their patron saint. Saint Sara is suspect as a Catholic saint; she may be none other that *Sarapis*, the Egyptian God of the Dead. (In France, there is a tradition that the shrine of Sara rests upon an ancient altar dedicated to Mithras, the Persian Sun God.)

It is generally accepted by scholars that the earliest playing cards originated in China and Korea, where examples have been found dating back to at least the 11th century. The design of these cards appears to have been based on paper money, which evolved during the T'ang dynasty (A.D.618–908). A Chinese dictionary, Ching-tze-tung , claims that playing cards were invented in A.D.1120 for the amusement of the Emperor's concubines.

Some believe that the cards originated in India. The four-armed Hindu diety, *Ardhanarishvara*, an androgynous figure combining the right half of the god, *Shiva*, with the left half of his consort, *Parvati*, is sometimes depicted holding a cup, a sceptre, a sword and a ring. The monkey god, *Hanuman*, is also at times shown holding these same emblems, which bear a close resemblance to the four suit signs of the Tarot pack: Cups, Wands, Swords, and Coins (Disks).

Unfortunately, there is no evidence to reveal how old these symbols are or whether they ever appeared on Indian playing cards, which are generally circular and bear little resemblance to European cards.

From the time of the Islamic Empire, roughly A.D. 900–1100, Egypt had been singled out in many wizards' minds as the place where the most potent magical secrets had originated. The word *alchemy* itself derives from Arabic, meaning *the art of Khem*, or Egypt. Egyptian origin is the oldest theory, and was actively evolved by 18th century occultists who rediscovered the Tarot.

It is possible that the four Tarot suits refer to four castes of Hinduism: Cups being priests/Brahmin; Swords, warrior overlords or Kshatriyas; Coins, merchants or Vaisyas; Batons or Wands, serfs or Sudras.

Both Chinese and Indian notions are fine theories, but when one compares the decks, one finds very little symbolism in common, especially where the Major Arcana are concerned. Any similarity is limited to 56 cards of the Minor Arcana.

The general climate in Europe in the 14th century, when Tarot made its first appearance, was one in which Christianity reigned supreme, but paganism still lurked in obvious forms, resulting in terrible persecution of heretics. There was a rise of heretical Christian sects, which today are grouped under the collective title of *Gnosticism.*

The word *Gnostics* is derived from Greek and implies much the same as the Anglo-Saxon words *wizard* or *witch*, or *someone who knows, a wise man,* or *initiate.* Gnosticism mixed together Indian, Caldean, Persian and Egyptian magical doctrines and seasoned them with Greek philosophy and Hebrew Cabalistic beliefs. These unorthodox Christian sects were called Waldenses, Cathari, Albigenses, Bogornils, and the monastic order known as the Knights of Templar.

Alexandria became the center for Gnostic learning around 2nd century A.D. and Coptic Christianity absorbed many of the old Gnostic symbols dating from that period. It is from this welter of Gnostic cults that the occult arts of the West appear to derive: alchemy, astrology and the images of the Tarot cards themselves. Popular demand for cards far outweighed religious opposition to them, and by the mid-15th century, card-making workshops were thriving in many cities of Italy, France, Germany and Belgium.

In 1781 – eight years before the French Revolution – Antoine Court de Gebelin, a French occultist and archeologist, proposed the theory that the gypsy Tarot was the remains of an ancient Egyptian book of magical widom, still treasured by the Romany peoples since their exodus from their native land of Egypt. He published a nine-volume book: *The Primitive World Analyzed and Compared to the Modern World.* The effect of this work was to almost overnight cause the Tarot to became the tool of the Rosicrucian sages, and it was feted as the bible of all true occultists.

Eliphas Levi, a French Rosicrucian writer and cabalist, inspired an 18th century occult revival. He discovered an apparent link between 22 letters of the Hebrew alphabet and the cards of the Major Arcana and he was the first to give elements to suits.

There evolved a secret society, *The Golden Dawn,* founded by three erudite scholars, Wynn Westcott, S. L. Macgregor Mathers, and Dr. William K. Woodman. This was a blend of theosophy, Eliphas Levi's magical cabalism, and Egyptian Rosicrucian ceremonies typical of the 17th and 18th centuries. The purpose was basically for the achievement of mystical illumination and magical power. The chief symbol that the group used for its teaching was the cabalistic glyph known as the *Tree of Life,* based on the medieval philosophy of Spanish Judaism known as *Cabala.*

From *The Mind of a Mnemonist,* written by A. R. Luria, and translated from the Russian by Lynn Solotaroff (N.Y., Discus Books, 1969), there is a theory that Tarot may have been a mnemic device for monks; perhaps a visual filing system to remember all that they were to record on their manuscripts.

In an article in *ASTROLOGY* (Vol. 51, No. 2, Summer 1977), Ian Macfarlane Smith suggests that the origin of Tarot may be found in the constellations: i.e., The Fool (Orion); The Magician (the constellation Ophiuchus); and The Hanged Man (the constellation Hercules).

TheTarot as a Book of Wisdom and a Map of Consciousness

The Tarot is a visual map of consciousness and a symbolic system that offers insight into professional contribution, personal motives, and spiritual development of each individual. As a map of consciousness, the Tarot represents a facet of the total life experience incorporating the "practical-everyday world" with the spiritual growth and evolution of each person. Basically, the Tarot reflects the opportunity that each individual has to visually see that life is a process of "walking the mystical path with practical feet."

The Tarot operates primarily through the symbolic, nonrational aspects of consciousness, the same state from which dreams communicate. The quality and accuracy of the Tarot interpretation depends solely upon the *querent's* own ability, because it is only a reflection of the focus or level of consciousness of the inquirer. The Tarot is an excellent teacher, for as the user advances in expanded awareness, it reflects this expansion and responds uniquely to each individual, never teaching more than the person is capable of receiving.

No one knows the origin of the Tarot cards. Teachers of metaphysics often refer to the ancient Egyptians and the Hermetic School as the originators, but the earliest decks thus far discovered are either Egyptian or European.

The Tarot deck consists of the Minor Arcana, which has four suits, each with fourteen cards, an ace through ten, a knight, queen, prince, and princess of each suit; and the Major Arcana, with twenty-two cards, which bear the zero and Roman numbers I through XXI.

The Major Arcana reveals life principles, universal laws, or collective experiences that all humankind have. Just as the I-Ching is the *Eastern Book of Changes*, the Tarot is the *Western Book of Changes*. The I-Ching hexagrams represent changes in literary and nature metaphors; whereas, the Tarot is a visual representation of internal and external changes that are possible for an individual to experience.

Tarot is symbolic behavior or vision consciously performed. Those who participate sense that they are doing an act that has symbolic meaning, and they consciously seek to transform that act into an active, dynamic symbol which is represented in the Tarot symbol reflected back to them. The meaning thus attributed reflects a movement that has the power of making "a symbol-in-motion" carry or bridge an inner world into a visible and physical form. (Johnson, 1986)

Without thinking about it in psychological terms, ancient and primitive cultures have always understood instinctively that ritual and symbols had a true function in their psychic lives. (Johnson, 1986) They understood symbol and ritual as a set of formal acts and visuals that brought them into immediate contact with the gods. Symbol served many purposes: it allowed them to show respect and reverence to the great Powers; and it permitted them to touch the Power. The Power did not overwhelm them or possess them because the exchange was contained within the safe limits of symbol and ritual. Symbols allow us to reclaim the language that enables us to approach the soul, which is reflected to us in our dreams and contemplative states.

The Tarot deck psychologically reveals different visual portraitures of psychological states. For example: the suits as they are represented here mirror what is happening as far as mental beliefs, ideas and quality of thinking as revealed by of the Swords. Swords are pictures of our thoughts. Cups represent the emotional psychological factors, which would include our responses, reactions, and our feelings. All of the Cups indicate different qualities of love and emotional states that range from happiness and satisfaction to disappointment, anger, fear, and inertia are represented by the Cups. Wands represents quality of vision, insight, perception, energy, vitality and spontaneity. Disks – or Pentacles, as they are often referred to in other decks – represent the external reality or ability to manifest what we want in the outer world in the arenas of health, finances, work, creativity and relationships.

Just as psychological and spiritual information is revealed to us in our dreams or in contemplative states, the Tarot functions as an outer mirror of external experiences and internal psychological states as well. In using the Tarot and looking at it from a humanistic and psychological perspective, these symbols can teach us a lot about our own psycho-mythology. Much of the psychological world is concerned with psycho-pathology, or looking for that which needs to be fixed or healed within the nature. The DSM-III manual is a diagnostic tool that is used primarily to facilitate therapists in diagnosing people's psycho-pathology. There is not yet a psychological manual to describe states of wellness. Perhaps Tarot is a visual map of both states of well-being and pathology. Tarot has the opportunity to be used by therapists as well as by the individual to assess one's own psycho-mythology.

Psycho-mythology is the psyche which is comprised of two components, *Logos* and *Eros*. Logos is the inherent wisdom within the psyche; *Eros* is the inherent love nature in the psyche; and *mythos*, or mythology, is associated with the inherent life purpose or life myth. Tarot has the opportunity to reveal to us individually, collectively and therapeutically, the quality of our current *Logos* and *Eros*, and how we are using both in actualizing our own life purposes or mythos. Basically, Tarot is a psycho-mythological tool which can be used to reveal and acknowledge the inherent gifts and talents that are represented within the psyche as well as reveal, through the challenge symbols, personal psycho-pathology.

Psycho-pathology can be viewed as neurotic states, or those issues that we see as character flaws, or under-expressed parts in our nature, or what Jung called the "shadow-parts." Within the Tarot there are only thirteen symbols out of the seventy-eight that are seen as shadow-states, neurotic states or psycho-pathological states. So the inherent value of Tarot, if it were used within a therapeutic context, could be as a counterpart to the DSM-III Manual, which is a psycho-pathological diagnostic manual defining categories of dysfunctional behaviors, whereas the Tarot could be used as a psycho-mythological manual. It supports and serves as a diagnostic mechanism enabling persons to recognize their inherent wisdom, which is logos, their love nature, which is eros. Tarot reveals how both eros and logos are working within their life purpose, which is mythos, and how their basic nature is revealed to them in multiple positive symbols. Tarot portrays the basic health and well-being of an individual. It reminds us that the thirteen challenges or shadow aspects are countered by sixty-five states of love (Eros) and wisdom (Logos).

The use of Tarot as a pyschological and mythical portraiture of oneself is validated by the ancient saying of Novalis: *The seat of the soul is there, where the outer and the inner worlds meet.* When an individual selects a Tarot symbol, the card itself represents an outer mirror of an internal process, and in that moment, one could say that the seat of the soul or the human psyche is revealed in the connection between the outer portraiture of the Tarot and its synchronistic appearance reflecting back an internal process.

Tarot from a Psychological, Mythical, and Cross-Cultural Perspective

The use of Tarot as an outer mirror for internal and external processes aligns with the basic functions of mythology, or the essential services that mythology provides for human growth and development, and as a resource for self-revelation and self-reclamation processes. In his book *The Inner Reaches of Outer Space: Metaphor as Myth and as Religion,* Joseph Campbell cites that "The first and foremost essential service of a mythology is this one, of opening the mind and heart to the utter wonder of all being. And the second service then is cosmological: of representing the universe and the whole spectacle of nature, both as known to the mind and as as beheld by the eye,..." (Page 18).

So the symbols found on each Tarot card function as a way that the mind and heart can be opened to the utter wonder of what's going on with the individual, internally and externally at that moment in time. The Tarot also represents a symbolic matrix, wherein symbols function simultaneously to reveal and conceal a representation of the outer universe and our own internal nature. This is further demonstrated in the examples that for every outer major discipline that we have, there is an equivalent internal discipline that corresponds. For example, if one is drawn to the outer discipline of astronomy, the internal discipline that corresponds with astronomy is astrology. If an individual is drawn to physics, the internal esoteric discipline that corresponds with physics is alchemy. If an individual is drawn to the outer discipline of mathematics, its internal equivalent as a discipline is numerology, and if an individual externally is drawn to science, the internal discipline that corresponds is symbols. Perhaps it is the function of the qualitative disciplines to reflect and explore the principles of affirmation, negation and limitation. And perhaps it is the function of the quantitative disciplines to support the principles of unity, plurality and universality. Myths and symbols, by our recognition of what has meaning in them, show us our own states of unity, plurality and universality, and also function as agents of affirmation or negation and limitation dependent upon the meaning that we place upon them or the sense of recognition experienced at that moment in time. (Campbell, 1986)

The mythic figures in Tarot reflect universal principles and processes that each human being, regardless of cultural imprinting or family conditioning, will experience at different times in his or her life and in different arenas of life. That is why it is very important not only to include Tarot as a psychological and mythological mirror and tool, but also to look at Tarot from a cross-cultural point of view, allowing us to see particularly in the Thoth deck, how it is that a universal principle or process may have a different garment in the Orient from what it does in the West, and yet be the same principle at work in multiple existence. In looking through the Tarot literature, it became apparent that the many interpretations of the Tarot symbols were interpretations from the particular author's viewpoint or bias. What is important to remember is that symbols are a universal language that bridge invisible and visible worlds. Within symbolic structures, there are mythic figures that reveal inherent psychological processes of a universal nature. Carl Jung referred to these as the *archetypes of the collective unconscious.* This particular deck, the Thoth deck, reveals the universal principles that are experienced cross-culturally, not only from a Western point of view, but from an Oriental, Egyptian, Greek and Medieval point of view. In working with Tarot from a cross-cultural point of view, one is able to see how universal principles, symbols and myths are outer representations of a deep collective psycho-mythology that is working inherently throughout the human species.

SECTION III

THE MAJOR ARCANA

**TWENTY-TWO UNIVERSAL PRINCIPLES,
LAWS, TEACHINGS, AND ARCHETYPES**

INTRODUCTION

The Major Arcana or the twenty-two universal principles or laws, are represented by the symbols that are discussed thoroughly in this section. Major Arcana means major teachings or universal principles, laws that we will experience in different aspects of our life at different times of our life. Jung called these principles *major archetypes* or those universal experiences that are collectively experienced, regardless of cultural or family imprinting. This section deals with twenty-two ways that we grow, evolve and deepen.

Regardless of our cultural background or family conditioning, there will be times in our lives during which we experience the state of "no fear" (The Fool). Daily we are practicing the art of communication (The Magician), which includes our self-trust and insight (The High Priestess), as we extend love with wisdom (The Empress), and incorporate our own power and leadership for the purpose of empowering others (The Emperor). It is through our life's lessons and challenges, that which we learn and teach others, that reveals to us our sense of faith and deep spirituality (The Hierophant), and which allows us to explore the different kinds of relationships (The Lovers). In all aspects of tranformation, we are faced with the effects of what we cause (The Chariot), and are required to make creative changes that simplify, clarify and balance the human experience in fair and just ways (The Adjustment card). Through introspection and contemplation, and trusting our experience (The Hermit), we are able to turn our lives in more fortunate, positive directions (The Wheel of Fortune), which places us in arenas where we can express our strength and luster (Lust), and which allows us to break patterns that bind, limit and restrict us (The Hanged Man). Breaking old patterns (The Hanged Man), requires us to let go and move forward (The Death card), and experience the state of detachment. Following the process of letting go, we are required to integrate our experience (Art/Temperance); it is that integration, or the temperance process, that we are able to retain and regain our sense of humor (The Devil card) and look at our bedevilments from a place of sure-footedness and stability. Through sustaining our humor and sense of balance, we are able to renovate and restore our authenticity (The Tower), and to dismantle that which is artificial and false-to-fact. When we have awakened to our own inherent nature (The Tower), we radiate our self-esteem and confidence (The Star) as we make choices about leaving old known worlds and go through the gates to explore new worlds (The Moon). Making choices that honor our authenticity rather than our dutifullness (The Moon), we are able, then, to be natural generators, motivators and stimulators (The Sun) in teamwork, partnership, and collaborative endeavors. Through utilizing good judgement and looking at the history and the whole of our relationships and creative endeavors, we are able to transform the judge to the fair-witness (Aeon/Judgement). Once we have moved through self-critical patterns and are more objective about our professional contribution and personal relationships, we are able to build new worlds within and without (The Universe), and have a sense of our own individuality and wholeness.

It is important as you move through this section that you realize that you are being educated in the twenty-two universal experiences that every human being experiences within his or her life-time, in multiple areas of each life, and within each self.

Fear Not.
What is not real, never was and never will be.
What is real, always was and cannot be destroyed.

- Bhagavad Gita

THE FOOL

The Fool

THE PRINCIPLE OF COURAGE;
STATE OF NO FEAR;
ECSTACY AND PEAK EXPERIENCE

is the universal principle that is associated with the state of consciousness that we experience before birth and after death. In life's experience, this state of consciousness is often labeled or experienced as being mystical, transcendent, ecstatic, and transpersonal in its nature.

The portraiture of the Fool is represented by Dionysus, the Spring-time god who is wrapped with four coils of a large umbilical cord. With his Bacchus horns and grapes, Dionysus represents the creative power of giving birth to new forms from a state of wonder and anticipation, rather than from fear. The Oriental symbol of fear is the tiger. Fear attempts to gnaw at his leg yet Dionysus doesn't give any power to fear. He looks straight ahead; therefore, fear (the tiger) cannot make a dent.

The Fool's rich capacity to give birth to various forms is represented by his green tunic and the different swirls of the umbilical cord. The first swirl of the umbilical cord goes around the heart as a symbol of the Fool's nature to give birth to new feelings; the second swirl has four symbols resting upon it as ways of giving birth to new ways of health and well-being (the caducei, the winged serpents facing each other); birth to new ways of transforming (the butterfly); birth to new ways of setting limits to vulture-like people and situations (the vulture); and birth to new ways of being compassionate with one's vulnerabilities and sensitivities (the dove). The third swirl of the umbilical cord reveals two people intertwined in an embrace which represents our capacity to give birth to new forms of relationship; and the last coil of the umbilical reveals the Eygptian Crocodile God, Souchos. At one period in Egypt, crocodiles were thought of as oracles and were embalmed when dead (*Leach* and *Fried*). The crocodile represents the power to give birth to creative vision in our work and creativity.

The Fool is the alchemist who holds fire in one hand and the upside-down cup in the other hand. He unifies feelings (water) with energy and vision (fire) to create original and innovative ideas (steam, the white drops in the background). The Fool uses his multiple talents (the astrological signs on the coins) to generate abundance (the bag full of coins) and fruitfulness (the grapes). With his sun-belt, he commits himself to bringing creativity into solid usable matter. The Fool represents the ecstatic adventure of growing and unfolding in our own journey of the hero and the heroine (the flowers between his legs in their different stages of growth and unfoldment).

For those individuals whose birthday adds up to the number 22, the Fool represents their life-time personality symbol. The number 22 is the twenty-second symbol of the Major Arcana and is also the number zero (2 − 2 = 0). Persons born with this number are seen by others as being highly creative and in need of variety. *Fool* people are not foolish or fool-hardy. They are courageous and risk-taking. They come across fearless even though they might feel fear gnawing within them. They are drawn toward and tend to explore the mystical, transcendent, and transpersonal realms of consciousness. They inspire the sense of adventure and courage within others. Their sense of wonder and anticipation is contagious.

The Fool as Life-Time Symbol

The Fool is an excellent symbol to use as a visual affirmation to enhance courage, risk-taking, and the creative expression that is needed to give birth to new parts of one's life. The Fool represents the energetic essence of who we are, the essence of ourselves which is always whole, healthy, and without fear. This symbol reveals the spirit of who we are, that spirit so often expressed and experienced in those states of wonder, awe, curiosity, and anticipation. This is an excellent card to meditate upon if one is experiencing a lot of fear.

The Fool as a Visual Affirmation and Meditative Symbol

I am a radiant being.

I am a living treasure.

I deeply honor and value the unlimited resource of courage that is within me

I respect the nature of who I am.

There is noting to fear.

Sample Affirmations To Use while Looking at The Fool

Whenever you are drawn to the Fool or might pull it from the deck, it represents your ability to give birth to new forms from a place of courage, wonder, and anticipation. The Fool indicates that you are operating from the essence of who

The Fool as an Outer Mirror

you are. Somewhere in your life you are experiencing the courage to be who you are without fear. This is also a creative time to implement the creative transcendent energy that is moving through you now.

Other Symbols which Are Aspects of The Fool

The Fool is the external expression of the Emperor *(See the Emperor constellation in Section VI)* and his combined leadership tools: the Four of Swords (truce), the Four of Cups (emotional luxury), the Four of Wands (completion), and the Four of Disks (power). The transpersonal aspects of who we are (The Fool) can be expressed outwardly in the world through our leadership skills (The Emperor) by expressing ourselves powerfully (Four of Disks) with emotional fullness and luxury (Four of Cups) in a complete (Four of Wands) and truce-making manner (Four of Swords). Operating from the fullness of all these symbols, we are able to let go and move forward (Death, Rebirth).

The Gifts and Challenges for Persons whose Life-Time Personality Symbol is The Fool

Gifts:	Challenges:
(The Fool) Transpersonal expression of courage through:	To Trust To Release Fear
The Four of Swords (Truce) The Four of Cups (Luxury) The Four of Wands (Completion) The Four of Disks (Power) The Emperor (Leadership) Death/Rebirth (Detachment/Creation)	

Note: Special Reminder about Fool and Magician:

The Fool is the state of ecstasy and wonder experienced by all humankind. It is an inherent resource we all have that is waiting to be remembered and utilized. Therefore, the number 0, The Fool, does not come up as a Growth symbol. The Fool and The Magician are both incorporated resources for every human being to access and use everyday. The Fool and The Magician are never Growth symbols. They are resources we draw upon daily. (See Section VII: Growth Symbols).

*Language shapes consciousness,
and the use of language to shape consciousness
is an important branch of magic.*

- Starhawk, *Dreaming the Dark*

THE MAGICIAN

represents the universal principle of communication. The golden figure of Mercury, the winged messenger from Greek mythology, represents communication that is inspired, resilient, and well-timed. This symbol represents an individual's capacity to communicate equally well in both oral and written communication (the floating book).

The Magician is surrounded by ten tools, each of which is the Magician's way of picking the appropriate tool or tools for communication that would best serve a particular context: 1) the coin represents the ability to communicate in ways that can assist finances and practical endeavors; 2) the floating kerub, the lighted lantern, represents communication which like Adaddin's lamp inspires or evokes the Genii or "genius" within one's communication and nature; 3) the ibis or phoenix wand in the Magician's hand is a symbol of being able to communicate from a philosophical, religious, or spiritual base; 4) the arrow moving toward the winged eye of Horus represents direct and honest communication which is well-timed; 5) the winged eye of Horus with the dove within it is a symbol of inspired vision which is articulated; 6) the floating scroll or book is the power of communication that is written; 7) the winged egg reminds us that all communication is prompted from our essence (the wings) and is constantly being reformed and delivered (the egg); 8) the cup with the coiled serpent represents the transformative power (serpent) to communicate the range of one's feelings (the cup); 9) the sword symbolizes the ability to articulate ideas and thoughts clearly and succinctly; and 10) the golden monkey represents the Egyptian God of Wisdom, Thoth, who transforms himself into a golden monkey to demonstrate that in commu-

**PRINCIPLE OF
COMMUNICATION
AND TIMING**

nication we must be flexible and aware of all communication lines that we have executed personally and professionally (the communication lines in the background).

The double serpents rising from Mercury's head are another rendition of Mercury's staff of communication which depicts the power of communication that is balanced, healing, and transformative.

The Magician as Life-Time Symbol

For those individuals whose birthday adds up to the number one, the Magician represents their life-time spiritual symbol. This symbol represents gifts and talents which are magical, particularly in the arena of communication. These persons are generally skilled in any arena where communication is required and would function easily in teaching, counseling, consulting work, media, design, film, photography, T.V., public relations, diplomacy, negotiation, management, music, and writing.

The Magician as a universal archetype is a representation of the gift of communication that is within the nature of us all. Persons with the Magician as their life-time symbol have the inherent ability through verbal, non-verbal, or written skills to inspire and motivate people through artful timing and clarity of communication. In Buddhist terms, the quality of combining right speech with right action is an art known as "skillful means."

The Magician as a Visual Affirmation and Meditation Symbol

The Magician is an excellent symbol to use as a visual affirmation to improve and support communication skills. By looking at this symbol or visually bringing it into one's memory, the archetype of Mercury, the winged messenger of communication, will enhance clarity of thought and feeling. The Magician organizes communication patterns by picking the appropriate tools or content and combines it with well-timed delivery. Blunt communication is communication which lacks correct timing. Confused communication is communication which lacks appropriate content, yet may be well-timed in delivery but poorly organized. The wizard-like quality of the Magician is to artfully combine good timing with clear content and appropriate context.

Sample Affirmations To Use While Looking At The Magician

I communicate effectively

I create magic when I use my inherent gifts and talents

I deeply honor and value the unlimited resources of skilled communication that are within my nature

The Magician as Outer Mirror

When you pull this symbol or find yourself continually drawn toward it, it represents that your communication skills are high during this period of time. The Mercury within you, the winged messenger, is expressing itself with skilled timing, clarity and inspiration. This is a good time to deliver important communication with impeccable timing. The Magician supports and enhances communication which will transform difficult situations that you may be experiencing personally or professionally.

The four aces are the Magician's tools. They represent the power of communication working on different levels of consciousness: the Ace of Swords represents the power of the Magician expressing itself in the mind through *clear thinking*; the Ace of Cups is the Magician working within the *emotional* nature in order to communicate feelings clearly; the Ace of Wands is the Magician working within our *spiritual* nature so that we might communicate our authenticity and truth; and the Ace of Disks represents the *alignment of inner and outer* communication which contains no double message.

The four tens in the deck are aspects of the Magician (10 adds up to 1, the Magician's number). Two states of consciousness can block our creativity and communication: Ten of Wands (oppression or holding back) and the Ten of Swords (fear of ruin). Following what has heart and resonance for us (Ten of Cups) and communicating in healing and inspirational ways can generate abundance (Ten of Disks). The Magician reminds us to creatively transform the Ten of Wands and the Ten of Swords so that we can express the Ten of Cups and the Ten of Disks. The Wheel of Fortune (X, or 10) is the Magician's creative power that transforms any blocks or obstacles to creative expression and clear communication.

The Sun (XIX, or number 19, which adds up ultimately to the number 1) represents the dance of creativity and communication that is being powerfully expressed in the outer world. The Sun represents the archetypal power of the Magician being externally expressed in teamwork, partnership, and collaborative efforts. *(See Magician constellation in Section VI.)*

Other Symbols which Are Aspects of The Magician

Gifts:	Challenges:
The Magician	Ten of Wands (Oppression; Holding Back)
The Wheel of Fortune	Ten of Swords (Fear of Failure)
The Sun	
The Ace of Swords	
The Ace of Cups	
The Ace of Wands	
The Ace of Disks	
The Ten of Cups	
The Ten of Disks	

The Gifts and Challenges for People Whose Life-Time Personality Symbol is The Magician

Note: Special Reminder about The Magician:

The gift of communication is an universal resource used daily; therefore, this symbol is never a specific Growth symbol. The Fool and The Magician are the only two Major Arcana symbols that are not used as specific Growth symbols. (See rules in Sec. VII.)

For self is a sea boundless and measureless.

- K. Gibran, *The Prophet*

THE HIGH PRIESTESS

THE PRINCIPLE OF INTUITION, SELF-TRUST AND SELF-RESOURCEFULNESS

or High Priest represents the universal principle of intuition, independence, self-trust, and self-resourcefulness. This is an androgynous figure who archetypally represents balance. From the navel up, the figure is all curved lines, soft, magnetic, *ying*, and receptive. From the navel down, this figure is all straight lines, strong, dynamic, *yang*, and assertive. This archetype serves as a reminder that we are not to sacrifice our strength for our softness or our softness for our strength. The High Priestess with her sun/moon crown represents each person's commitment to have equal balance in strength and softness.

The crystals represent the multifaceted aspects of intuition that are present at each level of consciousness: mental intuition (the triangular crystal); emotional intuition (the round crystal); spiritual insight (the diamond crystal). and physically registered information (the octagonal crystal). Intuition is like "the great still lake" – reflective, contained, deep, and always present, waiting to be accessed and trusted.

The High Priestess is represented in different cultures in some of the following ways: in Egyptian mythology, she is Isis, the Goddess of Intuition; in Oriental mythology, she is Kuan Yin, the Goddess of Compassion; and in Greek mythology with her bow and arrow, she is Artemis, the Nature Goddess getting in touch with her own nature. Mythically, this archetype also represents *the journey homeward* or the *return to oneself*. The camel within the oasis symbolizes the return to the inner oasis or garden within. The camel also represents self-resourcefulness in its capacity to go long barren distances, yet always find the oasis.

For those individuals whose birthday adds up to the number 2, the High Priestess represents their life-time spiritual symbol. These persons strongly value independence and self-resourcefulness. They have a deep regard for balance and harmony and are unusual people to know in that they are equally as dynamic as they are receptive. They are very tenacious and are able, like the camel, to go long, barren distances but invariably, they find the oasis. They are very perceptive and can quickly assess what is working and what is not working. High Priestess people can immediately tell one what is out of balance and can supply the creative solutions to bring situations, projects, or people back into balance. Anyone with the High Priestess as a life-time symbol would be an excellent negotiator, consultant, or diagnostician. Such persons would be highly gifted in arenas in which their visions, perceptions, and insights would apply.

**The Priestess
As Life-Time
Symbol**

Whenever one has the High Priestess as a growth symbol, there is the beginning of a long, nine-to-ten-year cycle that emphasizes the process of creative self-sufficiency and individuation. During a High Priestess year, one evaluates who one is and who one is not. It is a year in which there is need for balance and harmony, requiring trust in one's own independence, self-resourcefulness, and perceptions. Often during a High Priestess year, an individual will experience the emergence of a new identity. This year marks a period of independence during which one has little tolerance for being limited, restricted, or restrained. One may find that there is a need to be on one's own or it may be that circumstances force one to be on one's own. It is a year during which one could be drawn to water areas and have a deep need to remove oneself from disharmonious situations.

**The High Priestess
As a
Growth Symbol**

The High Priestess is an excellent symbol to use as a visual affirmation to enhance self-trust, independence, and resourcefulness. This symbol, more than any other, reinforces the trusting of one's intuition.

**The High Priestess
As a Visual
Affirmation and
Meditative
Symbol**

I deeply value and honor the human being that I am.

I am a very perceptive and intuitive human being.

I trust myself and value my sense of integrity.

**Sample Affirmations
To Use while
Looking at
The High Priestess**

When one pulls this symbol or finds oneself continually drawn toward it, it represents that one is in a state of harmony and independence. The High Priestess within one is working easily and effortlessly. There is a sense of self-containment and self-trust. One's perceptions are insightful and one trusts what it is that one sees internally and externally. There is a strong feeling of spiritual depth and resourcefulness.

**The High Priestess
As an
Outer Mirror**

Other Symbols that Are Aspects of The High Priestess

The four twos in the deck are the High Priestess tools: the Two of Swords (peace of mind); the Two of Cups (love); the Two of Wands (dominion and balance); and the Two of Disks (expansive yet stable change). Intuition and its various ways of expressing itself are also pictured by the four twos: inspired things (Two of Swords); picking up on other persons' feelings and moods or kinds of love expressed (Two of Cups); trusting the core of oneself (Two of Wands); and sensing information through the body (Two of Disks).

Lust/Strength (the number 11, which adds up to 2) is an example of the High Priestess being expressed externally. When we are in our strength or full *lustre*, we come across as the High Priestess: strong, balanced, and lustrous. Lust/Strength is the capacity to trust oneself fully. It is the High Priestess within that provokes our demonstration of strength and radiance in the outer world.

The Aeon/Judgment symbol is another external representation of the High Priestess. The Aeon (the number 20 adds up to 2) represents our capacity in daily life to utilize good judgment by looking at things in holistic ways rather than in getting caught or fixated in details or parts of the whole. The High Priestess within us provokes us externally to look at the historical history of our experience (the Aeon) in our families and in our career. The Aeon is the High Priestess's reminder that we can transform the *critic* within us to the *fair witness* if we are willing to trust the deepest core of who we are. NOTE: *See High Priestess constellation in Section VI.*

The Gifts and Challenges for Persons whose Life-Time Personality is The High Priestess

Gifts:	Challenge:
The Two of Swords (Peace)	To Trust Intuition
The Two of Cups (Love)	Transform Critic to Fair Witness
The Two of Wands (Dominion)	
The Two of Disks (Change)	
The Aeon (Good Judgment)	
Lust/Strength	
High Priestess (Independence)	

Love is the will to extend one's self for the purpose of nurturing one's own or another's spiritual growth.

- Scott Peck, *The Road Less Travelled*

THE EMPRESS

is the principle of love with wisdom. She is a symbol of humankind's ability to extend love and to receive love. The Greeks referred to this symbol as Demeter, the Earth Mother. Mythically, this archetype is also seen as Venus, the Goddess of Love, Beauty, and Creative Power. In Jungian psychology, she is the *anima*, the feminine nature. Behind the Empress, the Moon shines through the veils that fall from her crown. The Moon is the Western symbol for feminine, magnetic nature. She is the Goddess principle, or what the Orientals would refer to as the power of *yin* energy.

The Empress holds the blue lotus blossom of wisdom as a reminder that when we approach life from an attitude of love combined with wisdom, we will resist the need to over-give or push to make things happen emotionally; nor will we protect, or hold ourselves back emotionally. The Empress represents the trusting, balanced heart rather than the controlling, protective heart. She gives in equal proportion to her capacity to receive and is as comfortable in receiving love as she is in extending love. In her right hand, she holds the lotus blossom with its four points which indicate her capacity to give mentally, emotionally, physically, and spiritually as appropriate; and she holds her left arm in a curved position as a symbol of her willingness to receive that which is extended toward her in a loving and wise way. The Empress illustrates the healing power of love that is nurturing, comforting, and supportive. She reminds us that *love with wisdom* is the capacity to nurture and support ourselves in equal proportion to how we nurture and support others.

The large crystalline bubbles touching each other on the card represent the unity

**THE PRINCIPLE OF LOVE
WITH WISDOM:
THE EARTH MOTHER**

of mind and heart. This is the only symbol in the deck which shows heart and mind having equal balance and proportion. Another way that the Empress symbolizes the unity and strength of heart and mind integration is in the color of her burgundy robe (the depth of emotional expression) combined with all the birds which represent the mental realms of consciousness. Cross-culturally, birds are seen as spiritual messengers in the majority of myths. Birds are creatures of the air, and in alchemy, birds and air are associated with the mind, or the mental realms of consciousness. Birds represent spiritual messages that have been cognized or brought into conscious awareness.

The Empress faces the dove or kiwi bird, both are prophetic birds or birds that remind us that wisdom is within and remind us, therefore, to listen to inner guidance. She brings with her the precious memories of the past (the small sparrow or bluebird that sits to the back of her head). Her commitment to change and to become even more of who she is is represented by the swan with her four baby swans. The swan is a Western symbol for transformation; "from the ugly duckling to the beautiful swan" is a metaphor for transforming our own underdeveloped parts (the four baby swans) into awakened and expressive parts of who we are. The double phoenix on the Empress's shield is the Eastern bird that, like the Western swan, is associated with change and transformation. The mythical double phoenix facing each other reminds us that we are simultaneously changing internally as well as externally. Universally, every winged creature is symbolic of spiritualization. The Empress reminds us through all the birds on this symbol that love with wisdom is a way in which we can practice, as well as listen to, our own divine natures within.

Bumble bees are found on the robes of the Empress, Emperor and Art/ Temperance symbols. They represent ways of seeing, or varied forms of perception. According to the Greek Delphic tradition, the second of the temples built in Delphi was erected by bees to assist the oracular vision of the Delphic Oracles (*Cirlot, 1962*).

The globe in the Empress's crown represents the ability to explore internal and external worlds with equal agility and personal confidence.

The *fleur-de-lis,* the three-petaled flowers located at the bottom of the Empress symbol is also found at the bottom of the Emperor symbol. In the West, the *fleur-de-lis* is associated with royalty and leadership. In Tibet and some Eastern cultures, this same symbol is often referred to as the "three-pronged flame" representing the union of mind, heart, and spirit.

The crescent moons interfacing with the Earth on the Empress symbol illustrates the magnetic pull of the feminine nature and its necessity to offer love with wisdom. Just as the Earth is pulled toward the Moon magnetically, so are we pulled to people and situations that offer love with wisdom.

The Empress as Life-Time Symbol

For those individuals whose birthday adds up to the number 3, the Empress represents their life-time spiritual symbol. If one is born with the number 3 one is like the Empress in one's capacity to love, nurture, comfort, support and heal others. It is through one's own mother that one defines who one would be and who one would not be.

For both men and women, this archetype reveals their deep love nature. This archetype reveals their power to receive and to give love with wisdom. For a man, the Empress is his *golden lady* within, or what in Jungian psychology is referred to as the man's *anima*. With the Empress as their spiritual essence, both genders have an extraordinary capacity to heal, comfort, and nurture others. With this gift they would do well in any of the professions concerned with nurturing others like the medical profession or the healing arts; animal husbandry, farming, and veterinarian work, architecture, design, landscaping or any of the arts that contribute to beautification like being a fashion designer, gardener, artist or superb chef.

Their greatest challenge is to nurture, comfort and support themselves in equal proportion to how they support and nurture others. They have an enormous capacity to model to others the beauty of what it is like to have a balanced, wise, and trusting emotional nature. Because love with wisdom is their greatest gift, they may need to monitor a tendency to over-give or push to make things happen that are emotionally important to them or, because they feel so deeply, they may protect themselves or hold back emotionally for fear of being hurt. These tendencies may surface in times of stress or may announce that they are not nurturing themselves in equal proportions to how they are nurturing others.

The Empress as a Growth Symbol

During Empress years (see Section VIII), individuals experience a need to clarify what is emotionally important and what is not. There will be people in their life during this year who will show them what is emotionally important to them and what is not. This is one of the best years to do the following: 1) break patterns of over-giving or over-protecting oneself emotionally; 2) resolve motherhood issues, or heal issues surrounding one's own mother or maternal figures in one's life; 3) excel in professions and in leadership positions where one can model the power of the mind and heart working in tandem; and 4) bring more beauty, harmony, nature, and receptivity into one's life.

When the Empress begins a growth cycle (see Section VIII), this begins a nine year cycle that is one's Creative/Venus Cycle or the Path of the Heart. It is nine years ruled by Venus, the Empress or Earth Mother archetype. This is the best cycle during which to follow whatever has one's passion and heart. *Shoulds* of any kind will not work in this cycle. It is a cycle where the heart is saying "it is my turn." The Empress cycle is a time where some kind of creativity becomes a passion. It is also a time where one connects with deep emotional relationships; and is the best time to heal relationships with important women in one's life.

The Empress as a Visual Affirmation and Meditative Symbol

The Empress is an excellent symbol to use as a visual affirmation to enhance emotional balance, wisdom, and trust. For all women in motherhood roles or for others who are in positions of nurturing and comforting others, this is an important symbol to use as a visual reminder of giving and receiving love in balanced and appropriate ways.

**Sample
Affirmations
To Use While
Looking at
The Empress**

I give wisely and I receive wisely.

*I enjoy leadership positions where I can model
ideas and feelings that are equally honored and respected*

I value the healing power of beauty, harmony and love.

*I realize that the capacity to receive is equally as
powerful as the capacity to give.*

**The Empress
As an
Outer Mirror**

Whenever one is drawn to the Empress symbol or pulls her from the deck, she represents one's capacity to extend and receive love. She reminds one that one's emotional nature is currently in balance and that one is bringing into balance issues surrounding important women in one's life: one's mother, maternal figures, female authority figures, colleagues, friends, or deep emotional relationships. Regardless what form one's outer mirrors take, this symbol represents the power of one's owning one's own maternal and loving nature within.

**Other Symbols
that Are Aspects of
The Empress**

The Empress is the internal motivating energy for expressing love in the world (the Universe, as the number 21, adds up to 3) and for breaking destructive patterns which bind and hold back our self-love and expression of love toward others (The Hanged Man, as the number 12, adds up to the number 3). The major challenge toward expressing love is sorrow held in the mind (the Three of Swords). The Three of Swords is the tendency of the mind to rework old wounds or sorrows tied with the past or with unhappy triangular relationships one has experienced in the past. The threes in the decks are the Empress's tools. Everyone experiences sorrow in his or her life-time. It is by using the Empress's tools that we are given ways in which to overcome past sorrows or ways of preventing unexpected sorrows in our lives. For example, if we are clear in our priorities (the Three of Disks), we will be able to communicate the abundance of feelings that we have (the Three of Cups) from a place of honesty and integrity (the Three of Wands). The experience of sorrow is often the result of having abandoned ourselves, or from not communicating our feelings accurately, or from being unclear about where and with whom our priorities and commitments lie.

Once we break patterns that bind us (The Hanged Man) we are able to contribute to our community and to the world (The Universe) from a place of love with wisdom (The Empress). NOTE: *See The Empress constellation in Section VI.*

**The Gifts and
Challenges for
Persons whose
Life-Time
Personality
Symbol Is
The Empress**

Gifts:	Challenge:
The Three of Disks (The Works; Priorities)	Three of Swords
The Three of Cups (Abundance of Feelings)	(Sorrow)
The Three of Wands (Virtue; Integrity)	
The Hanged Man (Breaking Limiting Patterns)	
The Universe (Expression of Love in the World)	
The Empress (Love with Wisdom)	

Enlightened leadership is service, not selfishness.
The leader grows more and lasts longer by placing
the well-being of all above the well-being of self alone.

- John Heider, *Tao of Leadership*

THE EMPEROR

represents the universal principle of power and leadership. This symbol is the pioneer, the leader, the builder, the doer, and the visionary. Like Aries, the Ram, The Emperor is the explorer whose curiosity and initiative is always on the forefront of human experience. He is the traveler with the globe in his hand who has the ability to make things stable, solid, and secure for himself and others (the coins on his throne).

The Emperor symbol is totally the color of fire. Aries, the Ram, doubled twice behind the Emperor is a fire sign and represents adventure and exploration. Behind the Emperor, the sun rises as a symbol of Nature's source of light. Shamanic societies view this symbol as the power of the sun and see humankind's imitation of the sun in its creation of fire. In Oriental cultures, the Emperor represents dynamic, initiatory power known as *yang* energy. Jungian psychology refers to this symbol as a representation of the *animus* or masculine energy. In Greek mythology, this symbol is Zeus, the father or the patriarch.

The bees on the Emperor's cloak reminds us that all leadership requires vision. Bumble bees are found on the robes of the Emperor, Empress, and Art/Temperance symbols. They represent ways of seeing, or varied forms of perception. According to the Greek Delphic tradition, the second of the temples built in Delphi had been erected by bees to assist the oracular vision of the Delphic Oracles (*Cirlot, 1962.*)

The *fleur-de-lis*, the three-petaled flowers located at the bottom of this symbol, is associated with royalty and leadership. In Tibet and some Eastern cultures, the *fleur-de-lis* is often refered to as the "three-pronged flame" representing the union of mind, heart,

IV

TRUMPS

♈ The Emperor ♈

PRINCIPLE OF PERSONAL POWER AND LEADERSHIP

and spirit. The *fleur-de-lis* on the Emperor card reminds us that effective leadership requires the union of mind, heart, and spirit in making decisions and taking action. The Emperor represents the kind of leadership that is strong yet sensitive to negotiation and peace-making (lamb with flag, which is also a symbol for the Christian Agnus Dei, *lamb of God)*. The double phoenix on the Emperor's shield is the Eastern bird that, like the Western eagle, is associated with change and transformation. The mythical double phoenix facing each other on the Emperor's shield reminds us that leadership is a quality that is constantly changing both internally and externally. Both the shield and the *fleur-de-lis* are found on the Empress card, which is the feminine counterpart of the Emperor.

The Emperor as Life-Time Symbol

For those individuals whose birthday adds up to the number 4, the Emperor represents his or her life-time spiritual symbol. If you are born with the number 4, you are like the Emperor in your capacity to inspire and motivate others. You have strong leadership ability, and often people will put you in a leadership position whether you want to be there or not. You have a natural ability to go into business on your own or to work in organizations or institutions where you could be the head of a program or department.

For both men and women, this archetype reveals your relationship to power and leadership. The Emperor is a symbol of the father or the patriarch, so it might be that through your own father or through other paternal figures in your life you may have defined who you would be and who you would not be. The Emperor requires that ultimately you own your own power and authority and that you don't abandon your own authority or give your power away to others. It is generally known that if you are testing external authority figures or have difficulty with authority figures, that you have not yet fully owned your own power and leadership qualities.

For a woman, The Emperor is your *golden man* within, or what in Jungian psychology is referred to as the woman's *animus*. With this symbol as your life-time spiritual symbol, it reminds you that you have strong leadership ability and the resourcefulness to work well on your own. Since your own inner masculine nature, the *animus,* is well-developed internally, you need men around you who are as strong as you are, if not stronger; otherwise, you become easily bored or lose respect for those who are not as strong as you are. For a man with this symbol as your life-time spiritual symbol, it is important that you surround yourself with people who are as strong as you are, especially in teamwork and partnership endeavors; otherwise, you, too, will lose respect for or become easily bored and impatient with those who are not as capable as yourself.

Both genders with this life-time symbol have a deep love for the creative process, setting something new in motion, and capacities to implement visions, dreams, and ideas in practical ways. They could start their own business, depart-ment, or program. They could be gifted in anything associated with engineering, design, construction, or photographic or film work. They could be interested in the travel industry, in international work, or could find themselves traveling quite extensively in life, either for personal or professional reasons. Creative interests might include the arts, building models of their ideas, chemistry, physics, writing, and sports.

If the Emperor is your life-time symbol, your greatest challenge is to manifest your leadership and visionary gifts. You have an enormous capacity to model for others the quality of leadership that empowers others and serves to benefit the continued, or renewed quality of excellence, in a family, organization, community, or country. Like the element of fire, you are warm, nurturing, electric, vital, and energetic in those activities that are meaningful and challenging to you.

The Emperor as a Growth Symbol

During Emperor years (where your birthday and the current year add up to the number 22 or 4), you may experience a need to relocate or remodel; to travel; to start new ventures and interests; to resolve issues with your own father or with paternal people in your life; and to experience leadership positions. The Emperor year is the best year for important negotiations and truce-making. It is also an ideal year to resolve issues with Aries people (March 21 – April 20) in your life or to take your relationships with Aries people in new directions. It is a year to be open to significant opportunities coming from important older men or Aries people in your life; or the month of Aries (March 21 – April 20) may be a good time to start new projects or be open to new opportunities that might arise. Ultimately, the Emperor year requires that you move in new directions where you can own your own power and leadership.

When the Emperor begins a growth cycle (see Section VII), this begins a cycle which is called your Creative-Leadership Cycle. This cycle requires that you initiate change and move in new directions where you can demonstrate your capacities for responsibility and accountability. The Emperor cycle is an opportunity to build a foundation for yourself. It is often a cycle where you find out what is easy for you and what is difficult; and is also a time when you might find yourself discovering old patterns that you repeat, such as finding yourself in similar situations only with different people playing the parts. Regardless, it is a good time to begin a new project, business, or interest. The Emperor cycle requires that you do not abandon yourself and that you own your own authority. It is one of the best cycles to demonstrate your leadership abilities, and to break patterns that no longer serve you in constructive ways.

Emperor cycles are the best cycles to resolve and heal relationships with important men in your life. For men, these cycles are good ones in which to become fathers or to resolve whether they want to be fathers or not. Basically, the Emperor cycle requires that you demonstrate your ability to communicate, to produce, to empower yourself and others, to negotiate, and to explore what has meaning and challenge for you.

It is important to remember that everything that has been mentioned or described for the Emperor cycle, your Creative-Leadership Cycle, is experienced in depth during your Emperor year.

The Emperor as a Visual Affirmation and Meditative Symbol

If you have difficulty asserting yourself or setting limits, or knowing what your limits and boundaries are, the Emperor is an excellent card to meditate upon for personal and professional empowerment. Whenever you are drawn to this card, it mirrors to you your own leadership, creativity, and ability to be responsible. For leaders and fathers, it is an important symbol to use as a visual reminder of how to model the use of power and leadership in ways that empower yourself and others.

**Sample
Affirmations
To Use While
Looking at
The Emperor**

> *I enjoy starting and initiating projects.*
>
> *I value and honor my leadership ability.*
>
> *I am a good facilitator.*
>
> *I am a responsible and creative human being.*

**The Emperor
as an
Outer Mirror**

When you are drawn to the Emperor symbol or pull it from the deck, he represents the power of your owning and demonstrating your own leadership and paternal gifts. The Emperor indicates your ability to take care of yourself mentally, emotionally, spiritually, physically, and financially.

He represents your ability to be responsible for your life style, career, and personal life. Basically, it is a good time to move, travel, resolve fatherhood issues or issues with Aries or paternal people in your life, to start new ventures, and to be open to new opportunities. It is an important time to stay in your power and not abandon yourself in anyway, yet experience new opportunity.

**Other Symbols
Which are
Aspects of
The Emperor**

The Emperor is the motivating energy for expressing vision and leadership that comes from within. The Emperor is the number 4. Other symbols which add up to the number 4 are the four essential qualities that are needed in any leadership situation: the Four of Swords (truce), the negotiating mind; the Four of Cups (luxury), making sure that internal feelings match external statements in order to produce luxurious results; the Four of Disks (power), the ability to set limits and boundaries and to know what your limits and boundaries are; and the Four of Wands (completion), trusting your intuition to allow for the sense of completion or to know when it is important to complete what needs to be done before moving in new directions. The Death/Rebirth symbol, which adds up to the number 4, and The Fool, which is the number 22, are both outer manifestations of the Emperor. Every leader must have the capacity to let go and move forward (Death/Rebirth) and every leader must have the courage to risk and try the unfamiliar or initiate creative and *new* approaches (The Fool) without fear or resistance. Note: *See Section VI for The Emperor constellation which reveals all the symbols associated with The Emperor as they are described above.*

**The Gifts and
Challenges for
Persons whose
Life-Time
Personality
Symbol Is
The Emperor**

Gifts	Challenges
The Emperor (Leadership)	To use
The Fool (Courage; No Fear)	leadership skills
Death/Rebirth (Letting Go; Moving Forward)	
The Four of Swords (Truce)	
The Four of Cups (Luxury)	
The Four of Wands (Completion)	
The Four of Disks (Power)	

"As you teach so will you learn."
If that is true, and it is true indeed, do not forget
that what you teach is teaching you.
– Course in Miracles

THE HIEROPHANT

represents the universal principle of learning and teaching that is experienced within our families and in life challenges that require us to trust our faith. Faith is asked for in different parts of human experience, and yet for many human beings the test of faith and individuality is often challenged and experienced within family situations. The concept of family is represented within the Hierophant symbol by the central figures which symbolize the universal representations of the family: father, mother, child. In pre-Christian times, the central male figure was Osiris, the Egyptian god of wisdom. Osiris married Isis, the Goddess of Intuition, who strongly believed in the properties of intuition which she held in each hand: the septre of wisdom and the staff of crescent-moon instinct. Isis is pictured at the bottom of the card. Osiris and Isis gave birth to the star-like child, Horus, the Egyptian God of Perception and Vision. Christian interpretations on this same theme see these figures as the Papal figure with the Virgin Mary and the Christ Child. The modern day version represents the family of father, mother, child. From a psychological perspective, the Hierophant connotes the inner family that is expressed outwardly in our own dynamics with family members or extended family. Archetypically, these figures represent different aspects of our nature which require faith: faith in exploring spiritual teachings of any kind (represented here by the papal figure); faith in trusting our intuition (the feminine figure at the bottom of the card); and faith in following our child-like innocence and curiosity (the child in the star). Metaphorically, this symbol represents our capacity and need to learn how *to walk the mystical path with*

PRINCIPLE OF LEARNING AND TEACHING

practical feet. The Hierophant is that part of ourselves that knows how to directly apply the sacred, that is within all of us, into the outer world. This same concept is also represented by Taurus, the Bull. This is the Taurus card and Taurus is the sign which is committed to putting into form internal and external experiences.

The Hierophant also represents the initiator. This symbol reflects current tests or challenges that we might face in order to grow and develop further as human beings. Every initiation expands our awareness (the five petaled lotus blossom behind the Hierophant's head) and demands that we renew and regenerate ourselves (the snake coiled around the lotus blossom). The nine sacred thorns reminds us of events, people, tests, and opportunities that have not only intitiated us but have required that we change our beliefs, our identities, or life-styles in order to become even more of who we are.

The four creatures in the four corners of this symbol represent the four gifts that we can apply within any initiation, family system, or organization: 1) Taurus, the bull, reminds us to implement and take action on our ideas and bring them into form, the Eastern symbol of Taurus is the elephant which serves as the same reminder on this card; 2) Leo, the Lion, is a symbol of expansive and unlimited creativity that waits to be utilized; 3) Aquarius, the human face, is humankind's desire to be original, futuristic, and pioneering; and 4) Scorpio, the Eagle or Phoenix head, represents loyalty and committment towards anyone or anything that has heart and meaning for us. These four creatures remind us that in order for anything to come into form, it requires the creativity of Leo, the practicality of Taurus, the originality and vision of Aquarius, and the passion and committment of Scorpio. These four creatures are found also on the Chariot and Universe cards where they represent the same concepts that are necessary in times of handling change (The Chariot) and in building new worlds (The Universe).

The Hierophant holds the staff of committment which reminds us that any committment requires that our mind, heart, and action all share the same intention and focus (the interlaced circles on the Hierophant's staff). Committments that are kept and sustained are those where mind, heart, and action are consistently aligned and integrated. Committments that are broken are those where there is non-alignment among mind, heart, and action, when one or more of these parts are not willing to participate fully.

The Hierophant as Life-Time Symbol

For those individuals whose birthday adds up to the number 23 or 5 (2 + 3 = 5), the Hierophant represents their life-time spiritual and personality symbol. These persons strongly value family and wherever they go they create a personal and professional support system or extended family. They are loyal, practical, and community-minded people. Learning and teaching situations are important to them. They are well-suited in being in an active or receptive mode in arenas of teaching, counseling, consulting and management situations. Hierophant people want to see how ideas can be implemented and applied. They are drawn to the creative arts as a tangible way of expressing creative ideas in a variety of forms. For this reason, Taurus people become important mirrors for Hierophant people because Taurus is the sign known for producing and bringing beauty and creativity into tangible forms.

Often Hierophant people experience music as a way of renewing and regenerating themselves. The elephant heads on this symbol are associated with deep capacities to listen and remember through aspects of sound.

Spiritual work is important to Hierophant people and at different times in their life they will find themselves assisting others with inner work and exploration or will find themselves exploring their own internal realms. Hierophant literally means *spiritual teachings* or *bringer of the light* so Hierophant people often have a deep philosophical nature and strong sense of faith in themselves and others.

During a Hierophant year, you may find yourself wanting to resolve family issues or may find yourself assessing whether you want to have a family or not. It is the best year for attending to unresolved family issues, or for breaking old family patterns and conditioning.

Often persons will find themselves wanting to go back to school or to get additional training; or they may find themselves teaching, training, counseling, and consulting others.

Hierophant years support internal growth and development, so individuals may find themselves exploring contemplation, meditation, dreams, and spiritual practices during this time.

It is definitely a year to implement creative ideas or to make one's life more stable, solid and secure through one's own productivity. During a Hierophant year, you face and confront old fears of defeat (the Five of Swords), resolve old disappointments (the Five of Cups), realize that anxiety is produced by holding back (the Five of Wands), and release old worry patterns (the Five of Disks).

The Hierophant as a Growth Symbol

The Hierophant is an excellent visual to use to reinforce your capacities to produce and implement that which is important to you. It can assist you in resolving family issues and concerns. The Hierophant is the best symbol to use to increase your faith and ability to do deep spiritual work. It is the archetype that most facilitates you in any teaching, counseling, or consulting work. If you are wanting to bring important creative ideas into some tangible form, this symbol can assist that process immensely by your looking at it daily with your desired intention and affirmation, or by envisioning it within your meditation and asking for the inner guidance and direction needed to support any of the issues stated above.

The Hierophant as a Visual Affirmation and Meditative Symbol

I am inspired by learning/teaching situations

I honor the sacred within me.

I deeply honor and value the unlimited resource of faith that is within me.

I am a creative and productive individual in my professional and family life.

Sample Affirmations To Use While Looking at The Hierophant

**The Hierophant
as an
Outer Mirror**

When you pull this symbol or find yourself continually drawn toward it, it represents a committment to trusting your leadership, intuition, and child-like curiosity. It is a time of learning and teaching for you, and a time to trust your deepest faith in arenas of family and extended family. It is a good time to be productive and stabilize things in your life. Also, you may be involved in learning-teaching situations with Taurus people in your life (anyone born April 21 – May 21), or you may need to resolve issues that you might have with Taurus people.

In all arenas of your life, when you pull this symbol, it is a time to listen and to trust deeper parts of yourself.

**Other Symbols
that Are Aspects of
The Hierophant**

The four five's in the deck are challenges that everyone faces during life: the Five of Swords (fear of defeat); the Five of Cups (disappointment); the Five of Wands (strife or anxiety) and the Five of Disks (worry). These are the *tests of faith* which the Hierophant symbol has mastered and overcome in different parts of his or her life. Whenever you pull one of these cards, it is a reminder that within five weeks or five months, you are determined to resolve family issues involving fear, disappointment, anxiety, or worry; or that you are no longer willing to be the lineage bearer or tradition bearer of family patterns which include fear of defeat; disappointment, anxiety or worry.

The Art card (the number 14 card, which adds up to 5) is another expression of Hierophant energy. In other decks, this symbol is referred to as Temperance. An aspect of the Hierophant is the ability to integrate and synthesize polarities and oppositions in such a way that it tempers and reveals the inherent artistry that is found in one's strengths and weaknesses. This is the Art card. When you have brought light into your own darkness (fear, anxiety, worry, disappointment), you begin to integrate the light (gifts, talents, and resources) into your life in a balanced way. This is Art or Temperance, the synthesis or integration of the light and dark within; or the union of polarities, oppositions, and paradoxes internally and externally. When you have integrated both your strengths and weaknesses with equal comfortability, you reveal to others *the artistry* of who you are. Others get to see the whole of who you are.

When you pull the Art card, it represents that you are manifesting Hierophant energy in the world. You have integrated your challenges with your strengths. *(See Hierophant constellation in Section VI)*

**The Gifts and
Challenges for
Persons whose
Life-Time
Personality
Symbol Is
The Hierophant**

Gifts	Challenge
The Hierophant (Strong Faith; Family Oriented)	The Five of Swords (Fear of Defeat)
	The Five of Cups (Disappointment)
Art-Temperance (Integration, Synthesis, Synergy)	The Five of Wands (Strife, Anxiety)
	The Five of Disks (Worry)

*The value of the personal relationship to all things
is that it creates intimacy and intimacy creates understanding
and understanding creates love.*

 —Anais Nin

THE LOVERS

archetype represents the universal principle of the art and craft of relationship. Everything upon this symbol is paired: there are two children; there is the couple facing each other; there are the young man and the older man; there are the older woman and the younger woman; there are the eagle and the lion; there are the Cupid and the Orphic Egg, the egg that is wrapped with a snake. In astrology, this archetype is associated with Gemini, which symbolizes a universal motif that's found in all cultures, called the *journey of the twins.* In America, the journey of the twins is Raggedy Ann and Raggedy Andy; in Germany, it's Hansel and Gretel; and in every other culture we have the myth of the two brothers or the two sisters, the prince and the pauper – all the famous couples in history and in modern time reflect this archetype of the Lovers.

The Lovers reminds us that in every relationship, whether it be a friend, family member or a colleague, or a deep-love one, what is required is: child-like innocence, curiosity and playfulness, represented by the children on the card; loyalty and commitment, represented by the couple facing each other; and the gift of spaciousness – the allowing of space for contemplation, introspection and the need for being alone, necessary for any relationship – which is represented by the Hermit, who is giving the couple a blessing. This is the only symbol, other than the Hermit symbol itself, where the Hermit appears. In the background of the card are iron gates, symbolizing the Lovers' need not to be limited, restricted, barred or restrained in their relationships, and also symbolizing a line from the *I Ching,* the Oriental Book of Changes, which says: *But when two people are at one in their inmost hearts, they shatter even the strength of iron or*

PRINCIPLE OF ART AND CRAFT
OF RELATIONSHIP
THE JOURNEY OF THE TWINS

bronze; and when two people understand each other in their inmost hearts, their words are sweet and strong, like the fragrance of orchids.

Cupid, at the top of the card, reminds us that there are two kinds of love: love as passion, and love as compassion. These are the two extreme poles of the Lovers card, the Gemini card, and the two extreme poles of Gemini. Eros, the God of Love, represented by Cupid in Greek mythology, is both the eldest and the youngest of all the gods, and is represented by the older man and the younger man, and the older woman and the younger woman. Eros also reminds us that there are five kinds of love or five kinds of relationships where love is expressed: first, there is love of servant to master, which is often the professional or collegial relationship that we know today; second, there is love between friend and friend; third, there is love between parent and child; fourth, there is love between husband and wife, or spouses; and five, there is passionate and illicit love. The Lovers symbol represents to us the different kinds of relationship lines or the different kinds of bonding that we can experience within our life, and the responsibility that is incurred with different relationship lines. Regardless of the type of relationship that we have, either with people, ideas, or our creative projects, we will be faced in any of our relationship lines with the principle of duality, or the principles of good and evil that are found within our nature. Another way of representing good and evil would be the light or the dark, or that which is known or unknown within us, or that which is considered positive or negative within us. The principle of duality is represented by the children at the base of the card, symbolizing the *Yin* and the *Yang* within our nature, or the dynamic and magnetic within our nature, or the light and the dark within our nature.

In the *I Ching* hexagram of Break-Through, we have an important statement about how to resolve the struggle of good and evil, or opposites, that might be apparent within our natures. The *I Ching* says: *Even a single passion still lurking in the heart has power to obscure reason. Passion and reason cannot exist side by side. Therefore, fight without quarter is necessary if the good is to prevail. In a resolute struggle of the good against evil, there are, however, definite rules that must not be discarded if good is to succeed. First, resolution must be based on a union of strength and friendliness. Second, a compromise with evil is not possible: evil must under all circumstances be openly discredited. Nor must our own passions and shortcomings be glossed over. Third, the struggle must not be carried on directly by force. If evil is branded, it thinks of weapons, and if we do it the favor of fighting against it blow for blow, we lose in the end because thus we ourselves get entangled in hatred and passion. Therefore, it is important to begin at home, to be on guard in our own persons against the faults that we have branded. In this way, finding no opponent, the sharp edges of the weapons of evil becomed dulled. For the same reasons we should not combat our own faults directly. As long as we wrestle with them, they continue victorious. Finally, the best way to fight evil is to make energetic progress in the good.*

The energetic progress of the good within our natures is represented by the four tools that are held by each of the children. In times of darkness, which is represented by the child that is the dark figure, it is important that we trust our intuition, which is represented by the club or the wand; and that we have right attitude in our beliefs and in our thinking, which is represented by the spear or the sword that he holds. In times of positivity, it is important that we follow what has heart and meaning, which is the cup held by the child that is the white figure; and that we also through our action and behavior, implement what has passion and heart for us, which is symbolized by the cluster of pine cones or flowers that the other child holds, representative of the disks in the Tarot deck.

The animals at the bottom of the card remind us of three principles that are present in all relationships that we have: one, all relationships require us to be creative, like Leo the Lion; two, all relationships require that we are clear on our loyalties and priorities, which is represented by Scorpio, the eagle or the bird; and three, all relationships are a transformative experience, represented by the Orphic Egg, the egg wrapped with the snake, so that physically in relationships, we change like the egg, and spiritually, we transform and let go of old identities, like the snake shedding an old skin. Each relationship has an internal or spiritual connection, which is represented by the wings that are attached to the egg.

Essentially, the Lovers archetype reminds us that fundamental sincerity is the only proper basis for forming relationships of any kind.

For those individuals whose birthday adds up to the number 6, the Lovers represents your life-time spiritual symbol. If you are born with the number 6, you are like the Lovers in your capacity to inspire and motivate people of all ages and all generations, pictured by the children, the couple, the older people, the younger people on the symbol. It also indicates that you have the ability to work well with persons on a one-to-one basis, as well as to work with people in groups. This is the most peopled card in the entire deck, and teaches persons the art and craft of relating, either to ideas, creative projects or to human beings. If 6 is your number, you have the inherent gift of establishing relationship lines and perceiving what's working and what's not working in relationships. Your greatest abilities are people skills and in choice-making, especially weighing choices either between two situations, two issues, two people, or choices in how to bring two situations, two people or two issues together in order to create a greater whole. This symbol of the Lovers represents Buckminister Fuller's concept of the synergetic principle, which was that two or more parts that came together would create something greater than the two parts that initially came together. Basically, with the Lovers archetype as your spiritual life-time symbol, you have the inherent gift of synthesizing, integrating polarities, oppositions and paradoxes. You are gifted in putting together ideas, situations, issues or people that other people had not readily thought of as workable. You have the insight or perception to see what's workable and what's not workable as far as relationship lines are concerned on a one-to-one basis, or in group situations. Because of your sensitivity to people and to relationship lines, it is important at different times that you give yourself space, like the Hermit, to integrate your experience; also, at different periods in your life, you'll find yourself wanting to be alone, and not to be so people-oriented. This phase or cycle of your life will be much more targeted to the Hermit figure that is on this card, which is associated with contemplation, introspection and needs for emotional space and psychological space.

**The Lovers
as Life-Time
Symbol**

**The Lovers
as a Growth
Symbol**

During Lovers years (where your birthday and the current year add up to the number 24 or 6), you may experience a need to reassess all of your relationships – friends, family, colleagues, deep emotional relationships. It is a time of assessing whether you have the kind of support system that you need and want, or the kind that you do not need and want. It is a year where you want to deepen and expand certain relationships, and where you may want to distance, shed, or split apart from other relationships which you feel you have outgrown. During Lovers years, as a growth symbol, many people consider marriage or divorce, or moving in or moving out. It is the Gemini symbol, and so it is a weighing between two – either two options, two issues, two directions, two people, or two situations – and weighing which would be the better choice; or how to bring two or more choices together in order to create a greater whole in your life, either personally or professionally. It becomes apparent during Lovers' years that you're no longer willing to support relationships that are not equal and special. We all know what it is like to have equal relationships, this often is the colleague and professional relationship, it's an equal relationship but it is not *special*. We all know what it is like to have a special relationship that's not equal. And in a Lovers year it is often realizing the fact that you want more equal and special relationships in your life, rather than the disparity which is so apparent in having either equal, but not special, relationships or special, but not equal, relationships. What becomes clear during the Lovers year is that you emotionally know what you need and want, and what you do not need and want.

This archetype or symbol peaks in the month of Gemini, which is May 21st to June 21st, at which time there could be definitive choices made about relationships; or during a Lovers year, when Gemini people in your life could function as mirrors of choices that you are making personally and professionally, or choices that you are making about your support systems and what you need and want, and what you don't need and want. Often, the Lovers year is a choice-making year, either between two issues, two people, two situations, two places, two directions, and either weighing those choices, or attempting to creatively bring two or more choices together to create a greater whole. Often the Lovers symbol is a turning point within any cycle of change that you are experiencing.

**The Lovers
as a Visual
Affirmation and
Meditative Symbol**

The Lovers archetype is an excellent symbol to use for meditation or for affirming relationships and people skills. If you are a person who has difficulty in relating to people and would like to relate to people more skillfully, the Lovers card would be an incredibly good card on which to meditate as a visual affirmation. Also, the Lovers card is excellent for choice-making, or increasing one's choice-making ability, in bringing two or more things together to create a greater whole or in making definitive choices between two issues, or two situations or two people in one's life. The Lovers also affirms one's capacity to work with people of all ages – children, contemporaries, older people. Also, the Lovers archetype is an incredible visual portraiture of someone who knows how to deepen and expand certain relationships, and also knows which relationships have served their purpose or have been outgrown.

I enjoy working with people of all ages.

I have inherent people skills.

*Emotionally, I am sure about what I need and want,
and what I don't need and want, in the area of relationships.*

*I deeply honor and value the principle of friendship and the
quality of love that I bring into my life and that I express in my life.*

**Sample Affirmations
To Use While
Looking at
The Lovers**

Whenever you are drawn to the Lovers symbol or you pull it from the deck, the Lovers represents your current skills with people of all ages, and the Lovers indicates that you are in a period of making choices about important relationships in your life, especially those that you would like to deepen, expand; or those that you feel that you need to distance or shed or split apart, for a temporary time. The Lovers also indicates your desire not to be barred or limited in relationships. The Lovers symbolizes your desire to work with people on a one-to-one basis, or to work with people in groups, because there are inherent skills in these areas. Often, this symbol represents issues surrounding marriage or divorce, or deepening and expanding relationships, or moving in or moving out. The Lovers also represents choices that could be necessary to be made about children or important older people in your life. Regardless, it could also be choices about how to integrate two or more situations or issues, or how to make a definitive choice between two or more situations or issues. Since it is the Gemini card, it could also indicate choices about important Gemini people in your life – that is, anyone born May 21st to June 21st – or in the month of Gemini, you might be making important choices, especially emotional choices that are important to you about important people in your life.

**The Lovers as an
Outer Mirror**

The Lovers card is the basic principle that is associated with expressing and extending the art and craft of relating in all of our relationships. The Lovers is the number 6; and the other symbols which add up to the number 6 represent the four qualities that are essential and needed within any relationship: the Six of Swords (science), this is science of mind, the objective mind, the fair-witnessing mind, and in every relationship, it's important to have the attitude of objectivity and of looking at things realistically as they are rather than as we want them to be; the Six of Cups (pleasure) is another quality that is necessary in all relationships, especially pleasure that is healing (represented by the copper cups) revitalizing (represented by the orange lotus blossoms) and renewing and regenerating (represented by the snakes that are coiled within the cups) for it is important in every relationship for us to extend fun and pleasure, and not always to wait for fun and pleasure to be extended to us; the Six of Wands (victory) – the elemental victory is the victory which is a win/win, rather than a win/lose one and every relationship

**Other Symbols
that Are Aspects of
The Lovers**

requires that each individual within it be concerned that the relationship is a win/win for both parties involved, for a win/lose situation is never really the ultimate victory that is pictured on the Six of Wands; and the final ingredient that is required in any relationship is the Six of Disks (success) for on this symbol, we have the formula for success, in relationships or in creative projects or in our profession. The formula has six steps to success, which are pictured by the astrological symbols within the six spheres on this card. In order to be successful in anything, we must do things step-by-step, not push or hold back, which is the lesson of Saturn; we must be open and flexible and resilient, like Jupiter; we must follow our heart and what has meaning, like Venus; we must stay in our honesty and integrity and not abandon ourselves, like the Moon; we must communicate effectively, with artful timing and prepared content, which is the message of Mercury; and in all relationships, we must give consistent energy, which is the lesson of Mars.

The other symbol which is related to the Lovers card and is an outer external expression of the Lovers, is the Devil, or the Pan symbol, which is the number 15. The number 15 adds up to the number 6. Whenever you pull or draw the Devil card, or Pan, the merry goat, Capricorn, it is an indication that you are manifesting the Lovers card outwardly. The Pan within us requires that we look at whatever is bedeviling us or troubling us in relationships with the stability of Capricorn, the goat, and the mirth and humor of Pan, the smiling goat. Taking things too seriously sets us off balance, and so Pan, the merry goat, Capricorn, reminds us that through humor and through stability we are able to manifest objectivity in the mind (Six of Swords), pleasure in the heart (Six of Cups), victory in the spirit (Six of Wands), and success in the external world and in our relationships through our actions and behavior (Six of Disks). **Note:** *(See the Lovers constellation in Section VI.)*

The Gifts and Challenges for Persons whose Life-Time Personality Symbol Is The Lovers

Gifts:	Challenge:
The Lovers (Art and Craft of Relating)	To model
The Devil/Pan (Mirth; Stability)	the art and craft
The Six of Swords (Science; Objectivity)	of relationships and to
The Six of Cups (Pleasure)	utilize inherent
The Six of Wands (Victory)	people skills
The Six of Disks (Success)	

THE CHARIOT

*Motion or change and identity or rest are
the first and second secrets of nature: Motion and Rest.
The whole code of her laws may be written on the thumbnail.*

-Emerson

represents the universal principle of change and causation. Taoist philosophy states that change is successful when both "the great rooted tree by the flowing river" are combined within a natural setting. This Oriental nature metaphor is a reminder that during times of change it is necessary to incorporate in equal proportion the qualities of quietude (the great rooted tree) with activity (the flowing river). The Chariot depicts a figure in contemplation or quietude sitting within a chariot readied for activity.

The Chariot illustrates that change is pervasive in that it touches every individual multi-dimensionally, which is pictured by the four pillars, the four wheels, and the four animals – all of these symbols represent the four elements or the elemental aspects of who we are mentally, emotionally, physically, and spiritually. The charioteer holds the Wheel of Fortune in his or her hands reminding us that through choice we have the ability to select fortunate, positive, and abundant changes for ourselves. In times of contemplating the changes that we want to make, it is important for us to assess which changes will assist our growth and evolution and which ones will be nurturing, comforting, and supporting to us at this point in time. The choice of selecting change that is fortunate and nurturing is not only revealed by the spinning Wheel of Fortune, but it is also represented by Cancer, the crab, which is sitting on the charioteer's head. The ten crystals on the figures's golden armor also serve as reminders of clear choices made in the past. The number 10 corresponds with the Wheel of Fortune; therefore, the ten crystals are fortunate changes that an individual has made and thus carries past memories of those changes within the heart and torso of

VII

ꓩ The Chariot ♋

PRINCIPLES OF CHANGE
MOVEMENT
COMBINATION OF STILLNESS-ACTIVITY

self. These crystalline motivating memories remind us that change is an opportunity for creating new realities that expand and deepen our nature.

The four animals in front of the chariot are symbolic representations of the essential ingredients that are necessary for implementing the kinds of changes that are important personally and professionally. These ingredients are: 1) like Taurus (the bull's head and feet), it is important to see tangible results; 2) like Leo (the lion's head and feet), all change requires that we access qualities of our creativity that we have not touched before, and the mutation of combining the bull's head with the lion's feet and the lion's head with the bull's feet illustrates that creativity (Leo, the lion) always wants to come into some tangible and useable form (Taurus, the bull); 3) like Aquarius (the human's head and feet), all changes demand that we risk and initiate something new; and 4) like Scorpio (the bird's head and feet), successful change requires that we follow what has heart and meaning. The mutation of combining the human head with the bird's feet and the bird's head with the human's feet illustrates that in initiating anything new (Aquarius, the human head and feet), it is important to follow what has heart and meaning (Scorpio, the bird).

Change is magical, like the *Abracadabra* writing on the canopy of the chariot. When we combine our emotional nature (the blue, oceanic canopy) with our mind and life force (the white air and uncontainable wind), we can produce tangible results (the earth animals) that have been fired and stimulated by the motivating force of intuition (the fire chariot).

Change is for the purpose of reminding us of who we really are. The yellow brick road is the royal road of spiritual growth and evolution. Our choices during times of change are ultimately correct and motivate a deeper committment to the original purpose of personal and transpersonal existence.

The Chariot as Life-Time Symbol

For those individuals whose birthday adds up to the number 16 or 7, the Chariot represents your life-time spiritual symbol. Chariot people need variety and are successful in executing multiple tasks at the same time. If this is your life-time spiritual card, change and variety are necessary components in your life. For you, it is not a question of what it is that you want to do, but how many things you can do simultaneously. You can stay in one situation, personally or professionally, if it provides the variety and challenge that you need and want. You are constantly balancing your needs for quietude and activity, and implementing changes in your life that are both nurturing and fortunate.

There are five times out of the year where it is essential that you experience movement, change, and acitivty in your life which are represented by Cancer, the crab and the four animals in front of the chariot. Those months of the year are: 1) *Aquarius* (January 21 – February 21), which is the most restless time of year for you; therefore it is a good month to initiate new projects or do something entirely different. This is represented by the human head and human feet in front of the chariot. 2) *Taurus*, the bull (April 21 – May 21) is your most active and productive month. It is a time to implement and produce in tangible ways that which is important to you. 3) *Cancer*, the Crab (June 21 – July 21) is an important time to actively nurture, comfort, and support yourself. It is an essential time to support your needs for quietude, nurturement, and reconnection with family and extended family. 4) *Leo*, the lion, (July 21 – August 21) is the time to be open to new creative opportunities, to explore avenues of your creativity that have been dormant, and to dynamically express your creativity without reservation. 5) *Scorpio*, the bird (October 21 – November 21) is the best time of year to make emotional decisions or to act upon what has heart and meaning for you. The Scorpio month allows you to make emotional decisions that are important to you which ignite and motivate the need for new experiences in Aquarius, find you busy and productive in Taurus, actively nurtured in the month of Cancer, and open to new opportunities and creative expression in the month of Leo.

With the Chariot as your life-time spiritual symbol, you enjoy family and home for the stability that it provides; you love to travel, and do multiple things at the same time. You are a natural generator, motivator, and stimulator. You have an equal love for quietude and activity. If things become too boring in relationships or in work, you will generate change to break the monotony. For you, movement and quietude in combination are essential. Too much quietude is intolerable and dull. Activity that produces unseen results is anxiety-producing. Change is important as long as it produces some kind of tangible result.

During the Chariot year (a year where your birthday plus the current year adds up to 7), is the best year to move, relocate, travel, or make career changes. Persons in their Chariot year experience changes tied with the family and the home, which could be a move, or to remodel or redecorate the house or to have people move in or out of the home. Career changes or promotions are not unexpected events during a Chariot year. In hindsight, the changes that take place during a Chariot year are ultimately positive and expansive changes which further personal and professional growth and development.

Your Chariot year requires that you make changes that are nurturing and fortunate in all arenas of your life. Cancer people, anyone born June 21 – August 21, will function as mirrors to you as to what is needed for your personal and professional growth; or, the month of Cancer could be a time where it is important for you to entertain activities which support and nurture the deepest core of who you are.

The Chariot as a Growth Symbol

The Chariot supports the integration of quietude and activity in your life. It is the best symbol to use to support desired changes that involve moving, traveling, or making career changes. If you desire to make changes that are positive and nurturing, the Chariot is an excellent symbol to use in meditation or within creative visualization exercises to assist your process.

The Chariot as a Visual Affirmation and Meditative Symbol

I stimulate and motivate others positively.

I am responsible for what I cause.

I accomplish things effortlessly and well.

I enjoy the combination of quietude and activity

Sample Affirmations To Use While Looking at The Chariot

**The Chariot
as an
Outer Mirror**

When you pull this symbol or find yourself continually drawn toward it, the Chariot represents an inherent need to combine quietude with activity. It is a time where you may be contemplating making changes tied with the family or home or with Cancer people in your life (anyone born June 21st to July 21st.) In the next seven weeks or the next seven months, you may take an important trip or travel. You may relocate or move – if you don't, you will remodel or redecorate. It is a time where you will want to resolve ideas tied with the family or the home; or make career changes. If you stay within the same career, you will want to progress or express yourself differently either through promotion or using your combined skills in a different way.

**Other Symbols
that Are Aspects of
The Chariot**

The four seven's in the minor arcana represent the ways in which we block change or movement or can assist it. The three ways in which you block change in yourself is represented by the Seven of Swords (Futility), the Seven of Cups (Debauch or Indulgence), and the Seven of Disks (Fear of Failure). The Seven of Wands (Valour) represents the way you can support growth and change in yourself. Through valour or your willingness to stay by what you value, you can facilitate the process of growth and evolution within yourself and others.

The Tower (which is the number 16, which adds up to 7) is the outer representation of the Chariot card. The Tower represents the willingness to dismantle that which is artificial and false-to-fact in order to restore and renovate that which is actual and true within one's nature. If you pull the Tower card or have it as a life-time personality symbol, you are an individual who is committed to renovating yourself, ideas, people, environments and things. The Tower is a symbol of waking up to the essential nature of who you are. *(See the Chariot constellation in Section VI for additional information.)*

**The Gifts and
Challenges for
Persons whose
Life-Time
Personality
Symbol Is
The Chariot**

Gifts	Challenge
The Chariot (Gift for Combining Quietude with Creativity; Gift for Doing Multiple Tasks)	Seven of Swords (Futility)
	Seven of Cups (Debauch, Indulgence)
Seven of Wands (Valour)	
The Tower (Restoration; Healing)	Seven of Disks (Fear of Failure)

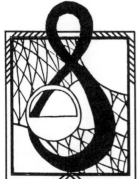

ADJUSTMENT/ JUSTICE

Know thyself. Nothing in excess.
The Self is required to balance the self.

– Ralph Blum,
Book of Runes

symbol represents the universal principle of alignment and balance. In most Tarot decks, this symbol is known as the Justice card, reflecting the principle of negotiation and truth. In the central portion of the symbol is a figure that stands in a diamond, having pierced the webbed veils of illusion, delusion, and deception. In Egyptian mythology, this central figure portrays Maat, the Goddess of Law, Truth, and Justice. This Egyptian goddess played an important part in the judgment of the dead, either herself or her feather was placed in the scales opposite the heart of the dead person in order to test its truthfulness.

In astrology, this symbol represents Libra, the scales. Within the scales are the Greek letters *Alpha,* representing beginnings, and *Omega,* symbolizing endings or completions. The principle of balance requires that whatever is initiated or begun (*Alpha*) must be completed at some time (*Omega*). The scales are also symbols of legalities, financial balance, and business acumen.

The perfectly shaped circles or balloons are symbols representing formulated ideas or thoughts. This is the integrating, balancing and synthesizing mind which is often expressed through writing, research, and design. The Adjustment card is also the only card where the Ace of Swords appears on another symbol other than its own card. Here the Ace of Swords is facing downward, symbolizing the application of creative ideas in tangible, useful ways. The Ace of Swords in its own card represents the inspired, creative, and original mind. Within this symbol, the Ace of Swords (the creative mind) is being directly applied and brought to earth in realistic and practical ways.

VIII

♄ Adjustment ♎

THE PRINCIPLE OF BALANCE:
JUSTICE / REALIGNMENT

The four elongated pillars in the background of the card represent balance of health: mentally, emotionally, physically, and spiritually. The eyes of the figure are masked, symbolizing that ultimate guidance for balance and staying within one's center comes from within.

The Adjustment/Justice as Life-Time Symbol

For those individuals whose birthday adds up to the number 17 or 8, the Adjustment/Justice symbol represents your life-time spiritual symbol. If this is your life-time spiritual symbol, you highly regard beauty, balance, and harmony in your life. You want things to be direct, simple, clear, and you have very little tolerance for situations that are complex, covert, and filled with intrigue. At different times in your life, you will attend to bringing balance into two arenas of your life (the scales) either in health or finances, or in presenting proposals in which other people can invest. Writing, editing and research will be another avenue that you might explore; or you might present original creative ideas in such a way that they can be used by many people. Inventions that would assist law, health, finances, and publications interest you, especially if they make things easier for people.

You will be drawn to Libra people (anyone born September 21 – October 21) because they mirror to you your own inherent love of balance and simplicity. Clarity is a quality that you reflect and also respect in others. Often this quality of clarity is reflected back to you by the Libra people in your life.

Nature is an important regenerating resource for you. The combination of water, greenery and sunlight is very healing to you at the core of who you are. This is symbolized by all the blue, green, and yellow on this card.

The Adjustment/Justice as a Growth Symbol

Whenever you have the Adjustment/Justice card as a growth symbol, it is the best year to bring what has been out of balance into your life back into balance. It is a good time to balance financial and legal considerations (the scales), attend to health (the four elongated pillars in the background of the card), and to implement new ideas in practical ways (the sword touching the ground).

Adjustment years are good years to simplify your life. Often you might find yourself cleaning out basements, garages, closets for the purpose of letting go of clutter or unused items in your life. Clarity, order and balance become increasingly important to you during this year. Your own illusions, delusions, or self-deceptions will become intolerable, as will your ability to tolerate the deceptions or illusions of others. Truth and authenticity are qualities that you reclaim for yourself during this year.

Nature and being in nature becomes a healing and rejuvenating resource for you. The combinations of water, greenery, and sunlight bring a sense of balance and healing within your own nature. Spending time outdoors becomes a priority for you.

Libra people (anyone born September 21 – October 21) function as important mirrors and teachers to you during this year. It is the best year to resolve issues with Libra people in your life; or to learn from Libra people about the art and craft of balance that can restore simplicity and healing in your life.

The Adjustment/Justice symbol best supports your intention to bring more clarity, balance, and simplicity into your life. Through meditation and creative visualization, The Adjustment/Justice symbol assists you in breaking though veils of illusion, delusion or deception. It is an archetype which can assist balance in healing, writing, legalities, and finances.

The Adjustment/ Justice as a Visual Affirmation and Meditative Symbol

I am balanced and centered.

I value being truthful in difficult situations.

 I honor my word and commitments.

The abundance and beauty of Nature is a reflection of my own nature.

Sample Affirmations To Use While Looking at The Adjustment/ Justice

When you pull this symbol or find yourself continually drawn toward it, it represents in the month of Libra, or with Libra people in your life, that you are determined to restore balance, harmony, and simplicity in specific arenas of your life.

Within the next eight weeks or months is a good time to balance health, finances, and legal issues. It is an excellent time to present proposals, do grant writing, or execute and finish writing, editing and research projects.

Basically, it is important for you to simplify and balance that which is out of balance or chaotic in you life. It is a time where you desire and achieve clarity on important issues that you have been considering.

The Adjustment/ Justice as an Outer Mirror

The four eights in the deck are reminders of ways to stay in balance and ways where imbalance can be experienced. Ways to stay in balance are reflected by the Eight of Wands (swiftness) and the Eight of Disks (prudence). The Eight of Wands reminds us that any problem or block in your life can be handled by doing two things: by communicating directly and by taking swift action. The Eight of Disks reflects to us that the "harvest tree" is available if we are willing to use prudence and wisdom rather than pushing to make things happen or by resisting or holding back.

Imbalance is created by over-analyzing or doubting oneself (the Eight of Swords, interference) and by over-extending and depleting oneself (the Eight of Cups, indolence). The Eight of Swords is that tendency to create doubt, confusion, and uncertainty by over-analyzing everything. This mental pattern serves only to

Other Symbols that Are Aspects of The Adjustment/ Justice

take us off balance. The Eight of Swords reminds us that during times of doubt and confusion, we must wait for clarity rather than to take action. The Eight of Cups reminds us that patterns of over-giving or over-extending outselves will lead only to states of depletion, inertia, and indolence. Both the Eight of Swords and the Eight of Cups are mental and emotional patterns which can take us out of balance.

The Star symbol (the number 17, which adds up to the number 8) is an example of the principle of balance, justice, and clarity being expressed externally. The Star is a portraiture of what each individual is like when essential clarity and balance is radiating from within and is observable and appreciated externally. The Star is a symbol of internal self esteem that is externally viewed as radiance and charisma that is neither inflated or deflated. It is that state of deep balance, harmony, and authenticity which is healing, clear, and inspirational. *(See Adjustment constellation in Section VI for additional information.)*

The Gifts and Challenges for Persons whose Life-Time Personality Symbol Is The Adjustment/ Justice

Gifts:

Adjustment/Justice
  (Balance; Clarity)
Eight of Wands (Swiftness)
Eight of Disks (Prudence;
  Wisdom)
The Star (Self-Esteem; Radiance)

Challenges:

Eight of Swords (Doubt;
  Interference)
Eight of Cups (Indolence;
  Patterns of Over-Extension)

The finest thing in the world is knowing how to belong to oneself.

– Michel de Montaigne, *Of Solitude*

THE HERMIT

represents universal principle of completion, contemplation, and introspection. This is the archetype of the wise person. The Hermit is the lantern-bearer, the way-shower and the wise leader who draws upon internal wisdom and life's experience as invaluable resources for assisting others through life's processes.

The Cerberus, the three-headed jackal, is the Greek watch-dog and guardian of the Underworld. The Cerberus represents the part of our nature that wants to make sure that things are complete (one head of the dog turning backward) before we initiate or move our attention forward (the other two heads of the dog). In all states of introspection and contemplation, the Cerberus reflects the dark and unknown parts of self that are necessary to explore and incorporate before the experience of wholeness or individuality can be actualized. In states of introspection, it is essential to own and express the inherent values and ethics that are within, in order to be able to express them externally. This quality of expression is reflected by the Hermit's burgundy cloak, an Egyptian symbol of the color of blood which represents the inherent integrity and honesty within each individual.

The Hermit is the *Virgo* card which is symbolized by all the wheat in the background of this symbol. Virgo is the astrological sign that is committed to attending to details, organization, and beauty. Contemplative states remind us of the beauty and *the pattern integrity* of who we are. How we attend to details and organizing our lives reveals the basic nature of who we are and who we are not.

The Orphic Egg (the egg wrapped with a serpent) represents the capacity to give birth to new physical and spiritual forms. The

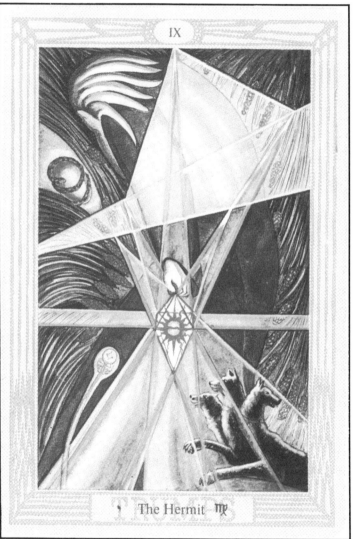

THE PRINCIPLE OF COMPLETION, INTROSPECTION AND SPACE

Cerberus asks us to complete unfinished business tied with the past so we are free to give birth to new forms in the present (the Orphic Egg). The Hermit represents transitional states of completion and initiation that are experienced both internally and externally. This symbol is that state of consciousness associated with introspection and contemplation. It is not so much the need to be alone as it is the need for emotional, psychological, and environmental space. The lighted wheat kernel or illuminated spermatozoa reflects the Hermit's need to experience that which is meaningful and significant, or if not, would prefer to be alone. The Hermit is the wise person who leads and facilitates others in the outer world from that which has been directly experienced.

The Hermit as Life-Time Symbol

For those people whose birthday adds up to the number 18 or 9, the Hermit is your life-time spiritual symbol. You have a deep regard for order and harmony in your life which is represented by the Virgo aspect of this symbol. You have a deep love for quietude and time spent alone. You can be around many people and situations as long as you have a feeling of psychological, emotional, and environmental space. You will withdraw and be like a Hermit under two conditions: 1) whenever you feel limited, restricted or restrained, you will leave and take the space that you need; claustrophobic situations are unbearable for you; and 2) whenever situations become too chaotic, disharmonious, and disorganized, you will remove yourself because of the inherent love of balance, beauty, and harmony that you revere and desire in your life.

People will put you in leadership positions whether you want to be there or not because of the respect and integrity that you command and model. You are unwilling to communicate or lead in any situation where you have not had direct experience of some kind.

You want to make sure that old business from the past is complete before you move forward, which is symbolized by the three-headed Cerberus. You are gifted in assisting others in making transitions either in completing and ending situations (the Cerberus) or initiating and starting new beginnings (the Orphic Egg, the snake wrapping the egg).

Virgo people in your life (anyone born August 21 – September 21) reflect your abilities for creating beauty, organizing and systemizing things, and bringing balance and harmony into situations. Older people in your life represent the inherent archetype of the wise person which is an important part of your basic nature. At different times in your life, older people will appear to present important opportunities or will be important mentors to your growth and development.

You are a natural way-shower and lantern-bearer to people in transitions and in helping others to discover and honor the internal essence of who they are. Hermit people live and model their spirituality and are not prone to talk about spiritual issues randomly. You are deeply philosophical and value the time that you have to be alone in activities that give you comfort and nourishment.

Whenever you have the Hermit as growth symbol, it is a good time to complete any unfinished business from the past. Hermit years involve unexpected desires to create times for retreats, silence, and contemplation. It is a time to organize things, attend to details, and release that which you have outgrown or that which is no longer useable.

During a Hermit year, you may want to resolve old and new issues with Virgo people in your life; or in the month of Virgo, you might find yourself completing and initiating projects or relationships. New opportunities from older people in your life or from Virgo people may present themselves for your consideration.

The Hermit year is an especially good year for expressing yourself through your hands, either through creative endeavors or through healing. This will also be a year where you will be asked to inspire and motivate others, or may be seen as a lantern-bearer or wayshower; or the exact opposite may be true, this may be a period where you may want to be alone or experience time for indepth work or contemplation.

The Hermit as a Growth Symbol

The Hermit best supports the process of completing unfinished business tied with the past. It is the archetype that assists contemplation and honors individual needs for space. If you choose to bring more beauty, balance, and organization into your life, the Hermit is the symbol that can motivate you to execute those qualities in your life. Through meditation and creative visualization, the Hermit allows you to get in touch with the inherent wise person within.

The Hermit as a Visual Affirmation and Meditative Symbol

> *I enjoy the feeling of completion and resolution.*
>
> *I enjoy exploring my inner worlds in meditation and times alone.*
>
> *I value that which is meaningful and significant.*
>
> *I will not compromise that which is important to me.*

Sample Affirmations To Use While Looking at The Hermit

Whenever you pull this card or find yourself continually drawn toward it, it represents a deep desire to follow that which is extremely meaningful and heartfelt for you. The Hermit reminds you to complete unfinished business and to reorganize and structure your life in ways that will be more harmonious and aligned with your basic nature. This symbol can represent your need to either complete or initiate things with important older people or Virgo people in your life who are significant. You will want things to be meaningful or significant, or you would rather be alone. It may be a time where it is important for you to assume leadership positions only if you can draw upon and reflect your own direct experience and wisdom.

The Hermit as an Outer Mirror

**Other Symbols
that Are Aspects of
The Hermit**

The four nines of the deck are aspects of the Hermit. States of contemplation and introspection will always have us confront the inner critic and judge which is reflected by the Nine of Swords (self-cruelty). Once we are able to face, embrace, and confront the critical nature within, the rewards are emotional happiness (the Nine of Cups), spiritual strength (the Nine of Wands), and external gain in all aspects of our external life (the Nine of Disks).

The Moon (the number 18 which adds up to the number 9, the Hermit's number) is the external expression of the Hermit into the world. The Moon is the major symbol of the power of daily choosing either to be authentic and true to your self-expression or to be dutiful and perhaps abandon yourself. This choice is represented by the two pillars on the card. The Moon reminds us that we will shine in our unedited brilliance if we choose to honor the core of who we are, which is represented by the Hermit. When we honor the core of who we are, everyone sees the full glory and light of who we are, our authentic selves which is reflected by the Moon symbol. *(See the Hermit constellation in Section VI for additional information.)*

**The Gifts and
Challenges for
Persons whose
Life-Time
Personality
Symbol Is
The Hermit**

Gifts:	Challenges:
Nine of Cups (Happiness)	Nine of Swords (Self- Cruelty; Criticalness)
Nine of Wands (Strength)	
Nine of Disks (Gain)	
The Moon (Authenticity)	
The Hermit (Introspection)	

WHEEL OF FORTUNE

All prosperity begins in the mind and is dependent only upon the full use of our creative imagination.

– Ruth Ross, *Prospering Woman*

is the universal principle of abundance, prosperity and expansion. In astrological terms this is Jupiter, the planet of luck, opportunity, and abundance. This symbol reminds us that like the goddess Fortuna in Roman mythology that we can turn our lives in more fortunate and positive directions by being objective like the Sphinx, flexible like the monkey, and reaching for new opportunities and ways to express our creative power like the crocodile. The stars exploding into lightning bolts represent the experience of awakening to the possibilities that can turn our lives in more positive and expansive directions. Often these experiences are referred to as the *aha!* or peak experience or that light bulb effect where we expand and feel inspired. The swirls in the background are a reminder that expansion and abundance come with the willingness to change and keep things moving by taking risks and being open to new opportunities.

THE PRINCIPLE OF OPPORTUNITY, BREAKTHROUGH AND PROSPERITY

**The Wheel of
Fortune
as Life-Time
Symbol**

The Wheel of Fortune is the life-time creative symbol for people whose birthday adds up to 19 or 1. With this symbol as your life-time creative symbol, you are stimulated by that which is creative and original. You are inspired by doing something creative that has not been done before, or if it has been done before, you see ways in which that idea can be put into another context that has not been considered. Inherently within your nature is a desire to explore that which is pioneering, futuristic, and ahead of its time. Like a sixth sense, you can readily assess what is financially or creatively viable as an opportunity and that which is not. You are flexible and resilient like the monkey and are able to see new possibilities and opportunites for creative expression like the crocodile, and its keys.

**The Wheel of
Fortune
as a Growth
Symbol**

In your Wheel of Fortune year (any year where your birthday plus the current year adds up to 10), is the best year to open to unexpected opportunities, to turn your life in more fortunate positive directions, and to grow and expand in new ways. It is a year to actively turn your life in new directions and to be open to abundance in all aspects of your life. The only thing that could stop the Wheel of Fortune would be to adhere to old patterns of doing things the same way (the opposite of the crocodile), to be rigid and inflexible (the opposite of the monkey), and to be judgmental, opinionated and attached to certain beliefs and ways of doing things (the opposite of the Sphinx).

Financial opportunities or unexpected windfalls could occur in this year, but most likely they occur only because you are open to the possibility or are actively trying to create situations of more prosperity and opportunity in your life.

**The Wheel of
Fortune
as a Visual
Affirmation and
Meditative Symbol**

The Wheel of Fortune is the best symbol to use to reinforce the intention of increasing abundance, good fortune, and prosperity in your life. It is the archetype that can allow your life to turn in more fortunate positive directions if you are willing to grow and expand. Through meditation and creative visualization, the Wheel of Fortune assists your affirmation and intention of multi-level prosperity in your life internally and externally.

**Sample
Affirmations
To Use While
Looking at
The Wheel of
Fortune**

I am a prosperous individual.

I enjoy manifesting internal abundance externally.

I am flexible during periods of change.

I am a flexible, objective, and open-minded individual.

Abundance which created me is what I am.

When you pull this symbol or find yourself continually drawn toward it, it represents that you are actively open to turning your life in more fortunate and positive directions. During the next ten weeks or the next ten months, you have Jupiterian possibilities of creating new possibilities and fortune in your life. It is a time to be open to unexpected creative and financial opportunities. You are reminded that only your fixed opinions, routine habits, and unopenness will create lack rather than abundance.

The Wheel of Fortune as an Outer Mirror

The Wheel of Fortune is an important aspect of the Magician constellation. The Wheel of Fortune (the number 10 adds up to 1, which is the Magician) reflects to us the opportunities and abundance that are available to us by using our communication skills (The Magician). Abundance and opportunity abound when we express our ideas clearly (The Ace of Swords); when we follow what has heart and meaning (The Ace of Cups); when we are authentic and expressive of the truth of who we are (The Ace of Wands); and when internally and externally we experience the unlimited possiblities of who we are (The Ace of Disks). The Wheel of Fortune is the accumulation of creatively expressing ourselves (The Magician) in unlimited and inspirational ways mentally (Ace of Swords), emotionally (Ace of Cups), spiritually (Ace of Wands), and physically (Ace of Disks). *(See the Magician constellation in Section VI for additional information.)*

Other Symbols that Are Aspects of The Wheel of Fortune

Gifts:	Challenges:
Wheel of Fortune (enhance creativity and fortune)	To trust and execute that which is original and could be fortunate for self and others
The Magician (Communication)	
Ace of Swords (Inspired Thinking)	
Ace of Cups (Love with Wisdom)	Ten of Swords (Ruin)
Ace of Wands (Truth; Authenticity)	Ten of Wands (Oppression)
Ace of Disks (Success)	
The Sun (Teamwork; Partnership)	

The Gifts and Challenges for Persons whose Life-Time Personality Symbol Is The Wheel of Fortune

To me, wholeness is the key to aliveness. It is more than just physical vitality, it is radiance, coming from being at one with yourself and your experience. Life then flows through you and radiates from you.

— Richard Moss,
How Shall I Live

STRENGTH/ LUST

is representative of the universal myth known as the "Beauty and the Beast." This symbol represents the beauty that we all possess in our gifts, talents, and resources which can quell the beasts or demons within our nature. Here is the picture of the beauty that has tamed and reigned the beasts within (the multi-headed lion). She has an inherent faith within herself which is symbolized by the fire-urn that she looks to and holds. She has overcome old fears tied with the past, the grayed and darkened figures and objects in the background of the symbol. She rides Leo, the lion, the astrological sign of creative power. It is through utilizing our creative gifts and talents, like Leo, the lion, that we can tame and reign the beasts within.

Lust comes from the root word *lustre*. We cannot be in our lustre and radiance if we are not also in our strength. People who exhibit strength also exhibit an inherent lustre or radiance. Strength and lustre are two qualities that are often inseparable. In other decks, this symbol is referred to as Strength, the beauty that tames the beast. Within Egyptian hieroglyphs, strength and lustre are synonymous, or aspects of each other.

THE PRINCIPLE OF STRENGTH, PASSION AND LUSTRE

The Lust/Strength Symbol as Life-Time Symbol

This is the life-time personality symbol of those people whose birthday adds up to the number 11. This is often the personality symbol of people who are 50 years and older or for people at this time who were being born in the late 1960's or 1970's. People with this archetype for their personality expression are creative. They are drawn to the creative and performing arts or may use their creativity in multiple arenas where they are in the limelight or highly regarded for the originality that they bring to traditional settings or situations.

Lust/Strength people are charismatic, radiant, and creative. They are determined to handle all situations creatively as possible. These people exhibit strength and unusual risk-taking. Often they hold strong beliefs that things will unfold like the flowers and renew and regenerate themselves like the snakes at the top of the card.

It is through your creativity and your strength that you are able to renew and regenerate yourself, like the haloed snake which serves as the lion's tail. This symbol is a reminder that the creative process, as well as our strength, is continually changing like the snake that sheds its own skin.

The Lust/Strength Symbol as a Growth Symbol

During your Strength year (any year where your birthday plus the current year adds up to 11), you may find yourself taming and reigning old beasts within. It is a year of renewed passion for all things in life, including the physical. You recapture and regain that sense of wonder and awe about life, and feel that you have overcome old fears tied with the past. It is a year where the creative arts or the performing arts may be of interest to you.

Leo people in your life become important mirrors about your own potentials for creative expression or you may find yourself directed to resolve old issues with Leo people (anyone born July 21 – August 21).

Your Lust/Strength year is a year where you tap unlimited resources of strength within your own nature. It is a year where you experience being even more of who you are.

The Lust/Strength Symbol as a Visual Affirmation and Meditative Symbol

The Lust/Strength symbol is the archetype that can assist your process of trusting that you have the strength to tame and reign the beasts within. Lust comes from the word *lustre* and in order to have lustre in your life you need to have strength, and visa versa. The Lust/Strength symbol facilitates creativity that honors and reveals our passion and strength. Through meditation and creative visualization with this symbol, you can assist your process of honoring and experiencing the inherent strength that is within your nature.

Sample Affirmations To Use While Looking at The Lust/Strength Archetype

I enjoy expressing my energy, vitality and enthusiasm in all that I experience.

I am an individual of character and strength.

I have unlimited creative resources from which to tap and express.

The Lust/Strength Symbol as an Outer Mirror

Whenever you pull the Lust/Strength card, it is a symbol that you are expressing your full creativity and strength. You have tamed and reigned the beasts within and have a strong faith and trust in your abilities.

With Leo people in your life, you have the ability to stay in your strength and not abandon yourself; or Leo people could mirror to you your own creativity that wants to be expressed unconditionally.

Other Symbols that Are Aspects of The Lust/Strength Symbol

Lust/Strength is an important aspect of The High Priestess constellation, which are all the numbers in the deck which add up to the number 2. Lust/Strength is the external expression of trusting one's intuition (The High Priestess) by utilizing good judgment (The Aeon) which comes from making choices that give us peace of mind (Two of Swords), trusting our feelings (Two of Cups – love), making expansive changes that are stable (Two of Disks – changes) and can create a greater sense of balance and dominion in your life (Two of Wands – dominion).

Strength is that capacity to radiate peace, love, and dominion as we make creative changes in our life by making good judgments. *(See the High Priestess constellation in Section VI for additional information.)*

The Gifts and Challenges for Persons whose Life-Time Personality Symbol Is The Lust/Strength Symbol

Gifts:	Challenges:
High Priestess (Independence)	To express one's strength creatively.
Two of Swords (Peace)	
Two of Cups (Love)	
Two of Wands (Dominion)	
Two of Disks (Change)	
Aeon (Good Judgment)	
Lust/Strength	

THE HANGED MAN

The world would have you agree with its dismal dream of limitation.
But the light would have you soar
like the eagle of your sacred visions.

– Alan Cohen

represents the universal principle of recognizing and awakening to repetitive patterns that bind, limit, and restrict our growth and evolution. The Hanged Man is the pattern-breaker. In order to break limiting patterns, it is often necessary to take a distinctly different posture, or stance, such as turning ourselves up-side-down to get another view of a restrictive pattern or stuck place in consciousness that is being experienced.

The Hanged Man represents that state of consciousness which requires that we move beyond ego and trust the deeper aspects of who we are. This is the state of surrender and acceptance which is the preliminary step required before we can free ourselves from destructive and limiting patterns that we experience in our lives. Often this symbol might be viewed as the crucifixion of the ego or of egoic patterns which are no longer constructive. The universal symbol associated with repetitive patterns is the labyrinth, represented by the squares within the squares within the background of this card. To use modern-day terms, the Hanged Man reminds us that our "hang-ups" can either prevent our growth and evolution or they can serve to teach us where we need to free ourselves from undue self-imposed limitations. This symbol ultimately teaches us that there are always many more options, solutions, and perspectives to consider than those in which we are currently invested.

Often, when we experience ourselves being bound or limited, there is a sense of being numb, asleep, depressed, or blind. The sleeping snakes remind us that nothing is renewed or regenerated when we are fixated or stuck. The Egyptian Ankh (the reversed cross holding the foot of the Hanged Man) is a

THE PRINCIPLE OF SURRENDER, BREAKING OLD PATTERNS

symbol of unlimited life force, constantly accessible for creative use. Self-imposed limitations or repetitive patterns can make us feel bound, or nailed, into impossible situations with the feeling of having no options, no way out. The solution is found in our willingness to surrender to a greater sense of faith and trust within our nature.

The Hanged Man as Life-Time Symbol

For those individuals whose birthday adds up to the number 12, this is your life-time personality symbol. For persons who are currently over the age of 50, and for the new-borns, this symbol is your personality symbol; a symbol of your outer expression. If this is your symbol, you will always be committed to looking at situations and persons from many different postures and perspectives. You will find it difficult to limit or restrict yourself in any way. You are a natural pattern-breaker. You will constantly assist others to look at life and their problems from different perspectives. Comedians are natural pattern-breakers. Through humor, as a comedian does, you may assist others to take a different view or perspective of their current fixations or stuck places. Or, like a psychologist, you may "reframe" a problem in such a way that the person can see the problem differently. Your greatest inherent gift will be that of constantly freeing yourself from self-imposed limitations and, as a result, you will have the ability to assist others in this process as well.

The Hanged Man as a Growth Symbol

The Hanged Man is your growth card during the year that your birthday, plus the current year, adds up to the number 12. During this year, people from the past will make contact with you. These people will function as important mirrors to show you those patterns from the past that you have or have not broken or released.

Hanged Man years are the best years to actively break destructive patterns that bind, limit or restrict your own growth and development. It is a year where you will experience greater compassion and acceptance of self by releasing limiting egoic needs and surrendering to the deeper love and wisdom that wants to be expressed within your spiritual nature.

The Hanged Man as a Visual Affirmation and Meditative Symbol

The Hanged Man reinforces the intention to break old patterns that bind, limit, or restrict your nature in any way. This is the best symbol to evoke in meditation or to use in creative visualization processes to assist your ability to take a different posture or stance on old issues. The Hanged Man, when consciously used, is an archetype that allows you to see who you are beyond ego. It is the symbol that facilitates freedom from limiting and unconstructive patterns.

Sample Affirmations To Use While Looking at The Hanged Man

I enjoy looking at the same situation from as many different perspeactives as possible.

I value breaking ineffective old patterns.

I trust and have faith in the deep essence of who I am.

I surrender to the higher design and to God's will.

When you pull this card or find yourself constantly drawn toward it, it represents that you have awakened to, and have recognized, limiting patterns that need to be broken. Since this is a trump card, you are determined to triumph in becoming unstuck or in releasing yourself from self-imposed limitations, fixed perspectives, and unresolved "hang-ups." Within the next twelve weeks or the next twelve months, you will see clearly restrictive patterns in yourself that you will be resolved to act upon and break. It may be a time when you may consider freeing yourself from destructive personal patterns or relationships. The Hanged Man represents a time to surrender and move beyond egoic needs in order to trust the deeper spiritual wisdom within your nature that wants to be expressed.

The Hanged Man as an Outer Mirror

The Hanged Man is the Empress archetype (love with wisdom) that is expressed externally toward ourselves and applied in the world without limitation or restriction. The Hanged Man reveals that part of ourselves that is willing to love ourselves enough to break limiting or destructive patterns within our personality. The Hanged Man is willing to sacrifice, or "make sacred," egoic needs in order to surrender to the inherent love and wisdom within us that wants to be expressed in the world in unlimited and undistorted ways. The Hanged Man (the number 12 adds up to 3) is the outer expression of the internal Empress (the number 3) that is within us. By releasing the wounded parts of the past that we still hold in our minds (Three of Swords), we are able to express our feelings abundantly (Three of Cups) from a place of knowing our priorities and commitments (Three of Disks). Love with wisdom (The Empress) comes from a place of integrity, which is the alignment of mind, heart, and action in all that we do (Three of Wands). When we release our limiting and destructive patterns (The Hanged Man), we are free to openly express our inherent love with wisdom (The Empress) in the world (The Universe). *(See The Empress constellation in Section VI for additional information.)*

Other Symbols that Are Aspects of The Hanged Man

Gifts:

The Empress (Love with Wisdom)
Three of Cups (Abundance)
Three of Wands (Integrity; Virtue)
Three of Disks ("Works"; Priorities)
The Universe (The Expression of Love in the World)

Challenges:

Three of Swords
  (Past Sorrow)
The Hanged Man
  (Breaking Patterns)

The Gifts and Challenges for Persons whose Life-Time Personality Symbol Is The Hanged Man

Birth and death are not two different states,
but they are different aspects of the same state.

— Gandhi

DEATH / REBIRTH

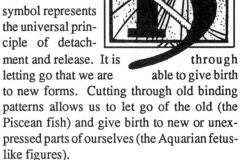

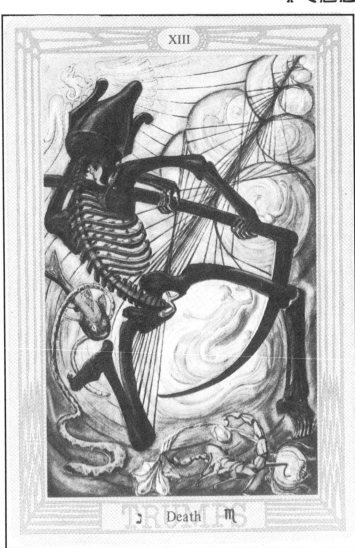

THE PRINCIPLE OF LETTING GO
AND MOVING FORWARD
RELEASE/DETACHMENT

symbol represents the universal principle of detachment and release. It is through letting go that we are able to give birth to new forms. Cutting through old binding patterns allows us to let go of the old (the Piscean fish) and give birth to new or unexpressed parts of ourselves (the Aquarian fetus-like figures).

Death is the *Scorpio* symbol in the deck. Scorpio has three symbols which represent three types of transformation, or death/rebirth, stages: the scorpion represents that part of ourselves that is willing to protect or take care of ourselves during times of change and letting go; the snake reminds us that in order to transform, we must let go of old identities in order to be able to express new ones, much like a snake that sheds its skin; and the phoenix, or eagle, reflects the over-all vision and perspective that is needed in order to become even more of who we are. The bird within our nature is the spiritual essence that is always free, vital, and irrepressible. It is the part of our nature that prompts us to let go so that we can give birth to greater parts of who we are.

The skeleton is the inherent structure within our body that allows movement and change within our self-expression. The bones of who we are represents our ancestral lineage and our present commitment to grow and evolve through repeated death/rebirth experiences.

The crown is a universal representation of expanded consciousness. It is humankind's imitation of the halo-effect. All cultures have crowns and headdresses. Here, the crown is the Egyptian funeral headdress with a phoenix emerging from it to remind us that death, itself, is a rebirth experience. The sickle, or scythe, is a harvesting tool. It has the capacity to cut through things for the purpose of yielding harvest. The Death/Rebirth experience is one that reminds us that by letting go (the wilted flower), we are able to allow some new life to emerge and express itself (the sea kelp).

For those individuals whose birthday adds up to the number 13, this is your life-time personality symbol. For people who are currently over the age of 50 and for new-borns, this symbol is your personality symbol, a symbol of your outer expression in the world. For you, you will always be committed to the process of transformation and change, particularly that aspect of letting go and moving forward. During your life, you may find yourself assisting others through divorce, handling the loss of loved ones, or encouraging people to initiate new experiences or, literally, midwifing the birth of babies.

Scorpio people in your life (anyone born October 21 – November 21) will function as important mirrors of your own commitment to deeply change beyond family or cultural conditioning.

For you, you recognize that detachment is a form of objectivity that includes caring. Since you know the pain and suffering that attachment can cause, you are willing to assist others in teaching or modeling how they can love objectively and let go when necessary. You have the ability to experience life and relationships deeply, and also have the ability to let go or release situations and people when it is no longer appropriate or *right action* to stay attached.

The Death Card as Life-Time Symbol

Death/Rebirth is the symbol for the year where your birthday and the current year adds up to the number 13. This year does not usually mean your own literal death; on the contrary, it is during this year that you can experience the death of an old identity, the ending of certain types of relationships (divorce may occur during this year), the closure of certain creative projects or types of work, and simultaneously the desire to initiate and start new relationships, projects, careers, and expression of new parts of oneself.

This symbol can represent the loss of a Scorpio relationship (anyone born October 21 – November 21) or in the month of Scorpio there could be the loss of important people in your life or the experience of relationship shifts and changes. More than anything else, this symbol as a growth symbol requires that you let go of that which you are unnecessarily attached to and give birth to new experiences in your life. It literally is the year for you to shed that which you have out-grown or over-worked.

The Death Card as a Growth Symbol

The Death/Rebirth symbol facilitates the process of letting go and moving forward. If you have difficulties in letting go, this symbol will assist your process of detachment. Through creative visualization and evoking the Death/Rebirth symbol in your meditations, this symbol assists your process of letting go of old identities, life-styles, relationships, and careers so that you can give birth to new forms.

The Death Symbol as a Visual Affirmation and Meditative Symbol

**Sample
Affirmations
To Use While
Looking at
The Death/Rebirth
Symbol**

I am excited about growing and becoming even more of who I am.

I let go of people and situations with ease and dignity.

Detachment is a form of objectivity that includes caring.

Every ending is an opportunity for something new to emerge.

**The Death Symbol
as an
Outer Mirror**

When you pull this symbol or find yourself continually drawn toward it, it represents your capacity to change and transform at deep levels. You are actively involved in an archetypal process of letting go of old patterns or relationships so that you can experience and express new parts of yourself.

This symbol can also represent that you may be in the process of restructuring your relationships with Scorpio people in your life (anyone born October 21 – November 21) or that in the month of Scorpio you may be required to let go of certain situations so that you can be free to move forward in new directions either personally or professionally.

**Other Symbols
that Are Aspects of
The Death/Rebirth
Symbol**

The Death/Rebirth symbol is the changing expression of personal power and leadership in the world. The Death card (the number 13 adds up to 4) is the externalized expression of the internal Emperor within us. In order to own our full power and inherent leadership (The Emperor), we must be willing to change and transform ourselves continually (The Death/Rebirth symbol). All change requires that we let go in order to experience the new or under-expressed parts of ourselves (Death/Rebirth). Our full power and leadership (The Emperor) is required during times of death/rebirth. It is during times of change that we must know what our boundaries and limits are (Four of Disks), that we be open to negotiation and truce (Four of Swords), that we follow what has heart and meaning (Four of Cups), and that we remember that we are essentially whole and complete (Four of Wands). *(See the Emperor Constellation in Section VI for additional information)*

**The Gifts and
Challenges for
Persons whose
Life-Time
Personality
Symbol Is
The Death/Rebirth
Symbol**

Gifts:

The Fool (Transpersonal
  Expression of Courage)
The Emperor (Leadership;
  Authority)
Four of Swords (Truce)
Four of Cups (Luxury)
Four of Disks (Power)
Four of Wands (Completion)
Death/Rebirth (Desire to Change)

Challenges:

Death/Rebirth
  (Detachment with Caring;
  Letting go and
  moving forward)

The point is...to unify and harmonize the opposites, both positive and negative, by discovering a ground which transcends and encompasses them both.

– Ken Wilbur, *No Boundary*

ART/ TEMPERANCE

symbol represents the universal principle of integration, synthesis, and synergy. In order to come into the artistry of who we are, it is important to balance the apparent paradoxes, oppositions, or polarities within our nature. Every symbol on this card represents the union of opposition which creates something new. Synergy is the union of two or more principles which combined, can create a greater whole. Art/Temperance is the integration of opposition in order to become even more of who we are. Fire and water are merged to create steam. This same metaphor is pictured by Leo, the lion; a fire sign drinks from the caldron with Scorpio, the eagle or phoenix, a water sign. Together they drink from the caldron which contains air, or the life force. On the caldron itself is another union of polarity represented by the bird and the skull – the union of life and death which is a prevalent experience for all humankind. In the background, the great sun disk unifies with its polar opposite, the crescent moons, from which the spinning stars at the top and sides of this card are created.

This is the *Sagittarius* symbol which is represented by the arrow going up the central part of the figure. Sagittarius reminds us it is through our life visions and dreams that we fully express the artistry of who we are as well as resolve any apparent conflicts or opposition within our nature.

The light and dark of our nature needs to be incorporated before we can fully express the whole of who we are. This is represented by the light and dark arms and faces which, when combined, create the balanced and tempered Being.

THE PRINCIPLE OF INTEGRATION; SYNTHESIS; SYNERGY

The Art/Temperance Symbol as Life-Time Symbol

For those whose birthday adds up to the number 14, Art/Temperance is a symbol that represents your life-time personality symbol, a symbol of your external expression in the world. Your inherent nature is one of bringing together polarities, oppositions, and paradoxes in order to create a greater whole. You will find that artistry of any kind holds within it the synthesis of many parts, which are simultaneously paradoxical, but when brought together create symmetry and balance. You are a visionary. You can see possibilities and combinations that many others would never consider. You are a natural alchemist constantly seeing that two or more is always a greater combination than one. For you, it would be important to merge or negotiate rather than stay in one fixed perspective or polarity. You have a natural ability to temper and balance situations which seem impossible.

Sagittarius people in your life (anyone born November 21–December 21) function as mirrors of your own dreams and visions that want to be applied in the world; or the months of Sagittarius could be inspirational and integrative times for you.

The Art/Temperance Symbol as a Growth Symbol

Art/Temperance is the symbol that you experience during the year where your birthday and the current year add up to the number 14. This becomes a year where it becomes important for you to temper and integrate seeming polarities and paradoxes in your life. It is a year when things begin to "fall into place" or that you have a feeling that "things are finally coming together."

Art/Temperance years may find you drawn to artistically expressing yourself in ways that you have not previously considered. It is definitely a year where beauty, balance, negotiation, and networking are important qualities that want to be expressed more fully in your life.

During this year, it is also the best time to resolve issues that you may have with Sagittarius people; or the month of Sagittarius (November 21–December 21) may be the best time to implement new dreams and visions.

The Art/Temperance Symbol as a Visual Affirmation and Meditative Symbol

The Art/Temperance symbol is the best symbol for supporting the integration and synthesis of polarities or oppositions in your life. If you are wanting to integrate two or more important issues, this is the archetype which reinforces the synergetic principle where two or more things coming together create a greater whole. Evoking the Art/Temperance symbol in meditation, or through conscious intention, can assist your process of experiencing your life as an art form that is both tempered and balanced.

Sample Affirmations To Use While Looking at The Art/Temperance Symbol

I am a creative, well-integrated individual.

I am as strong in my magnetic nature as I am in my dynamic nature.

I express the artistry of who I am in states of balance and integration.

I experience temperance when I equally value the light and dark within my own nature.

Whenever you pull the Art/Temperance symbol or find yourself drawn toward it, it symbolizes that in the next fourteen weeks or the next fourteen months would be an excellent time to bring two or more gifts and talents together in order to create something greater. It is a time to integrate and synthesize apparent polarities or oppositions that you are experiencing personally or professionally. You may find that aesthetics, integration, and the arts become important qualities that you want to incorporate more fully into your life.

Whatever life dream or visions that are important to you may be actualized, or may fall into place, within the next fourteen weeks or fourteen months, depending on your desire and intention to realize them.

During the month of Sagittarius or through Sagittarius people, you may find that you are able to bring two or more parts of your life together in ways that create a greater whole. It is also a good time to resolve issues with Sagittarius people in your life.

The Art/Temperance Symbol as an Outer Mirror

The Art/Temperance symbol is the externalized expression of the Hierophant card. (Art is the number 14, which adds up to the number 5, the Hierophant.) The capacity to integrate and balance varied parts of ourselves and our lives (Art/Temperance) is a result of listening to our inner teacher and instinctive faith which comes from deep within (The Hierophant). It is through the learning and teaching that we experience in our family and extended family (The Hierophant) that highlights what needs to be tempered and balanced in our life (Art/Temperance). We are tempered, and discover the artistry of who we are when we face and move through fear of defeat (Five of Swords), disappointment (Five of Cups), anxiety and strife (Five of Wands,), and worry (Five of Disks). The integration of our gifts and weaknesses (Art/Temperance) allows us to inspire and motivate others to face their challenges from their greater sense of Being (The Hierophant). *(See the Hierophant constellation in Section VI for additional information.)*

Other Symbols that Are Aspects of The Art/Temperance Symbol

Gifts:	Challenges:
Hierophant (Spiritual Faith)	Five of Swords (Fear of Defeat)
Art/Temperance (Integration/ Synthesis)	Five of Cups (Disappointment)
	Five of Wands (Anxiety/Strife)
	Five of Disks (Worry)

The Gifts and Challenges for Persons whose Life-Time Personality Symbol Is The Art/Temperance Symbol

The difference between a comedy and a tragedy is that in a comedy the characters figure out reality in time to do something about it.

– Bennett W. Goodspeed

THE DEVIL

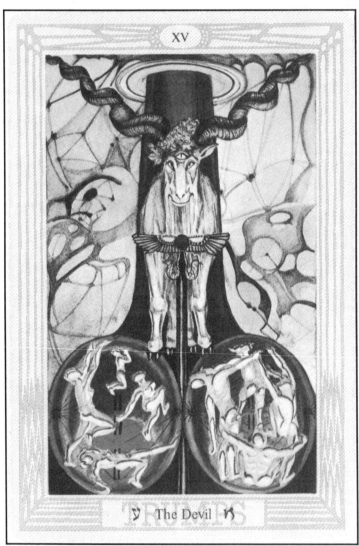

XV

The Devil

THE PRINCIPLE OF MIRTH/HUMOR AT WHAT 'BEDEVILS' US

represents the universal principle of mirth combined with stability. This is the only card in the entire deck which has undergone a transformation within itself. During Greek mythology, this symbol was Pan, half-man and half-goat, the God of Merriment and Sensuality. In Egyptian mythology, this symbol was Ra, the Sun Diety, a symbol of life force and energy. During the Middle Ages, there was a backlash to the panistic cults and the archetype of the devil was created. The panistic goat was changed into the devil; and, ironically, devil spelled backwards is *l-i-v-e-d*. During the Middle Ages the panistic activities of people "living-it-up" were considered hedonistic; therefore, in order to quell those activities they had to be rendered "evil" or made wrong in order to make way for new belief systems that were emerging at that time.

The Devil/Pan archetype represents the need to face whatever we might consider our bedevilments or problems with the tenacity of Capricorn, the goat, or with humor like Pan or Bacchus from Greek mythology. We can face and move through our bedevilments (the webbings on the sides of the card) with sure-footedness like Capricorn, the goat, and with the mirth and humor of Pan (the smiling goat). This symbol reminds us that if we take our problems or bedevilments too seriously that they can ensnare us and take us off balance. The Devil/Pan symbol represents the need to hold on to both the qualities of mirth, stability and our centeredness in facing real or imagined problems (the webbings or spider-like veils) so that we won't be thrown off balance.

Capricorn, the goat, is willing to look at internal issues (the third eye of the goat) and external bedevilments (both eyes open looking straight ahead). With the Eye of Horus staff, the Egyptian staff of vision and intuition, we can protect ourselves from other people's considerations about what we are doing or not doing (the figures within the circles at the bottom of the card). The four female figures and the four male figures at the base of the card also represent an inherent need during times of bedevilment to use both our magnetic, receptive abilities portrayed by the female figures as well as our dynamic initiatory abilities represented by the male figures. Creative power is the ability to combine both the genetic balances of magnetism and dynamism within our natures.

This symbol also represents the principle of sensuality and sexuality or the law of attraction and resonance. The phallus and the testicles represent the potency of creative power that is within each of us that wants to be expressed with mirth and tangibility. It is important in our lives to follow that which we are drawn toward or that which inspires us personally or professionally. The laws of attraction and resonance motivate and evoke unlimited creative energies within us that want to be used.

Saturn, the double ringed planet, rules the sign of Capricorn, the goat. The rings of Saturn are seen at the top of the card. Saturn is the planet most associated with balance, discipline, and doing things step by step. Capricorn is the astrological sign of the goat known for tenacity, productivity and achievement. It is in our capacity to follow our bliss or what has resonance for us that we can execute the discipline to bring into form our creative visions with mirth and tangible results.

For those individuals whose birthday adds up to the number 15, the Devil/Pan symbol represents your life-time personality symbol, or symbol for your external expression in the world. With this symbol as your life-time personality expression, it is important for you to maintain your sense of humor and your productivity. You are a practical person and yet you know how to have a good time. People will enjoy being around you, not only for your earthiness and appeal, but also for your sense of humor that is combined with practicality and productivity.

The Devil/Pan as Life-Time Symbol

You will be drawn to Capricorn people (anyone born December 21 – January 21) because they function as mirrors of your own capacities for achievement and for handling multiple responsibilities with grace. During Capricorn months, you are willing to face your own bedevilments or problems with mirth and sure-footedness as well as assist others with those that they may be facing.

You highly regard being able to face challenges by being open and receptive to creative options and by being dynamic and assertive in your execution of solutions. You are willing to look inward for guidance (the goat's third eye) and you are willing to see things as they are rather than as you want them to be (the fully opened goat eyes).

The Devil/Pan card is your growth symbol when your birthday and the current year add up to the number 15. It is the best year to resolve issues with Capricorn people in your life (anyone born December 21–January 21), or in the month of Capricorn it is important to handle personal or professional issues with humor and stability. It is also a reminder not to take things so seriously that they take you off balance. This is a year where you are required to maintain and sustain your sense of humor in all arenas of your life. It is a time where you find your creative

The Devil/Pan Card as a Growth Symbol

energies ignited to such a degree that you will find yourself attracted to creative people and to inspirational events or projects.

Devil/Pan years are years where you become more comfortable within your own body and sensuality. You may find yourself attracted to someone whereby you experience aspects of your sexuality that you had not previously experienced. It is a year where you discover that sexuality is a form of play and creative expression. Old beliefs about sexuality may be dropped during this year.

The Devil/Pan Symbol as a Visual Affirmation and Meditative Tool

The Devil/Pan symbol reinforces the ability to combine stability and humor in all aspects of life. If you are wanting to look at your *be-devilments* from a place of humor and solidity, this archetype assists your process of facing difficult issues in a centered way that carries with it the grace of humor. Through meditation or creative visualization, the Devil/Pan archetype can facilitiate the ability to move through challenging situations in a way that will not take you off balance. If you have a tendency to take things too seriously, this symbol reminds you of your ability to maintain a sense of humor about yourself and your process.

Sample Affirmations To Use While Looking at The Devil/Pan Archetype

I retain my sense of humor in areas of experience which be-devil me.

I enjoy my sensuality.

I am a vital, joyful, and grounded person.

Whether my problems are real or imagined, I can handle them realistically and mirthfully.

The Devil/Pan as an Outer Mirror

When you pull this symbol or find yourself continually drawn toward it, it represents that you are currently facing your bedevilments or problems with humor and sure-footedness. You may be resolving issues with Capricorn people with grace and humor and less willing to let yourself be thrown off balance by taking things too seriously. The month of Capricorn may be a time where you are required to maintain and sustain your sense of humor in all arenas of your life.

During the next fifteen weeks or the next fifteen months, you may find yourself attracted or drawn to creative people, projects, and inspirational events. It is the best time to follow your bliss and to trust that which has strong resonance and attraction for you.

The Devil/Pan symbol represents the externalized expression of The Lovers archetype. (The Devil/Pan's number is 15 which adds up to the number 6, The Lovers.) Many of our real and imagined problems and bedevilments occur in our personal and professional relationships (The Lovers). The Devil/Pan symbol reflects our willingness to look at our bedevilments in relationships with a creative and problem-solving attitude. By maintaining our sense of humor, we can continue to maintain balance within our relationships. Taking things too seriously will always take us off balance. If we can laugh at something that was once painful, we express the fundamental aspect of the Devil/Pan archetype. The Devil/Pan archetype is the reclamation of joy and the recommitment to that which inspires and uplifts our nature.

Relationships (The Lovers) always mirror to us internal relationships that we have with multiple parts of ourselves whether we are conscious of it or not. The relationship that we have with ourselves and others stays in balance and is successful (Six of Disks) if we maintain mental objectivity (Six of Swords), emotional playfulness (Six of Cups), and spiritual openness for co-created victories (Six of Wands). The Devil/Pan symbol reminds us that our relationships (The Lovers) are creative resources and invaluable teachers about our own internal and external bedevilments and talents. *(See the Lovers constellation in Section VI for additional information.)*

Other Symbols that Are Aspects of The Devil/Pan Archetype

Gifts:	Challenges:
Devil/Pan (Mirth; Stability)	Devil/Pan
The Lovers (Art and Craft of Relating)	(Bedevilments;
Six of Swords (Science of Mind)	Being too Serious)
Six of Cups (Pleasure)	
Six of Wands (Victory)	
Six of Disks (Success)	

The Gifts and Challenges for Persons whose Life-Time Personality Symbol Is The Devil/Pan

*I feel within me a consuming fire of heavenly love
which has burned up in my soul everything that was contrary to itself
and transformed me inwardly into its own nature.*

– William Law

THE TOWER

is a symbol of the universal principle of healing, renovation, and restoration. Because this card looks so violent, it has often been misinterpreted. The Tower is a symbol of the change and awakening that is required to dismantle that which is artificial, false-to-fact, or conditioned within our natures. The Oriental fire-eating dragon is the spiritual fire or life force that requires that we dismantle and restructure old forms within our personality (The Tower) so that that which is actual and true within our nature can be restored and expressed. Whatever is crystallized or not truly a part of our nature is burned or thrown out of our personality (The Tower). The four figures flying in the air are representative of old mental, emotional, intuitive, and physical ways of expressing oneself that are outmoded and are no longer a part of the authentic or essential Self.

The Eye of Horus, the opened and radiant eye at the top of the card, is an Egyptian symbol for the God of Perception. It represents the state of awakening and of seeing the deeper and authentic aspects of self. Once we begin to awaken we are required to come into alignment with the greater Being of who we are, which is symbolized by the Oriental fire-breathing dragon. Simultaneously, this process is one of restructuring old, artificial and out-grown forms of self in order to heal, renovate, and restore that which is actual and true within our nature. The haloed snake reminds us that renovation often is a process that is similar to that of a snake shedding an old skin in order to express more fully its new and expanded nature. The Egyptian snake with a halo reminds us that as we expand our consciousness (the halo) we are required to shed out-grown parts of ourselves like the snake when it sheds its skin.

XVI

꒓ The Tower ♂

THE PRINCIPLE OF RESTORATION
RENOVATION
DE-STRUCTURING OLD FORMS

The dove with the olive twig is a symbol of the inner peace that comes when we return to the essential and authentic aspects of who we are. This symbol reminds us that during times of inner and outer restoration processes, it is important to remember this line from the Deserata: "Be Gentle with Yourself."

For those individuals whose birthday adds up to the number 16 or 7, this symbol is your life-time personality symbol, a symbol of your external expression in the world. Inherently you have a natural ability to heal, renovate, and restore ideas, people, buildings, organizations, and environments. You can see what is working and what is not working; and you desire always to repair, rectify, and restore people, things or situations to a point that is definitely more balanced, beautiful, and in harmony with its authentic expression. You believe very much in the Prigogine principle that once an organism experiences chaos and disorder as a means of dismantling itself, the organism always reassembles itself to a more evolved and expanded structure.

The Tower as Life-Time Symbol

For you, it is important to have what you see come into form. Internally you are a natural architect, designer, and builder of ideas, forms, and visions. With people, you inherently sense what is in or out of balance. Healing is an art or subject that may interest you during different parts of your life; or spending time in nature as a means of getting in touch with your own nature may become very important to you.

The Tower is your growth symbol for the year when your birthday and the current year add up to the number 16. It is the best year to buy or renovate old buildings, cars, ideas, and projects. It is a year where you could experience a mystical experience or have the experience of waking up to who you really are. As a result, you may, through diet, exercise, or meditation, begin the process of renovating yourself so that you feel that your outer expression is in alignment with your internal nature. Externally you begin to dismantle that which is artificial, false-to-fact, or outmoded in your life. You shed things, people, and situations in order to restore what is true within your essential nature. You are no longer willing to support the dichotomy of experiencing your life as being externally full and internally empty; or being internally full and externally empty. During this year, you are determined to experience the alignment of internal and external fulfillment.

The Tower Card as a Growth Symbol

The Tower is the best symbol to use to facilitate any process associated with healing, renovation, and restoration. If you choose to dismantle that which is conditioned or no longer useful in your life, the Tower will assist your intention of de-structuring old forms and restoring that which is actual and true for you in your life. Through creative visualization and meditation with the Tower, you can reinforce your intention of renovating and healing aspects of yourself and your life.

The Tower Symbol as a Visual Affirmation and Meditative Tool

**Sample
Affirmations
To Use While
Looking at
The Tower**

I have a commitment to actualize who I really am.

My body is a temple for my spirit.

*I have the ability to naturally restore and heal
myself at all times.*

Who I think I am is a belief to be undone.

I am not inside my body; my body is inside me.

**The Tower
as an
Outer Mirror**

When you pull this symbol or find yourself continuously drawn toward it, you may be renovating different parts of your life personally and professionally during the next sixteen weeks or the next sixteen months. This is a time when you might consider healing and restoring yourself through diet, exercise, excursions in nature, and inner work. It definitely is a period where you are determined to eliminate from your life that which is false-to-fact, artificial, and no longer useful. You find yourself committed to simplifying and restoring your life to match who you are internally. Either through varied synchronicities, peak experiences, or external "wake-up-calls," you clearly see who you are and what you want in your life regardless of family or cultural conditioning. You are actively bringing your internal and external realities into alignment during this period.

**Other Symbols
that Are Aspects of
The Tower
Archetype**

The Tower is the external manifestation of the internal Chariot that is within us. (The Tower number 16 adds up to the number 7, which is the Chariot.) External processes of change (The Tower) are motivated and ignited by internal changes (The Chariot). During processes of change and renovation, it is important to have the courage to stay by what we value (Seven of Wands), which will allow us to move through those blocks which inhibit or delay change: debauch (Seven of Cups); futility (Seven of Swords), and fear of failure or success (Seven of Disks). When we are deeply willing to change (The Chariot), the results are transformation and restoration (the Tower). *(See the Chariot constellation in Section VI for additional information.)*

**The Gifts and
Challenges for
Persons whose
Life-Time
Personality
Symbol Is
The Tower**

Gifts:	Challenges
The Chariot (Change)	Seven of Swords (Futility)
The Tower (Restoration)	Seven of Cups (Debauch)
Seven of Wands (Valour)	Seven of Disks (Fear of Failure/Success)

We convince by our presence.

– Walt Whitman

THE STAR

is the universal principle of self-esteem and confidence. It is the state of radiance and confidence that is neither inflated or deflated. The quality of looking within and trusting what is there is symbolized by the figure looking toward the guiding star within the cup she holds. The word confidence comes from the root base *to confide*. Confidence is the ability to confide in and trust oneself. This deep confidence allows us to fully radiate and be expressive of who we are. When we trust our inner guidance and direction, we see things more clearly (the multiple crystals) and become more spontaneous, like flowing water, with our feelings.

In major religions, the Star symbolizes the guiding light, like the Star of Bethlehem and the Star of David. In astrology, the Star is Aquarius, the water-bearer, symbol of the innovative and creative mind. The two seven-pointed stars that are spinning their way toward earth on this card represent the radiance and confidence of our inherent light or life force that has every intention of actualizing creative ideas on earth through our own natures. Perhaps the best description of the function of this archetype comes from the philosopher Heidegger when he said, " A Person is not a thing or a process but an opening through which the Absolute can manifest." The Star card reminds us that each of us is an opening for light, or a gateway through which the Absolute can manifest

XVII

The Star

TRUMPS

THE PRINCIPLE OF SELF-SUFFICIENCY
AND TALENT
RECOGNIZED BY OTHERS

To the side of the card, the flowers and butterflies or moths are symbols of unfoldment (the flowers) and of transformation (the butterflies). Through our self-esteem, which has three components (self-love, self-trust, and self-respect), we are able to unfold like flowers and grow more fully into our many-splendored expression (the butterflies).

The Star as Life-Time Symbol

For those individuals whose birthday adds up to the number 17 or 8, The Star is your life-time personality expression or symbol of your external expression in the world. People will see you as naturally radiant and confident. You possess a natural charisma and magnetism that pulls people and opportunities toward you. Often The Star symbol is associated with fame and recognition and, at different times in your life, you will be recognized for accomplishments that provide a contribution and service to others.

You have a natural ability to assist others with self-esteem issues. You instinctively know that arrogance and self-effacement are signals that low self-esteem is being experienced. You assist others to trust their inner guidance and intuition because work can build confidence, and the ability to confide in and trust oneself. You know that qualities such as arrogance and self-deprecation cannot continue to exist in the presence of self-love, self-trust, and self-respect.

Aquarius people (anyone born January 21 – February 21) in your life become mirrors of your own ability to be pioneering, innovative, and creative. You are a natural visionary (the crystals) who trusts your intuition (the star within the cup) and your feelings (the flowing water from the cups). You have an innovative and inspirational mind like Aquarius (the two spinning stars) with a deep commitment to actualize those ideas on earth (the planet in the background).

The Star as a Growth Symbol

The Star is your growth symbol when you add the month and day of your birthday to the current year, and the sum total is the number 17. This is the best year to resolve issues or initiate new projects with Aquarian people (anyone born January 21 – February 21) in your life; or, the month of Aquarius would be an excellent month for initiating new projects.

During this year, you could be recognized for services or accomplishments that have made a notable contribution. It is a year where you experience your self-esteem intact or are more confident in who you are. You no longer feel the need to inflate or deflate yourself and others.

The Star Symbol as a Visual Affirmation and Meditative Tool

The Star is a symbol that assists the process of sustaining and increasing self-esteem. If you desire to reinforce your self-esteem in any area of your life, The Star is the archetypal symbol that facilitates your inherent confidence and trust to manifest all of who you are. Through meditation with this symbol, or conscious intention, you can maintain and increase your own ability to confide in oneself, which is the true meaning of the word *confidence*.

If you are wanting to be pioneering or innovative with your ideas, The Star is a symbol that can assist you in actualizing those ideas.

I am a walking star on a giant star.

I value who I am.

I see what can be of benefit to people in the future.

I am a radiant lighted being.

Sample Affirmations To Use While Looking at The Star Archetype

When you pull this symbol or find yourself continuously drawn toward it, it represents a state of radiance and deep inner trust and confidence in oneself. Like Aquarius, the water-bearer, you are committed to implementing innovative and creative ideas that can serve the planet. During the month of Aquarius (January 21 – February 21) or with Aquarian people, you are determined to initiate new concepts, visions, and experiences for yourself and others.

The next seventeen weeks or the next seventeen months you find yourself increasing and maintaining your own self-esteem to such a point that you may find yourself assisting others with their self-esteem issues. During this period of time you may find that recognition comes your way for projects, services, or accomplishments that are noteworthy.

The Star as an Outer Mirror

The Star (the number 17) is the externalized expression of internal balance and clarity (Adjustment/Justice, the number 8). Self-esteem and internal radiance are apparent in the world when we are spontaneous, vital, and natural (The Star). Our self-esteem is a barometer of our internal balance or imbalance (The Adjustment/Justice symbol). Two conditions sabotage our balance and self-esteem: Over-extension or compensation patterns (Eight of Cups) and doubting ourselves (Eight of Swords). Two qualities rectify or reestablish our balance and self-esteem: taking swift action and communicating directly (Eight of Wands), and utilizing prudence and wisdom in our actions (Eight of Disks). Once we naturally adjust and realign to the clarity within (Adjustment) we are able to express who we are more fully (The Star). *(See the Adjustment/Justice constellation in Section VI for additional information.)*

Other Symbols that Are Aspects of The Star Archetype

Gifts:	Challenges:
Adjustment (Balanced; Clarity)	Eight of Swords (Doubt; Interference)
The Star (Confidence; Self-Esteem)	Eight of Cups (Indolence, Over-extension or Compensation)
Eight of Wands (Swiftness; Directness)	
Eight of Disks (Prudence; Wisdom)	

The Gifts and Challenges for Persons whose Life-Time Personality Symbol Is The Star

The Moon's gates reveal the unlimited splendor of the soul.

– Anonymous

THE MOON 18

is the universal principle of choice-making and authenticity. Often this symbol is referred to as the *karma* card, karma meaning "work that needs to be done." The ultimate work to be done each day is to choose whether we will support our authentic self or support our false persona or dutiful self. Every day we are at the gates making choices about leaving old known worlds or going through the gates to explore new worlds. The gates also represent the process of choosing either between our authentic expression or our false or dutiful expression. Choice has three functions. It is through choice that we can 1) create new realities, 2) sustain and maintain current realities, or 3) release and let go of realities that no longer serve us.

The guardians of the gate are the Ra kings from ancient Egypt, the Sun gods, who protect our life force and energy as we change and reclaim our authentic selves. The jackals (symbol of the Egyptian diety, Anubis) are reminders that we must let go of the old in order to go through the gates and experience anything new. In addition, the Egyptian beetle, or scarab, represents Khepri, the Egyptian God of Transformations. The scarab symbolizes "he who becomes." Before him, the scarab rolls the ball of the sun, pushing it into the Other World in the evening and over the horizon in the morning as the scarab beetle pushes before itself a ball of dung. For the Egyptians, the scarab-god represented the rising sun and symbolized the renewal of life and the idea of eternal existence.

THE PRINCIPLE OF CHOICE,
AUTHENTICITY vs. DUTIFULNESS

The Moon is the astrological representative of the water sign, *Pisces*. The two fish traditionally representing Pisces are symbolized here by the Anubis, or jackal-gods, serving as guardians of the gate, or symbols of Piscean commitment to evolution and transformation.

The Moon is also the universal feminine principle. Its magnetic force upon the waters of the earth remind us that the inherent power of our receptive nature is to open, expand, yield, and totally express our full power and nature like the Moon. The Moon reflects back to us the mystery of who we are, and in its relentless consistency and changing phases, reminds us of those qualities which are inherent within our authentic natures. Whether we are male or female the reclamation of the authentic self requires that we open, receive and go inward; and like the Moon, it is essential to reveal ourselves without holding back or censoring ourselves in anyway.

The Moon is the symbol most associated with romance. The Moon reminds us that during romantic involvements we can see our potential dreams and visions, and yet, in romantic involvements we are challenged to truly be ourselves rather than to pretend to be other than who we are. The romantic state can be one of inspiration, or illusion and deception. The Moon reminds us that through our choices we can either reveal or conceal who we are and are not.

For those individuals whose birthday adds up to the number 18 or 9, the Moon represents your life-time personality symbol. You have a great deal of magnetism as a personality, and like the Moon, often your personality has the capacity of bringing light into darkness. You are a romantic yet are willing to make choices that inspire rather than deceive you. Deception, whether it be your own tendency or of your being at the brunt of someone else's deception, is something that you will find difficult to handle at different points in your life. Your inherent nature is to reclaim the authentic aspects of your life so that your commitment to truth and self-disclosure can be expressed.

Even though many people will think that they know you and feel close to you because of your magnetism, it is only a few that you allow really close to you. Your emotional nature is like what the I-Ching refers to as the "great still lake." Since you feel very deeply, you establish trust and loyalty before allowing others to explore the depths of your nature. You will be drawn to Piscean people (anyone born February 21 – March 21) because they will function as mirrors of your own emotional depths and commitment to evolution and transformation.

You have a natural ability to make choices. Often life will present you with two or more choices to make at the same time. You will find yourself either combining two or more situations or choices together or you will carefully weigh one choice over the other. Since your inherent gift is to reveal and to make sound choices, you may find yourself assisting others to reveal more of who they are and to make choices in their life which will support their authentic expression.

The Moon as Life-Time Symbol

**The Moon
Card as a Growth
Symbol**

The Moon is your growth symbol for the year when your birth month and day plus the current year adds up to the number 18. The Moon as a growth symbol requires that you begin the process of opening and reclaiming the authentic aspects of who you are. During this year, you will be faced with your own intolerance of old illusions, delusions, and self-deceptions. The Moon year becomes a year where you make choices that support your inherent nature rather than making choices that support your false persona or dutiful self. It is a year where you are no longer willing to abandon yourself in order to receive someone else's love or acceptance, or in order to keep peace, balance, and harmony in your life. You are willing only to be yourself regardless of what issues that might cause for others.

This is the best year to resolve issues with Pisces people (anyone born February 21–March 21); or in the month of Pisces, you may resolve romantic issues or make choices that support your full creativity and expression in personal and professional arenas of your life.

The Moon year is a rite of passage, it is the year where you discover that you do have *the right* to make the kinds of passages in your life that support your becoming even more of who you are.

**The Moon
Symbol as a Visual
Affirmation and
Meditative Tool**

The Moon reinforces the commitment to be authentic rather than dutiful or false in any way. If you choose to no longer abandon yourself, the Moon can assist your commitment to authenticity. Through evoking this archetype in meditation or in creative visualization, the Moon enhances your capacity to be open and receptive. The Moon is the feminine principle within each man and woman which honors the ability to be like the bamboo reed – firm, yet yielding. This symbol allows you to realize that you are committed to leaving old known worlds so that you can go through the gates to experience even greater parts of who you are.

**Sample Affirmations
To Use While
Looking at
The Moon
Archetype**

I enjoy making important decisions.

I value honesty and integrity in relationships.

I like what is mysterious within me and within others.

Through choice I can change my experience.

I am willing to express who I am fully and openly like the Moon.

When you pull this symbol or find yourself continually drawn toward it, it represents your commitment to reflect yourself accurately in all aspects of your life. During the next eighteen weeks or eighteen months, you may find yourself confronted with making choices which will require that you drop old illusions, delusions, and self-deceptions in order to reclaim and express your own authenticity. This is the best time period to make changes that would support your basic nature. It is a time to reveal rather than conceal who you are.

You may find that Pisces people (anyone born February 21 – March 21) function as important teachers and mentors for you; or that during the Pisces month you want to make important changes in your life that will be more in alignment with who you are.

You become very clear about what you want romantically in your life and what you don't want. Women's issues or important women in your life mirror your need to go inward and trust the essential parts of who you are.

The Moon as an Outer Mirror

The Moon is the external expression in the world of the Hermit archetype. The Moon (the number 18) is the expression of the authentic self in the world. Authenticity and the expression of our essential nature comes from going inward and reclaiming ourselves through contemplation, prayer, and meditation (The Hermit, the number 9).

We are only able to reveal our true natures (The Moon) when we have been willing to go inward and explore and reclaim the essence of who we are (The Hermit). During the reclamation process, we will face our own self-judgments (Nine of Swords). Once we are able to release our own self-delusions and self-criticalness, we will begin to experience the qualities of our essential nature: happiness (Nine of Cups); strength (Nine of Wands); and our own unlimited abundance (Nine of Disks). The Hermit is the authentic self within us that wants to be openly revealed and expressed in the world (The Moon). *(See the Hermit constellation in Section VI for more additional information.)*

Other Symbols that Are Aspects of The Moon

Gifts:

The Moon (Reflection of Self)
The Hermit (Introspection)
Nine of Cups (Happiness)
Nine of Wands (Strength)
Nine of Disks (Gain)

Challenges:

Nine of Swords
(Self-cruelty)

The Gifts and Challenges for Persons whose Life-Time Personality Symbol Is The Moon

You who are the source of all power
Whose rays illuminate the whole world
Illuminate also my heart
So that it too can do your work.

– Book of Runes

THE SUN

is the universal principle of teamwork, partnership, and collaboration. The Sun depicts the life force and unlimited energy that is within us waiting to be used and expressed. This is the "cosmic dance of two on the green mountain of creativity." It is the inner dance of male/female energy that is within each of us that taps unlimited reservoirs of creativity. Integrating and applying our creativity in both magnetic and dynamic ways allows us to experience the unlimited aspects of who we are.

The life force of The Sun reveals our ability to be natural generators, motivators, and stimulators within our personal and professional lives. We can bring the exuberance and consistency of The Sun into our one-to-one relationships (the dance of two) or into group and organizational settings (all the signs of the Zodiac going around the outside of this card).

Teamwork and group work is a transformative experience which requires trust in spiritual and physical processes working simultaneously (the dancing, winged figures). Teamwork and partnership is often for the purposes of implementing a shared creative vision (the orange energy band around the mountain).

All creative processes are a form of play and exploration. It is the Divine Child within us that is always seeking to express itself in unlimited ways. Like the Eastern lotus blossom in the middle of the sun, our basic natures unfold and are revitalized within every creative process that involves the implementation of both our dynamic and magnetic expressions.

THE PRINCIPLE OF COLLABORATION, TEAMWORK/PARTNERSHIP CO-OPERATION

The small coins with figures within them at the bottom of the mountain are another duplication of the dancing figures that have been brought into form in a tangible way. The dancing figures represent the joy and excitement of inspiration. The encircled earth figures represent inspiration and joy coming into practical and useable form.

The Sun is your life-time personality symbol if your birthday adds up to the number 19. Your personality expression is like that of The Sun. You are a natural generator, motivator, and stimulator of people and situations. You are able to work with people equally as well on a one-to-one basis as you are in group situations. You are drawn to teamwork, partnership, and collaboration that is innovative and creative. You believe in the synergetic principle that two or more can create a greater whole. You will work on your own if you are not inspired by people and situations that are equal or more original in your creativity than you are.

It is important in different periods of your life to remove yourself from partnerships or teamwork efforts that become depleting, draining, and uninspirational. You need to be met by people and situations that have equal sun energy rather than constantly be the sun or life force for people who have lost their source of inspiration and look to you to provide it.

The great mountain is a symbol for Nature. Nature and Sun itself are important regenerative elements for you. It is important for you to incorporate greenery and sunlight into your life; both of these are nature metaphors for the essence of who you are.

The Sun as Life-Time Symbol

The Sun is your growth symbol during the year when your birthday and the current year add up to the number 19. This is the best year to enter partnership or teamwork efforts that are collaborative only if they are inspirational, creative, and innovative. It is important not to be involved in depleting and draining alliances during this year in either your personal or professional life. Sun years are the best years to magnetize people, opportunities, and situations that enhance and support your basic vital nature. The next nineteen weeks or nineteen months is the best year to generate new projects, relationships, and collaborative efforts, or to remove yourself from teamwork efforts that are depleting and unfruitful.

The Sun Card as a Growth Symbol

The Sun is a symbol that supports the ability to generate, motivate, and inspire others in teamwork and collaborative efforts. If you are wanting to energize yourself in partnerships that are personal and professional, the Sun is an archetype that reminds you to remove yourself from depleting alliances and move toward situations that offer inspiration and productive results. Through creative visualization or the incorporation of the Sun in your meditation processes, you can reinforce your intention to align yourself only with people and situations that energize you rather than deplete you.

The Sun Symbol as a Visual Affirmation and Meditative Tool

Sample Affirmations To Use While Looking at The Sun Archetype

> *I work well in teamwork situations.*
>
> *I enjoy making contributions to group efforts.*
>
> *I am a cooperative individual.*
>
> *I am a natural motivator, and stimulator of creative and original endeavors.*

The Sun as an Outer Mirror

When you pull this symbol or find yourself repeatedly drawn toward it, it represents the child-like innocence and curiosity within your creative nature that wants to be expressed in all aspects of your personal and professional life. You have the natural ability to generate and motivate others to claim their creative talents and resources. The Sun reflects your own ability at this time to be fully who you are in a very dynamic and creative way. Your abilities to contribute creatively in teamwork and collaborative efforts at this time is enormous.

Other Symbols that Are Aspects of The Sun Archetype

The Sun is the external creative expression of the Magician within. The Sun (the number 19) is the creative power that we have to express in our collaborative efforts our communication gifts (The Magician). The Sun is the external expression of the creative mind (Ace of Swords), love with wisdom (Ace of Cups), authenticity and truth (Ace of Wands), and manifested success (Ace of Disks). Through our communication (The Magician), we are able to express our creativity and life force (The Sun) *(See the Magician constellation in Section VI for additional information.)*

The Gifts and Challenges for Persons whose Life-Time Personality Symbol Is The Sun

Gifts:

The Magician (Communication)
Ace of Swords (Clarity)
Ace of Cups (Love with Wisdom)
Ace of Wands (Truth; Authenticity)
Ace of Disks (Success)
Ten of Cups (Satisfaction)
Ten of Disks (Wealth)

Challenges:

To place oneself in partnerships that are energizing
Ten of Swords (Fear of Ruin)
Ten of Wands (Oppression)

*Learn to look with an equal eye upon all beings,
seeing the one Self in all.*

– Srimad Bhagavatam, *Perenniel Philosophy*

THE AEON

symbol represents the principle of good judgment that is utilized in both personal and professional situations. Webster's dictionary defines the Aeon as *that state which represents a long, indefinite period of time.* The Aeon reminds us that all perceptions come from our ability to take a look at the whole; and that it is our inherent desire to consider longevity, history, and broad perspectives in all situations.

Within the central representation of this symbol, we find two powerful reflections of both family and profession. The concept of family is represented by the large giant-child figure of Osiris, the Egyptian God of Wisdom, who married Isis, the Goddess of Intuition. They gave birth to the body, mind, and soul of Horus, the God of Perception which is represented by the three floating fetuses. These central figures represent the family. Surrounding them is the Egyptian Goddess, Nut, the Sky-Goddess. She is the dark woman with elongated body, touching the earth with toes and fingers as she makes a back-bend in order to hold up the stars at night. She makes the shape of the Zodiac sign, Leo, which represents creative and professional power. Creativity that is properly used can make positive impacts in both family and career. The Aeon is the only symbol in the entire deck which incorporates the integration of the personal and professional aspects of our lives.

The Goddess Isis in the womb reminds us of our creative power to give birth to new forms (the floating fetuses). Osiris with his forefinger to his mouth reflects that wisdom comes from experience and is not randomly spoken. Camus in his book, *The Fall*, stated that the Last Judgment is faced in all the daily judgments we make of ourselves and

THE PRINCIPLE OF GOOD JUDGMENT
DISCERNMENT

others. The Aeon/Judgment symbol represents our ability to give birth to new forms in both family and career situations. The Aeon reminds us to look at the history we have shared and to forgive ourselves and others for the judgments we are making about what we are doing or not doing in our lives. The red-winged Eye of Horus at the bottom of the symbol represents inspired vision. Horus, the Egyptian God of Perception, was able to see the whole or over-view of situations. The perception of Horus is needed as we give birth to new forms in both family and career.

The Aeon as Life-Time Symbol

For those individuals whose birthday adds up to the number 20, the Aeon/Judgment represents your life-time personality symbol. This symbol represents your expression in the world. For you, it is important to be creative in both family and career. It would be very hard for you to be all family without creative and career endeavors; and, it would be very hard for you to be all career without family or important relationships. Externally in the world, it is important for you to be creative in all arenas of your life. The Goddess Nut symbolizes this desire by making a back-bend in the sign of Leo. Leo people in your life (anyone born July 21–August 21) mirror to you your desires to be creative and dynamically expressive in all parts of your life; or, in the month of Leo, you could initiate new opportunities or give birth to new forms in relationships and in professional activities.

Others will see you as very perceptive, insightful, and intuitive. You have the ability to see the history and longevity of any situation. You can readily assess what is workable and what is not workable; and you have the ability to communicate your perceptions in such a way that they can be received and heard. Your committment is to share what it is that you see in such a way that it inspires and motivates people rather than making them feel judged or diminished in anyway. With your gift of perception combined with communication, you could make an excellent consultant or critic in any of the creative arts or standard professions.

The Aeon as a Growth Symbol

The Aeon/Judgment card is your growth symbol during the year when your birthdate and the current year adds up to the number 20. This is the best year for you to go into teamwork or collaborative efforts with important family members or loved ones. It becomes a year where you find that you are creative in balancing both relationship and career issues. You may find yourself motivated to initiate new activities or new interests in your personal and professional life.

Leo people in your life (anyone born July 21–August 21) will mirror to you your own desires to manifest your creativity in all that you do; or it may be a time to resolve issues with Leo people or for giving birth to new opportunities that Leo people might present to you.

The Aeon/Judgment year is a time where you might consider having a family (the floating fetuses at the bottom of the card) or you might consider starting something new in your professional life.

The Aeon Symbol as a Visual Affirmation and Meditative Tool

The Aeon can be used as a visualization and meditation tool, particularly for increasing your ability to perceive situations from a broad perspective. This is the best symbol to use to transform criticalness or judgmentalism to an increase in your capacity for objective observation and communication. By meditating with this card in front of you, or by looking at it with conscious intention, you can enhance your ability to bring balance and creativity into both your personal and professional life.

I observe people and situations objectively and fairly.

I value the composite of my qualities and characteristics.

I commumicate what I see in such an objective and integral way that it can be received and heard.

I deeply honor and value the unlimited resource of creativity that is within me to express in both family and career situations.

Sample Affirmations To Use While Looking at The Aeon

When you pull this card or find yourself drawn toward the Aeon, it reflects your current ability to integrate both family and career issues. You are perceptive and are utilizing good judgment as you initiate new interests in your life. During the next twenty weeks or five months, you are determined to change judgmental attitudes you might hold in order to look at all situations that you are currently facing with more objectivity.

The Aeon as an Outer Mirror

The Aeon (the number 20) is the outer expression of The High Priestess (the number 2). We can only use good judgment or be objective (The Aeon) when we come from a place of self-trust and resourcefulness (The High Priestess). We are able to be creative and balanced in both our professional and personal lives when we manifest peace of mind (Two of Swords), love (Two of Cups), dominion (Two of Wands), and positive change (Two of Disks). The Aeon represents the observable expression of the qualities listed above. People are able to see our Strength and lustre as we give birth to new forms in relationships and in career. (*See High Priestess constellation in Section VI for additional information.*)

Other Symbols that Are Aspects of The Aeon Archetype

Gifts:

Aeon/Judgment
High Priestess (Self-Trust)
Two of Cups (Love
Two of Swords (Peace)
Two of Wands (Dominion)
Two of Disks (Change)
Lust/Strength

Challenges:

To transform
 criticalness to objectivity.
To communicate perceptions
 in such a way that they can
 be received and heard.

The Gifts and Challenges for Persons whose Life-Time Personality Symbol Is The Aeon

The universe resounds with the joyful cry I am.

–Scriabin

THE UNIVERSE

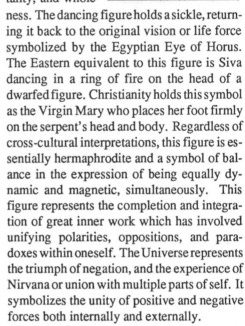

**THE PRINCIPLE OF TOTALITY,
INDIVIDUATION/WHOLENESS**

is the principle of individuation, totality, and wholeness. The dancing figure holds a sickle, returning it back to the original vision or life force symbolized by the Egyptian Eye of Horus. The Eastern equivalent to this figure is Siva dancing in a ring of fire on the head of a dwarfed figure. Christianity holds this symbol as the Virgin Mary who places her foot firmly on the serpent's head and body. Regardless of cross-cultural interpretations, this figure is essentially hermaphrodite and a symbol of balance in the expression of being equally dynamic and magnetic, simultaneously. This figure represents the completion and integration of great inner work which has involved unifying polarities, oppositions, and paradoxes within oneself. The Universe represents the triumph of negation, and the experience of Nirvana or union with multiple parts of self. It symbolizes the unity of positive and negative forces both internally and externally.

With the sickle, the figure cuts through limitations and restrictions and weaves them into a net to dance upon. In order to become free and more individuated, it is important to simultaneously let go and move forward. Like the regenerative diamond-back serpent, we are required to transform before we can experience new worlds internally and externally. Change requires that we grow and evolve like the spiral hair-do of the figure, and that we expand our awareness like the diamond-shaped halo.

The pantheon at the bottom is the Greek symbol for the home of all the gods and goddesses. When we fully express our totality or full individuality, we have the experience of being at home within ourselves. The Universe represents our capacity not only to be at home in the external world but also it represents our ability to be at home within ourselves.

The four animals in the corners of the card represent the four elements: earth (Taurus, the bull); fire (Leo, the lion); water (Scorpio, the bird); and air (Aquarius, the human face). These animals represent what it is like to be in our element or out of our element. It is important in order to fully express our natures that we express ourselves physically (Taurus), spiritually and creatively (Leo), emotionally (Scorpio), and mentally (Aquarius).

The Universe is your life-time personality symbol when your birthday adds up to the number 21. This is the symbol which represents your outer expression in the world. You are a natural explorer, adventurer, and builder of new worlds. You love travel and experiencing other parts of the country and other cultures. You are a natural visionary. Instinctively, you can see what needs to be re-built or designed in new ways whether it be environments, ideas, projects, or people. You have a natural ability to renew and regenerate yourself and others (the regenerative snake). People will see you as highly creative like Leo, the lion; practical and productive like Taurus, the bull; innovative and original like Aquarius, the human face; and passionately involved in what has heart and meaning for you like Scorpio, the bird.

The Universe as Life-Time Symbol

At different times in your life, you will be very ecologically minded and deeply concerned about the Earth and very active in making the universe a better place in which to live. You may experience yourself questioning the origins of the universe as a whole or contributing towards theories, projects, and services that assist universal understanding. National and international work will appeal to you, or travel that allows you and others to value cultural differences as well as honor inherent similarities found within the human species.

You will find it difficult to be limited, restricted, or restrained in any way. With your inherent ability to cut through things and get to the bottom of most situations (the sickle), you are able to build new worlds internally and externally. The concept of freedom at different times in your life will be very important.

The Universe is your growth symbol when your birthdate and the current year adds up to the number 21. During this year, it is important for you to place yourself in the world in an active way. It is a year where you see clearly what needs to be done and you do it. You may find yourself only willing to be creative, productive, and innovative in areas that have heart or meaning. You will not be able to tolerate "shoulds" of any kind during this year. You will find that you want to make a tangible contribution through service or volunteer work that is meaningful and assists your family, community, country, or planet in some way.

The Universe as a Growth Symbol

Travel and visiting other countries may be available or become a high priority for you in your Universe year. Through an important trip, you may be motivated to expand and build new worlds for yourself internally and externally. You definitely will see your life through a different perspective and be motivated to make changes that allow you to become more whole and expressive of who you are as an individual.

The Universe Symbol as a Visual Affirmation and Meditative Tool

The Universe symbol is an excellent symbol to use as a meditation or visualization tool to increase the sense of full uninhibited expression in the world. By meditating with this card in front of you, you can affirm or visualize expressing yourself in the world and making the contribution that you have come to make on Earth. This symbol reinforces universal understanding and global awareness. If you want to build new worlds internally and externally, this symbol is a visual portraiture of universal worlds that can be creatively maintained and supported.

Sample Affirmations To Use While Looking at The Universe

I love exploring the unknown.

I am excited about bringing ideas and creative projects into form.

I love to travel.

I deeply value making a contribution that makes the world a better place in which to live.

The Universe as an Outer Mirror

Whenever you pull this symbol or find yourself drawn toward it, it represents that you are currently expressing who you are in the world and that you are making a difference. You are building new worlds internally and externally, and the next twenty-one weeks is the time that you are determined to actualize or manifest the kinds of worlds that you want in all arenas of your life.

You may find yourself planning a special trip or may find yourself traveling extensively in order to make the kind of community or cultural contributions that you see are essentially needed at this time. In no way are you holding back any of your individuality or full expression at this time. The Universe reflects that your service and talents are needed at this time and you are actively involved in making a necessary contribution.

Other Symbols that Are Aspects of The Universe Symbol

The Universe (the number 21) is the outer expression in the world of the Empress symbol (the number 3). In order to make a contribution in the world with our inherent talents (The Universe), we must trust our ability to express love with wisdom (The Empress). Love with wisdom can be expressed in the world when we are willing to break limiting patterns (The Hanged Man), release old sorrows (Three of Swords), be clear on our priorities (Three of Disks), express our integrity (Three of Wands), and communicate respectfully (Three of Cups). (*See the Empress constellation in Section VI for additional information.*)

The Gifts and Challenges for Persons whose Life-Time Personality Symbol Is The Universe

Gifts:

The Empress (Love with Wisdom)
Three of Cups (Abundance)
Three of Wands (Integrity)
Three of Disks (Priorities; "Works")
The Hanged Man (Breaking Patterns)
The Universe (Expression of Love in the World)

Challenges:

Three of Swords (Sorrow)

SECTION IV

ROYALTY SYMBOLS

**Sixteen Types of Self-Mastery
Mirrored by Important People in Our Lives**

INTRODUCTION

General Meanings

The Royalty symbols are symbols which demonstrate mastery at certain levels of consciousness. The suit of each card will indicate which level of consciousness the mastery is occurring. For example, Swords always indicate activity that is occurring at the mental level of consciousness; Cups reveal emotional expressions of consciousness; Wands are symbols for intuitive and spiritual aspects of consciousness; and Disks are symbols for external reality – health, finances, relationships, creativity, and career. If a royalty card is selected, it indicates some level of mastery that has been obtained and is occurring at this time. The suit of the royalty card will indicate the level of consciousness where the mastery is currently occurring or is being demonstrated.

Basic Guidelines

The Knight and the Queen of any suit indicate older mastery, or mastery that has occurred for some time. The Prince and Princess of any suit reveal mastery that is new, yet obtained.

Activity at the different levels of consciousness is illustrated in the following ways: the Knight and the Prince of any suit indicate consciousness that is expanding and is in motion. The Queen and Princess of any suit indicate consciousness that is centered and is in the process of deepening. The suit of the Royalty card (Sword, Cup, Wand, Disk) will indicate where the processes of expansion and movement (Knight and Prince) are taking place; and where the processes of centering and deepening (Queen and Princess) are occurring.

Besides mastery, the Royalty symbols indicate important people in our lives who function as outer mirrors of our own levels of mastery. The Knight and the Queen of any suit will mirror to us people in our lives who are our age and older; and the Prince and Princess of any suit will mirror to us people in our lives who are our age and younger.

Ways of Identifying
Natural Gifts, Talents and Resources

Royalty symbols indicate inherent states of mastery, natural gifts, talents and resources. They reflect internal states of learning and teaching. To find your inner resources or the natural inherent quality of your own Inner Teacher, follow the directions below:

1) Write out your full name as it was given at birth. Count the letters in your name. If the total letters is higher than 16, add the double digit number together to reduce the total to a single digit. (Example: if the total letters in your name is 23, then add 2+3 together which equals 5; then, look for the number 5 on the chart at the top of the next page to find the symbol which represents your inherent mastery.)

2) Name changes indicate recognition of new talents, gifts, and resources being mastered and utilized. For various names that you have used, merely count the letters in the name and refer to the chart.

The Inner Teacher, the quality inherently present at birth, is the quality that we carry throughout our lives, regardless of what other qualities we choose to explore as a result of name change.

		K	Q	P	PR
Disks	(Physical)	1	5	9	13
Swords	(Mental)	2	6	10	14
Cups	(Emotional)	3	7	11	15
Wands	(Spiritual)	4	8	12	16

K equals Knight
Q equals Queen
P equals Prince
PR equals Princess

TYPES OF MASTERY REVEALED BY THE ROYALTY SYMBOLS

Each suit reveals four kinds of mastery at each level of consciousness

Knight of Swords:	Mastery of focus, will, intention, concentration, passionate thinking	**Four Kinds of Mental Mastery**
Queen of Swords:	Mastery of rational, objective thinking; *the mask cutter*	
Prince of Swords:	Mastery of creative, intuitive thinking	
Princess of Swords:	Mastery of practical, tangible thinking; *the mood fighter*	

Knight of Cups:	Mastery of emotional loyalty and commitment; *the Knight and the Holy Grail*	**Four Kinds of Emotional Mastery**
Queen of Cups:	Mastery of emotional integrity; self-reflection	
Prince of Cups:	Mastery of emotional desire; Eastern Tantric practice	
Princess of Cups:	Mastery of emotional objectivity and detachment	

Knight of Wands:	Mastery of inspired direction, vision, intuition	**Four Kinds of Spiritual, Intuitive, Visionary Mastery**
Queen of Wands:	Mastery of self-knowledge and transformation	
Prince of Wands:	Mastery of inspired creativity	
Princess of Wands:	Mastery of self-liberation and the capacity to release fear	

Knight of Disks:	Mastery of prosperity, harvest, and abundance	**Four Kinds of Physical, External World Mastery**
Queen of Disks:	Mastery of diet and nutrition; builder of fruitful worlds	
Prince of Disks:	Mastery of exercise and the body; designer and builder of new worlds	
Princess of Disks:	Mastery of giving birth to new forms; mastery of one's creativity	

TYPES OF MENTAL MASTERY

Knight of Swords

Queen of Swords

Prince of Swords

Princess of Swords

KNIGHT OF SWORDS

is a visual portraiture of a knight in the air flying over water. In alchemy, the element of air is associated with the mind, and water is associated with emotionality. Combining the elements of water and air, metaphorically, is a symbol for *passionate thinking*. Here we have a picture of the focused, intentional, determined mind.

The three swallows represent the union of mind, heart, and action all proceeding in the same direction. They serve as reminders that focus, will, and intention must be aligned and moving in the same direction before a goal can be obtained.

The Knight holds a dagger and a sword; each a symbol for the receptive and dynamic thinking required to execute a goal. In Oriental terms, the dagger would be a metaphor for *yin* (feminine) energy and the sword would be a symbol for *yang* (masculine) energy. The *yin/yang* symbol in Oriental philosophy is associated with the two energies that are required to create balance and unity.

Within the four wings attached to the Knight's helmet are written the words *north*, *south*, *east* and *west*. Each direction is a symbol for the four levels of consciousness: mental, emotional, spiritual and physical, which are combined as a picture for unified consciousness. At the center of the four wings is a six pointed star, a universal symbol associated with illumination, clarity, and spiritual guidance.

The Knight of Swords is associated with the air sign months of Aquarius, Libra, and Gemini, or with air sign people. Since this is a Knight, this could represent an older man or older mastery of passionate thinking and mental determination.

Knight of Swords

**MASTER OF
PASSIONATE THINKING
AND INTENTIONALITY**

Powerful fluid thinking is represented by the Knight's gold armor. Gold, in alchemy, was associated with malleability, fluidity, and spiritual radiance. The horse, pictured with all of the Knights, is a symbol of power and intuitive understanding. Horses, cross-culturally, are associated with intense desires and instincts. (*Cirlot*, 1962).

Range of Interpretation for The Knight of Swords

This is a symbol of the focused, determined, intentional mind. During the air sign months of Aquarius (January 21 – February 21), Gemini (May 21 – June 21), and Libra (September 21 – October 21), would be a good time to move in new directions with clarity of purpose and strong will. This is the state of mind that contains no doubt.

The Knight of Swords could be an air sign person or older man who is an Aquarius, Gemini, or Libra. This person could be an outer mirror of your own focus, will and determination to move in new directions with undaunted clarity. Or, in the air sign months, an older man could provide new opportunities that could take you in new directions, personally or professionally, in the air sign months of Aquarius, Gemini, or Libra.

The air sign months would be a good time to set things in motion, especially if there is clarity of purpose within all parts of your nature. The heart or emotional nature (water) supports the ideas, clarity and direction of the mind (air).

For women, the Knight of Swords may also represent an aspect of their *animus*, the internal masculine or dynamic energy that is expressing itself with relentless determination, focus and will.

QUEEN OF SWORDS

reflects the rational, objective, fair-witnessing mind. She sits upon a huge cloud in the air with a sword in one hand and a mask in the other. She is the *mask-cutter*. She holds a mask in her hand as a symbol of having cut through her own masks, roles, and defenses in order to retain her objectivity and clarity (the crystal crown) and her child-like innocence and curiosity (the child's head resting on top of the crystal crown). The Queen of Swords is the counselor or the consultant in the Royalty symbols. She has the ability to counsel and consult others and has the wisdom to seek counseling and consulting for herself when necessary. In Greek mythology, this symbol would be a picture of the goddess Athena.

This is mastery of the objective, rational mind which is centered and deepening in consciousness. It is the observing mind which is detached from roles and assists us in reconnecting with our child-like truth. It is the quality of mind that considers options fairly and demands authenticity and the abandonment of pretense.

For men, this symbol can reflect a quality of their own inner *anima* or feminine nature that seeks clarity, truth and authenticity beyond roles, masks and defenses. This is the counseling, consulting aspect that is witnessed when people ask for clarification or have the desire to get to the bottom of things.

Queen of Swords

**MASTERY OF
OBJECTIVE THINKING
AND CLARITY**

**Range of
Interpretation for
The Queen of
Swords**

The Queen of Swords represents the air sign months of Aquarius (January 21 – February 21), Gemini (May 21 – June 21), and Libra (September 21 – October 21), or important air sign people in our lives. During the air sign months, you may find yourself cutting through your own roles, masks and defenses to experience more of your own child-like innocence and curiosity; or you may seek counseling or consulting; or you may find yourself assisting others with your own consulting and counseling gifts.

The Queen of Swords may also mirror to you an older woman or significant air sign person in your life that you may want to consult, or it may mean an air sign person that might be seeking counseling and clarification from you. This symbol represents your desire to cut through any roles, masks or defenses that might be present within yourself or within your relationships with significant older women in your life – anyone your age, one to five years older, or significantly older. The Queen of Swords ultimately represents your desires to be authentic with important air sign people in your life; or it is the desire to demonstrate your authenticity in all that you do during the air sign months of Aquarius, Gemini, and Libra. It is a symbol which illustrates your current mastery of objective, rational and clear thinking.

RINCE OF SWORDS

is that aspect of the mind which has *newly* mastered creative-intuitive thinking. He represents the inspired mind that does not want to be limited, restricted, or restrained in any way. The desire for non-limitation during the creative-intuitive process is symbolized by the Prince who, with his two swords (a sickle and large sword), is determined to cut through any thoughts, attitudes, or beliefs that might reign the movement (the chariot) and expression of creative-intuitive thinking.

The Prince's curved sickle and elongated sword are symbols for the dynamic function of thinking. For women the Prince of Swords is an expression of an aspect of their *animus*, or internal masculine energy, that desires to express itself in unlimited creative and intuitive ways.

Prince of Swords

MASTERY OF CREATIVE AND INTUITIVE THINKING

**Range of
Interpretation for
The Prince of
Swords**

The Prince of Swords represents new mastery of creative-intuitive thinking which is expanding and is in dynamic motion. This symbol is associated with the air sign of Aquarius, which is a symbol for the creative, original, innovative mind. Aquarius is symbolized on the card by the three human bodies (inspired ideas) that want to be released and expressed. During the month of Aquarius (January 21 – February 21), you may experience limitations and restrictions being removed so that your creative-intuitive processes can be freed to move forward. Aquarius can also be a month where you experience the need for more creative problem solving in areas of your life that have become boring, routine, and predictable. Sometimes the Prince of Swords actually indicates a desire to literally move, relocate or travel. Regardless, it is creative energy that wants to be actively expressed.

The Prince of Swords may represent an Aquarius person or any younger man with whom you choose to restructure your relationship so that it moves in new directions that are unlimited and less restrained; or this may represent a younger person or an Aquarian person in your life that you might enjoy working with in creative endeavors; or someone that you might inspire to move in new directions where they might express more of their creative-intuitive thinking.

PRINCESS OF SWORDS

This symbol represents the ability to apply ideas in tangible and productive ways. The Princess of Swords is the *mood-fighter* who is determined with her sword (clarity of mind) to fight any moods (dust-storms) within herself. She actively prevents herself from getting engulfed in the moods of those around her. She is determined to apply her practical ideas in productive, useful ways (the mushroom pedestal covered with coins).

      The Princess of Swords is constantly regenerating her thinking (the spring-green color of her gown and her butterfly wings) to see how her ideas can be cost-effective (coins on pedestal) and nourishing to others beyond herself (the mushroom in the shape of a pedestal). This symbol reflects a need to act upon ideas rather than to just talk about them. The Princess of Swords is that state of consciousness where word and deed are aligned. Practical thinking requires that there be no difference between verbal commitment and external action.

Princess of Swords

MASTERY OF
PRACTICAL THINKING

Range of Interpretation for The Princess of Swords

The Princess of Swords is associated with the air sign months of Aquarius (January 21 – February 21), Gemini (May 21 – June 21), and Libra (September 21 – October 21), or with those persons that you know who are born during those months. The air sign months are the months to plant and incubate seeds externally and internally. During these months of gestation, it is important to fight your own moods and the moods of others so that you might attend to what it is that you want to produce in the areas of health, finances, work and relationships. These are also the months in which you will look to the action and behavior of others to see if they are in alignment with thoughts and ideas that they have expressed. The Princess of Swords suggests that the air sign months are productive months for you if you fight your own moods and the moods of others. The Princess of Swords indicates that younger women in your life might mirror your current mood-fighting processes or your own desires to be productive. If not younger women, then this process is demonstrated or reflected back to you by Aquarian people who are your age or younger. Ultimately, the Princess of Swords illustrates the recent mastery of practical thinking that is unobstructed and committed to quality and excellence.

TYPES OF
EMOTIONAL MASTERY

Knight of Cups

Queen of Cups

Prince of Cups

Princess of Cups

NIGHT OF CUPS

is a visual representation of emotional loyalty, generosity, commitment, and unconditional love. Mythically, this is the "Knight and the Holy Grail." Of all the Knights in the deck, this is the only one which is not helmeted: a symbol of openness, trust, and the willingness to be seen, the very qualities that are needed in order to be emotionally spontaneous, outreaching, and unguarded.

This is the winged Knight, who like Pegasus, the winged horse, offers emotional regard and spiritual upliftment. The white horse is a symbol of power coming from an integrated and spiritual source (the color white). The Knight of Cups wears the green suit which is symbolic of creative love. He holds the Grail, or loving cup, out of which a crab emerges. Cancer, the crab, is an astrological symbol that represents the quality of emotional loyalty and the ability to give emotional comfort, support and positive regard to others.

The Knight of Cups is rising out of the emotional waters above the peacock, which represents love that has moved beyond ego and vanity (the peacock) and offers unconditional love that is spiritually healing and uplifting (the Knight and the Grail). In the West, the peacock is a symbol associated with warding off evil and is also representative of vanity and ego. In the East, the peacock is associated with perception and vision and is seen as a healing omen; and in medieval hermeneutics, it was viewed as a symbol of the soul.

Knight of Cups

MASTERY OF EMOTIONAL LOYALTY AND COMMITMENT

**Range of
Interpretation for
The Knight of Cups**

The Knight of Cups represents mastery of emotional loyalty, generosity, and unconditional love. The Knight of Cups reminds us of the healing power of unconditional love, acceptance and positive regard.

During the month of Cancer (June 21 – July 21), or from now until Cancer, is an ideal time to be open to emotional rewards and opportunities presented to you by significant older men or from Cancer people in your life.

For women, this symbol can represent the loyalty and commitment found within their own *animus* or dynamic masculine nature within. For both genders, the Knight of Cups can represent a reassessment of priorities, loyalities, and commitments for the purpose of eliminating *shoulds* and moving toward that which has vitality, heart, and meaning.

Ultimately, the Knight of Cups is that quality of the emotional nature which can forgive and extend compassion.

QUEEN OF CUPS

is a symbol which represents mastery of emotional integrity. She is the woman with one hand on a stork, which represents her determination to express herself accurately as she gives birth to new forms, new talents, new identities, and new life (the stork). She is the expression of emotional authenticity and congruity about motherhood issues and issues surrounding maternal or female authority figures in one's life including one's own mother. The Queen of Cups represents the constant practice of owning one's feelings and expressing them without blame or judgment. She does not abandon, deny, or repress her feelings. She communicates her feelings accurately and openly. She does not use her feelings to attack others nor does she apologize for her feelings.

In her other hand, the Queen of Cups offers the crayfish shell as a reminder that she chooses integrity over illusion or deception (the fish standing on its tail making the sign of Neptune's fork). Neptune is a planetary symbol for inspiration or delusion. In Greek mythology, Neptune was the God of the Seas whose trident represents the three *vital impulses* of the spirit: conservation, reproduction and evolution (*Cirlot*, 1962). The Queen of Cups is committed to expressing Neptune's inspiration rather than Neptune's illusionary or delusionary qualities. The double reflection of the water is representative of her constant choice to reflect her feelings accurately, "as above, so below." Whatever she is feeling inside, she is determined to reflect accurately on the outside as a way of preventing any dichotomy between what is felt internally and what is being expressed externally.

Queen of Cups

MASTERY OF EMOTIONAL INTEGRITY

For men, the Queen of Cups represents the *anima* figure within his nature that is committed to expressing feelings honestly and responsibly.

Range of Interpretation for The Queen of Cups

The Queen of Cups represents the responsibility of communicating your feelings accurately during the water sign months of Pisces (February 21 – March 21), Cancer (June 21 – July 21), and Scorpio (October 21 – November 21), or to water sign people in your life.

This is one of the four motherhood symbols in the deck (the other motherhood symbols are The Empress, Aeon, and Princess of Disks). As a result, this symbol can represent issues surrounding motherhood and the need to express yourself honestly about motherhood issues, or issues involving female authority figures in your life, including your own mother.

The Queen of Cups also requires that you reflect yourself honestly as you make changes or give birth to new identities, new forms, new talents, or new life styles. It is important that you express yourself authentically to water sign people and in the water sign months as you make these changes or give birth to new parts of your life.

As a visual affirmation, the Queen of Cups empowers an individual to express feelings honestly and responsibly.

PRINCE OF CUPS

is the visual representation of the passionate heart and mastery of emotional desire. The symbols which specifically illustrate emotional desire and transformation are the snake emerging from the cup and the eagles – one pulling the chariot and the other sitting upon the Prince's helmet. The eagles and the snake both represent the astrological sign of Scorpio, a sign known for its emotional passion, desire, and transformation.

The Prince of Cups is *the lover* within each individual that expresses and experiences emotional passion deeply. Desire ignites the heart and propels us forward. This is a picture of an individual who is willing to face and experience his desire (the snake in the cup); and, at the same time, he is willing to let go of that which is desired when necessary to do so (the lotus held in his hand turned upside-down, ready to be released). Mastery of desire is the capacity to simultaneously move forward and let go.

For women, the symbol of the Prince of Cups is a visual portraiture of dynamic emotional desire which is expressed and mastered by the *animus* figure within.

Prince of Cups

MASTERY OF
EMOTIONAL DESIRE

**Range of
Interpretation for
The Prince of Cups**

The Prince of Cups represents the desire to follow the song of the heart and move in directions that are enlivening and passionate. During the months of Scorpio, the month of the snake and eagle, (October 21 – November 21) and in Pisces, the sea-shell chariot, (February 21 – March 21), there is symbolic support for moving, traveling and following one's bliss. Or, this visual rendition can represent moving your relationships with Scorpio and Pisces people in new directions that are emotionally enlivening.

The Prince of Cups can also represent someone your age or younger who inspires you to move in new directions; or, in the time frames of Scorpio and Pisces, you may want to inspire men your age or younger to move in new directions that are emotionally inspiring for them and for yourself.

The months of Pisces and Scorpio may also mark the months or time frames where important people enter your life or important emotional issues are resolved.

PRINCESS OF CUPS

is a portraiture of the emotional mastery that has worked through jealousy, manipulation, seduction, and possessiveness. The Princess of Cups has the capacity to offer emotional longevity and loyalty to others (the turtle in the seashell) in objective and non-possessive ways. She is emotionally secure (the swan coming from the top of her head) and is able to communicate her feelings, desires, and concerns in realistic and meaningful ways (the dolphin). The crystals on her seashell gown indicate her ability to look at things as they are rather than as she would like them to be. She allows the lotus blossom to go free, a symbol of the trusting heart rather than the controlling, possessive heart. Basically, this entire symbol represents the capacity to state feelings objectively and realistically and with a firm conviction not to abandon oneself emotionally.

Princess of Cups

MASTERY OF
EMOTIONAL OBJECTIVITY

**Range of
Interpretation for
The Princess of Cups**

This symbol is the visual representation of the objective, realistic heart. The Princess of Cups represents emotionality that is loving and realistic rather than attached and clinging.

The Princess of Cups is associated with the water sign months of Pisces (February 21 – March 21), Cancer (June 21 – July 21), and Scorpio (October 21 – November 21), or with people born within these time frames. Whenever this symbol presents itself, it represents the water sign months or water sign people in your life. It is important during these time frames to break patterns of jealousy and possession and to look at emotional situations realistically and objectively. The Princess of Cups reminds you that it is paramount that you don't abandon your feelings or repeat old reactive patterns.

For men, the Princess of Cups can represent their inner feminine nature, the *anima*, that is committed to offering emotional longevity and loyalty (the turtle) in realistic, and non-possessive ways. For both genders, the Princess of Cups can be reflected by a person who is one's own age or younger and who may be teaching one lessons about emotionally letting go.

Whenever anyone is drawn to this symbol, it is a picture of an individual who has worked through jealousy issues and is now able to love deeply, but in a more accepting and detached way. The Princess of Cups is the visual representation of emotional acceptance, authenticity, and objectivity. She has worked through old reactive patterns of insecurity, possessiveness, and jealousy. She has moved through issues surrounding fears of abandonment and loss. She is not willing to perpetuate or get involved in emotionally divisive situations.

TYPES OF
SPIRITUAL MASTERY

Knight of Wands

Queen of Wands

Prince of Wands

Princess of Wands

KNIGHT OF WANDS

is committed to the principle of spiritual growth and evolution. This is the visionary and energetic Knight who is unwilling to edit, rehearse, or hold back any part of who he is. He rides the unicorn horse, a symbol of vision and inspiration that has purpose and application. He represents the power of deep internal shifts and perceptions that are being dynamically expressed. This is the *Vision Quester* who has attained a significant vision and is mobilizing all energy to actualize it. The Knight of Wands holds the torch, the Ace of Wands, in his hand to burn out any blocks or obstacles that might stand in the way of his vision. He has the ability to shed old beliefs and to honor the changing perceptions he has of himself and others, which is symbolized by the reptilian suit that he wears. He charges forward, eager to share perceptions and insights which can assist deep changes internally and externally.

Knight of Wands

MASTERY OF
VISION AND VITALITY

**Range of
Interpretation for
The Knight of
Wands**

The Knight of Wands represents mastery of visionary goals and changes that are inspired from the deepest core of who we are. This symbol is associated with fire sign people and the fire sign months of Aries (March 21 – April 21), Leo (July 21 – August 21) and Sagittarius (November 21 – December 21). During these time frames, there is support to initiate something new or to move in new directions. Opportunities to begin new ventures or to apply one's vision in new ways can come through significant older men or fire sign people; or, a strong focus or directional clarity can be experienced in the fire sign months.

For women, the Knight of Wands can represent the dynamic part of their inner assertive nature, the *animus*, that is determined to apply an inspired vision without holding back in any way.

QUEEN OF WANDS

is the *knower of the Self*. This symbol represents self-mastery, and the process of self-reclamation. She wears the symbol of Pisces on her chest (the clasp on her cloak) as a symbol of the fluidity and the aspiration that is required to attain self-knowledge, an attribute often given to Piscean people. Her process of transformation and self-actualization is best described by the story she represents of a woman who, before she knew who she was, had black hair and walked with a panther by her side. As she began to discover who she was, her hair turned brown and the panther changed to a leopard. When she fully realized who she was and began to manifest who she was in the world with her pine cone wand, her hair turned fiery red. At this stage of self-knowledge, she pinched the growth marks of the leopard to prevent it from tranforming into a beautiful lion to match her self-knowledge because she wanted a reminder of the dark places from whence she had come (the spots of the leopard). This myth represents the process of self-discovery and the splendor of awakening to the deepest essence of who we are (the radiant crown).

Queen of Wands

**MASTERY OF
SELF-KNOWLEDGE**

Range of Interpretation for The Queen of Wands

If you are drawn toward the Queen of Wands as a symbol, you may be in the process of self-discovery or of experiencing more of who you are. This symbol represents the fire sign months of Aries (March 21 – April 21), Leo (July 21 – August 21) and Sagittarius (November 21 – December 21), or fire sign people in your life who may be your age or older and who mirror to you who you are and who you are not. During the fire sign months, you may manifest more of who you are and recognize how much you have grown in order to be where you are at this point in time.

The Queen of Wands, also, represents Pisces people in your life who may be your age or older or she can symbolize the month of Pisces. The astrological symbol of Pisces is shown as the clasp on her cloak. With Pisces people, or during the month of Pisces, it is essential that you demonstrate your self-trust and not abandon yourself in any way.

For men, this symbol can represent the inner *anima,* or magnetic part of their nature, that is committed to trusting internal and external experiences which have revealed self-knowledge.

PRINCE OF WANDS

is dynamic mastery of unlimited creative expression that is totally inspired from deep within. The reins are casually thrown over the Prince's hand as a symbol of inspired creativity that is not held back and is free to powerfully express itself. The Prince in this way demonstrates self trust in letting the creative process flow and not restrict it or restrain it in any way (the lion freely pulls the chariot). There is focus, concentration, and attention to manifest one's creativity which is shown by the contained fire within the chariot. The Prince of Wands represents a deep passion for one's creativity, which is the completely unfolded flower within the Prince's chest. With his phoenix wand and cape, he is committed to growing, expanding, and transforming himself through the creative process.

When people talk about "channelling information" or that they "feel lost for hours during a creative project", it is an acknowledgment of the inspired creativity that they have experienced which is represented by the Prince of Wands.

Prince of Wands

MASTERY OF
INSPIRED CREATIVITY

**Range of
Interpretation for
The Prince of
Wands**

The Prince of Wands is associated with the fire sign month of Leo, the lion; or with fire sign people (July 21 – August 21). When you are drawn toward this symbol, it represents your desire to move creatively in new directions with Leo people in your life; or it can mean that in the month of Leo that you might find yourself moving in new directions with inspired creative projects.

The Prince of Wands may also represent a younger man in your life – someone your age, one or two years younger, or significantly younger – that is inspiring you to move in new directions with your creativity. This symbol may also represent someone younger in your life that you may be inspiring or motivating to move in new directions to express his creativity. Sometimes this symbol can mean meeting someone important while traveling or relocating during the summer month of July 21 – August 21, or it can represent your meeting someone who inspires your creativity and might provide opportunities that could take you in new directions from the time that you pull the card to the month of Leo.

For women, this symbol may represent the inner part of their dynamic nature or *animus* that is moving powerfully in new directions in order to experience unlimited and inspired creativity that wants to be expressed.

RINCESS OF WANDS

is mastery of internal blocks, obstacles and obstructions. She has the tiger by the tail. The tiger in some Oriental mythologies is associated with fear or blocks experienced within the nature. The Princess of Wands is a symbol of the *free and liberated spirit* that is within each individual. She moves in new directions without fear; new directions that are energizing, like her sun-wand. She wears the Aries crown as a symbol of the pioneering and adventurous spirit that each of us possesses.

The spring-time is a season for renewal and new beginnings, which is represented by the ram's pedestal. The Princess of Wands has placed her old obstructions and fears on the altar and offers it as a Spring sacrifice. She can be totally exposed and defenseless because she has nothing to fear.

Princess of Wands

MASTERY OF
SPONTANEOUS EXPRESSION
AND LIBERATION

**Range of
Interpretation for
The Princess of
Wands**

The Princess of Wands is associated with Aries people in our lives, or the month of Aries (March 21 – April 21), as being an important time to express one's sense of freedom, adventure, and of initiating something new. From the time you pull this card to the month of Aries, is a time frame in which you could overcome old fears or obstacles with important Aries people in your life or with important younger women in your life.

If you are a man, this symbol can represent the spontaneous, free spirit that you experience within your own deep nature. It is the part of your *anima*, that does not want to be limited or obstructed by fear. This inner quality can be mirrored to you by spontaneous, adventurous, spirited younger women in your life.

When a person is drawn toward this card, it is an indication that some major fear has already been released internally and that there is an experience of renewed energy, spirit, and vitality.

TYPES OF PHYSICAL MASTERY

Knight of Disks/Pentacles

Queen of Disks/Pentacles

Prince of Disks/Pentacles

Princess of Disks/Pentacles

KNIGHT OF DISKS

demonstrates the capacity to manifest skills in the outer world in practical, observable ways. He is the *harvester* who, with his threshing tool in hand, is prepared to harvest that which he has cultivated. He is determined to achieve harvest in the areas of health and finances. The Knight of Disks represents the doctor or the healer in the deck, or the financier or invester in the deck. In the area of health, he monitors his diet like the horse eating the grains; and, in the area of finances, he creates and protects that which is financially necessary with his large coin shield. The Knight of Disks is the diagnostician, with his antlered helmet, who determines what is necessary in order to manifest abundance. He is the *manifester*. His work is not abstract. This is harvest that is the result of one's creative and diagnostic abilities combined. The creative aspects of manifesting harvest are represented by the lion's head (Leo) which appears on the Knight's coin shield.

Knight of Disks

MASTERY OF
ABUNDANCE AND PROSPERITY

**Range of
Interpretation for
The Knight of Disks**

If you are drawn to this card, it may represent that from now until Leo (July 21 – August 21) would be an excellent time to use creative and diagnostic abilities to manifest harvest in your life. The Knight of Disks can also represent harvest in areas of health and finances in the month of Leo (the lion's head on the Knight's shield) or through opportunities provided either by Leo people or from significant older men, who could be any sign of the Zodiac, and who may be connected with the medical professions or healing arts, or who are actively involved in finances and investments. Regardless, this symbol represents harvest that is to be experienced.

For women, the Knight of Disks can represent the dynamic assertive part of themselves, the inner *animus* that wants to sustain abundant health and financial well-being.

Disks, as a suit, also represent the earth sign months of Capricorn (December 21 – January 21), Virgo (August 21 – September 21), and Taurus (April 21 – May 21) which can also indicate particular people with those signs who could provide opportunities for harvest in your life. Or in the months of Capricorn, Virgo, and Taurus, you could experience more well-being and harvest in your life.

QUEEN OF DISKS

With the globe in her hand, the Queen of Disks builds new worlds through diet and nutrition. She wears a reptilian gown as a symbol of regenerating her body through diet and nutrition. She sits on top of a huge pineapple as a reminder of her commitment to build new worlds that are more fruitful and less bleak and barren than the deserts of the past. With her crystal wand, she sees with clarity what she needs nutritionally in areas of health, finances, work, and relationships. Like Capricorn (the goat) and Aries (the ram, her crown), the Queen of Disks pioneers stable diets for herself in all arenas of her life.

Queen of Disks

MASTERY OF
DIET AND NUTRITION

**Range of
Interpretation for
The Queen of Disks**

The Queen of Disks represents mastery in building new worlds that are nutritious and fulfilling. During the months of Aries (March 21 – April 21) to Capricorn (December 21 – January 21), you can address the need for new diets in all areas of your life; or, important people who are Aries or Capricorn can present new opportunities that can inspire new focus on diet and enhancing nurturing aspects in other areas of your life. The Queen of Disks represents the magnetic, organizing parts of yourself — the inner *anima* which desires to be nurtured in all areas of your life.

This symbol can also indicate that you may want to re-direct your relationships with Capricorn and Aries people in your life so that these relationships may be more nurturing.

The Queen of Disks can also represent deep appreciation for desert areas and tropical environments; or a desire to visit such environments from Aries to Capricorn of the current year.

The Queen of Disks is the aspect of yourself that pioneers (Aries) new ways that are nurturing and stabilizing (Capricorn – the crown that Queen of Disks wears). This symbol indicates the ability to manifest beauty, health, and fulfillment in specific and practical ways in those areas of your life where it is needed and necessary.

PRINCE OF DISKS

is the architect, the designer, and the builder of new forms. With steel-like determination (the chariot), he builds new worlds that are beautiful and abundant (flowers and fruits in the golden tapestry) and worlds that are less obstructive and difficult (the many little boulders on the back of the chariot).

He is the sportsman who through exercise has mastered the capacity to build and recreate structures, which include reforming the body through exercise. The Queen of Disks reforms the body through diet. The Prince of Disks reforms the body through exercise.

The Prince of Disks forges ahead like Taurus, the Bull, to implement structures and forms that are solid, abundant, and beautiful. He holds the double helix as a reminder of his capacity to build new worlds that can be implemented consciously (the winged-bull helmet) in concrete, aesthetic ways.

Prince of Disks

**MASTERY OF
EXERCISE AND
BUILDER OF NEW WORLDS**

**Range of
Interpretation for
The Prince of Disks**

The Prince of Disks represents mastery of the body, especially through sports and exercise. When you are drawn to this card, it is an indication that there is ability concerning physical activity, architecture, design, building, and sports.

During the month of Taurus or with Taurus people in your life, you have the capacity to move in new directions where new fruitful forms can be built. The Prince of Disks can also indicate a desire to travel or relocate either in the month of Taurus or from now until Taurus (April 21 – May 21). It can also mean meeting new people that inspire your moving in new directions as a result of taking a trip or relocating in a new environment.

The Prince of Disks can represent a younger man or Taurus person that you are inspiring to be more active in exercise or, you may be motivating him to move in new directions that are more fruitful for him. Also, a younger man in your life, or Taurus person of any age, might be a motivating force in your life at this time.

For women, this symbol represents the dynamic youthful part of yourself that loves activity. This is the inner *animus* of your nature that is determined to build solid and abundant structures.

RINCESS OF DISKS

is the pregnant lady who represents mastery of creative power. She is a woman who has been over the volcano and through the briar patch. She bears new life that has been gestating and incubating within her for sometime. She is fertile and abundant with either a new identity, life style, creative project, or human being. Her pioneer nature is represented by her Aries crown (the horns that she wears on her head). The snake on her shoulder, which transforms into an ermine cloak, represents her earthy and ancient passion to create.

The Princess of Disks desires to give birth to new forms that are in alignment with who she is (the lighted crystal wand). She is determined to manifest harvest (the pedestal of tied grains upon which she leans) in a balanced and organic way (the lotus blossom with the *yin/yang* center). She approaches motherhood issues or issues surrounding her own mother in creative ways.

Princess of Disks

MASTERY OF CREATIVITY AND BIRTH OF NEW FORMS

**Range of
Interpretation for
The Princess of Disks**

The Princess of Disks represents the capacity to give birth to new forms or resolve motherhood issues from the month of Aries (March 21 – April 21) to Scorpio (October 21 – November 21). This symbol indicates a desire to creatively resolve or restructure relationships with Aries and Scorpio people in your life.

When you are drawn toward this card, it can represent a desire to assist a younger woman in giving birth to new forms in her life, or in helping her resolve motherhood issues.

For men, this symbol can represent the creative part of your *anima* that desires to give birth to the new life that has been gestating within your nature for some time; or this symbol can represent the part of your nature that wants to resolve motherhood issues, or issues involving Aries and Scorpio people in your life.

SECTION V

THE MINOR ARCANA

**Symbolic Representations of
Life's Opportunities and Challenges**

INTRODUCTION

The Minor Arcana in the Tarot is the Ace through Ten of each suit. These are portraitures or pictures of life's lessons and opportunities, or possible experiences that we could have mentally, emotionally, spiritually and physically.

Swords will always indicate the mental level of consciousness. Anytime that you pull a Sword, it will indicate the quality of mind that is present in thoughts, attitudes, and beliefs.

Cups will always mirror to you the emotional level of consciousness, your responses and your reactions. *Reaction* comes from the root word, *to react, to redo*, so it's an habitual reaction to the situation rather than a response, which is spontaneous.

Wands indicates the spiritual suit. Other synonyms for spiritual would be *energy, life-force*. Also, Wands represents the intuitive function, insight, and perception. It illustrates what's important to the person at the core of who they are. Anytime that you pull a Wand, it indicates a core sensation, or the gut of who you are, or a picture of your own truth and authenticity. The Wands are associated with an unwillingness to abandon oneself.

Disks – or Pentacles in other decks – is always a portraiture of what's happening in your external reality; that which you can definitively point to. So whenever you pull a Disk, it's going to indicate an outer situation, whether it's health, finances, work, creativity, or relationships. Disks do not represent an abstract situation; they reflect outer situations that can be definitely seen.

In Egypt, there was both the Egyptian Book of the Dead, and the Egyptian Book for Living, reflecting all the possibilities of what one could experience in life in hieroglyphic or pictographic form. Egypt was one of the few cultures that had both a Book of the Living and a Book of the Dead. The Book of the Living was called the Book of Thoth, from which this particular Tarot Deck comes; it was also called the Book of Wisdom. Within that Book of Wisdom, there were thirteen challenges or tests, and twenty-seven gifts, talents and resources that could assist one in transforming what are called the Bardo states, or the problematic or challenging states of consciousness.

The beauty of this particular Tarot Deck is that in the entire seventy-eight cards, there are only thirteen real challenges that one faces, and these are pictured in the Minor Arcana. Also in the Minor Arcana, as in the Book of Thoth, there are twenty-seven positive states. If we remember the positive states, or the gifts, talents and resources within, these qualities are present to assist or transform the Bardo states. It is through choice that we can transform the Bardo states, or what Jung would call *the Shadow aspects of who we are*. In Jungian psychology, there is the statement, "the brighter the sun, the darker the shadow." Tarot reminds us that both states are present within our natures.

ACE THROUGH TEN
OF
SWORDS

Ace of Swords

ACE OF SWORDS

The Ace of Swords represents mental clarity, inventiveness, and originality. It is the mind that has no doubt. It is the mind that has moved out of doubt and confusion as symbolized by the clouds at the bottom of the card. The Ace of Swords represents creative thinking, the inspired and innovative mind. It symbolizes expanded awareness and consciousness. The creative mind is revealed by the green sword. The Ace of Swords represents the balanced and receptive mind, which is portrayed by the crescent moons on the handle of the sword. The creative mind is willing to express itself dynamically, which is represented by the suns, the two balls on the handle, and is constantly renewing and regenerating itself, which is represented by the snake on the handle of the sword.

The sword pierces the crown, a symbol of expanded awareness. The crown represents the *aha* experience, or the mind that has gleaned a new insight, a new awareness. This is the mind that has come out of the clouds of doubt and confusion, totally into the light, into a new place of clarity. In metaphorical terms, this is the mind that is like the clear blue sky. From a Tibetan point of view, or Buddhist point of view, this is the state of mind that is referred to as "diamond consciousness."

The Ace of Swords is associated with the air sign months of Libra (September 21 – October 21), Aquarius (January 21 – February 21), Gemini (May 21 – June 21). All of the Aces stand for a year's time, so whenever one pulls this card, the qualities that are associated with the creative, innovative, inspired clear mind are what wants to be utilized during the year. The Ace of Swords represents a good year in which to implement an original idea or an important dream or purpose that can be actualized. This symbol supports writing, editing, research of any kind and represents access to creative thinking, brain-storming, intuitive thinking, and decision-making.

The Ace of Swords suggests that the months of Libra, Aquarius and Gemini would be good times to execute ideas. It also represents a period during which there would be more clarity about important air sign people in your life, any Libras, Aquarius and Gemini people.

Mythically, the Ace of Swords is associated with King Arthur and the Round Table. The search for the Grail and the application of wisdom achieved from retrieving the sword lodged in the stone is reflected by the Ace of Swords.

TWO OF SWORDS

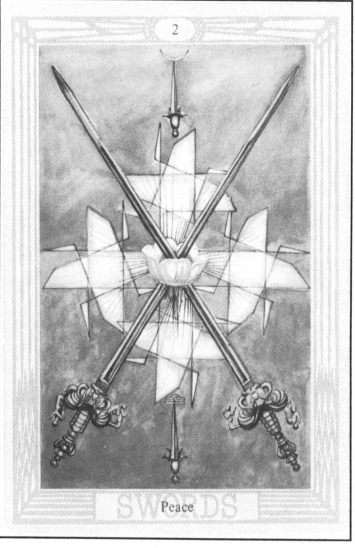

Peace

The Two of Swords represents peace – peace of mind. It is a picture of the meditative mind, or the mind that has made a choice, either between two issues, two situations, or two people, all of which is represented by the two swords piercing the blue lotus blossom of wisdom. This is the choice or decision made in the mind that generates the quality of peace, satisfaction, clarity. The four pinwheels in the back of the card indicate that there is resolution or peace of mind that pervades all levels of consciousness – mental, emotional, spiritual and physical. Peace that is experienced pervasively throughout the system is represented by the handles of the swords which have angels coming off of them. The handles of the swords also are very Scorpionic in their shapes, or look like Scorpio, representing peace that goes to a deep and substantial level, which is the essence of Scorpio. Scorpio is the sign in astrology that is most associated with transformation, and so this is a transformative peace of mind, or what we might refer to as a "vivid peace."

Astrologically, the Two of Swords is Moon in Libra, which is symbolized by the two small swords, one at the top of the card that holds a crescent moon, and the other at the bottom of the card which holds the sign of Libra. The crescent moon indicates that at a deep subconscious place, there is a sense of balance and peace, which is signified by the Libra symbol. This is peace that goes to a very deep spiritual place which is represented by the yellow on the card, and a peace that is renewing and regenerating, which is represented by the green on this card.

Whenever you pull this symbol, it indicates that there has been a decision made. Swords are always a representation of the mental level of consciousness; and the Two of Swords indicates a decision that will manifest peace of mind and resolution within the next two weeks or the next two months, represented by the number 2 at the top of the card. The Two of Swords is a portraiture of the meditative mind that contains the quality of bringing peace, clarity, and balance to the mental realms of consciousness. This symbol represents the integrative mind, or the mind that has been able to bring two or more issues together into a state of resolution, which is represented by the two swords piercing the blue lotus blossom of wisdom.

Sorrow

THREE OF SWORDS

The Three of Swords is a symbol representing sorrow. This is sorrow held in the mind, or reworked in the mind. It is, specifically, negative-thinking about the past, and particularly, the parts of the past that have produced sorrow. The Three of Swords represents events or sorrow that have pierced our nature to the core, which is symbolized by the swords piercing the lotus blossom to its core with petals falling from its stem. The Three of Swords reflects a tendency in the mind to rework the old bones of the past, and particularly the parts of the past that contain sorrow or negativity. This is sorrow that could have resurfaced in the last three months, or could go back to three years ago, or could go back as early as to when you were three years old. It could also be the first sorrow that was experienced within the family, the number 3 is associated with the original triangle, which is father-mother-child. How we handled that first triangle – which is represented by the three swords – is how we will handle subsequent triangles, whether they are friend-co-worker-friend, or friend-sibling-mate or friend-lover-mate. In whatever triangles that we have been involved, the Three of Swords reminds us to break family patterns and to release a tendency in the mind to hold grudges or to rework parts of the past in the mind that are hurtful and destructive. This symbol reflects the need to remove oneself from triangles that produce sorrow. There are many creative triangles and constructive triangles, but this is a reminder to remove oneself from triangulations that produce sorrow and that are not constructive. The symbol that represents the triangulation is shown by the two swords at the top being bent by the entry of a third sword. This often reflects that there is something to be resolved between three people. The central sword can also represent an event that bent and pierced the receptive and dynamic sides of a person's nature.

The astrological symbol or aspect that is represented on the Three of Swords is Saturn, the symbol at the top of the card, in Libra, which is the symbol at the bottom of the card. Saturn is the planet that reminds us to do things step-by-step, and in so doing, will bring balance, which is Libra, into our nature. Basically, the Three of Swords shows us that we can heal the memories of the past by ceasing to look only at those parts of the past that created sorrow, and by looking at the past as a whole. This symbol often represents the mind that has a limited view of the past, which is represented by Saturn, and that by expanding our view of the past, we can bring things into balance, which is Libra.

It is important to remember when you pull this card that the sorrow is only through negative thinking in the mind. This is a mental tape or an old way of thinking about the past. This is not sorrow that is held in the heart or in the body, this is a tendency in the mind to resurrect old parts of the past, particularly the sad and negative parts of the past. When you pull this card, it indicates that you are ready, in the next three weeks or the next three months, to change your perspective or thinking about the past by eliminating negative thinking which constantly reworks the past, particularly the parts of the past that have created sorrow. The Three of Swords also indicates that in the next three weeks or the next three months you may be making conscious choices to remove yourself from triangular relationships that produce sorrow, or situations which are not constructive learning experiences for you, or others. When a person is drawn towards this card, it is an indication that some past sorrow is affecting his or her current thinking, and that there is a desire to release an old pattern which is producing the current sorrow or sadness. With focus and intention, this state of consciousness can be released within the next three weeks or the next three months in a step-by-step balancing process. The Empress can be drawn upon for support in this process. The Empress is the Major Arcana card number III, which has already moved through aspects of sorrow tied with the past. This symbol may also represent that in the next three weeks or the next three months, that you may want to release negative thinking about disappointments or sorrows experienced with Libra people in your life, anyone born September 21 to October 21, which is represented by the Saturn in Libra aspect on this card.

Truce

FOUR OF SWORDS

The Four of Swords is the negotiating mind, the conflict/resolution mind, or the mediating mind. In order for any kind of negotiation to be successful, one must be open and flexible like the sign Jupiter at the top of this card, and committed to staying in balance and non-positional which is represented by the sign of Libra at the bottom of this card. The truce-making process is a four-fold process which is represented by the four swords and also the four tiers of the lotus blossom flower. The four-fold process is truce that's experienced on all four levels of consciousness: mentally, emotionally, spiritually, and physically, which is also represented by the integrating four swords into the four tiers of the lotus blossom.

Truce is an opportunity to move through conflictual issues, which is represented by all the webbing in the background of this card, and the states of complexity that need to be resolved. In order for negotiation or conflict-resolution to be successful, there are four peaceful principles that come from native traditions which is referred to as the four-fold way. In order for truce to be experienced, one must: first, show up; second, pay attention; third, tell the truth; and fourth, not be attached to outcome. When one is able to show up, pay attention, tell the truth, and not be attached to outcome – the results are renewal and regeneration, which is symbolized here by the yellow and the green colors on the card representing regeneration and renewal (green) from a very deep spiritual place (yellow).

Whenever you pull this card, it can indicate that in the next four weeks or in the next four months, there is opportunity for truce-making, conflict resolution, negotiation and resolution with important issues or people in your life. You have the flexibility and expansiveness of Jupiter, and the centeredness and the balance of Libra in which to accomplish resolution. Or, the Four of Swords can symbolize that in the month of Libra (September 21 – October 21), or with Libra people in your life, there could be truce-making and resolution in the next four weeks or in the next four months.

FIVE OF SWORDS

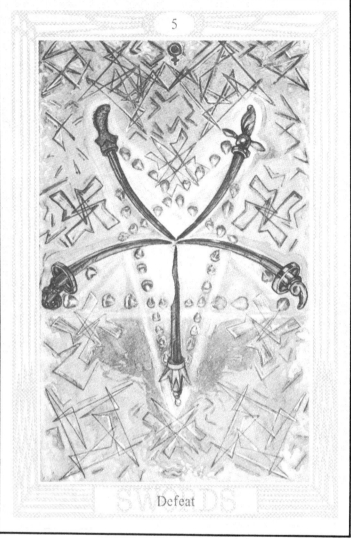

The Five of Swords is fear of defeat, or memory of defeat. Here we have five bent swords, one of which has a hankerchief that's red with blood dripping from it, which is representative of negative thinking that opens an old wound, and as a result of opening that old wound, there is an experience of fear. Fear has one function, which is to constrict. All the twisted lines in the background are showing the function of fear, which is to constrict, to distort, to bend one's perspective or way of thinking. This is a fear that history might repeat itself, or fear that one will be hurt again.

The astrological aspect of this card is Venus, at the top of the card, in Aquarius, the wavy lines at the bottom of the card. Basically, there are two fears held in the mind – one is fear that a new relationship may not work out (Venus in Aquarius), or two, having fear of moving in new directions that are emotionally important to you, the new directions are symbolized by Aquarius at the bottom of the card, and those directions being emotionally important to you, is symbolized by Venus at the top of the card. Venus in Aquarius also symbolizes the emotional fears of what you might not attain that's important to you in this new direction. The symbol that represents an old fear tied with the past is the red handkerchief from which blood is dripping, and this fear is also symbolized by the handle of the sword that holds the Pisces fish. Pisces as an astrological sign represents the past, the Piscean age, or that which is old, yet memorable. The function of fear is to distort and is based on events unknown or on past experience. When we move into states of fear, nothing is renewed or regenerated, which is symbolized by the sleeping snake on the handle of one sword; and we're unable to move in new directions, which is symbolized by Aries the Ram on the other sword. Basically, fear has us looking at things from a distorted perspective, which is symbolized by the handle of the sword that has the crown placed upside-down. The crown is a symbol of expanded awareness, and here it is upside-down, indicating that our awareness is not attainable or is distorted. Yet in the background, the greater aspect of who we are, represented by the white light and the star shape, is attempting to break through fear that is created in the mind through negative thinking about the past or future.

Whenever you pull this card it indicates that in the next five weeks or the next five months you are determined to release negative thinking that produces fear of defeat about either new relationships, or fear that new directions that are so heartfelt for you will not work out. It could also be old fears that have surfaced that may go back to the last five months, or may go back to five years ago or may be old fears that got imprinted when you were five years old. Five is the number of the Hierophant and the family, so it might be interesting to see which of your parents had a lot of fear about relationships not working out, or fears of defeat about moving in new directions. In pulling this card, you are no longer willing to be the lineage bearer or the legacy bearer of family fears of defeat held in the mind. Since this is also the Venus in Aquarius aspect, there could be fears of defeat about Aquarius people in your life, anyone born January 21 to February 21, that you choose to resolve in the next five weeks or the next five months, to release those fears. The Hierophant is the Major Arcana card that can be drawn upon for support at this time, because the Hierophant has the wisdom and the faith to move through these fears that are created or generated in the mind. The mind is the easiest to reprogram through creative visualization and affirmation.

SIX OF SWORDS

The Six of Swords is science of mind, the objective mind or the fair-witnessing mind. This is the very focused, intentional mind represented by the six cards coming to the center of the Rosicrusian Cross, which is a miniature representation of the cross that is on the back of all of these Tarot cards. This symbol is the rational, objective, fair-witnessing mind. It's the mind that considers the whole, which is represented by the circular crystalline shape, as well as the mind that is creative, which is represented by the diamond that surrounds the crystalline shape. The creative mind is represented by the diamond. The wholistic mind is symbolized by the circle, and the focused, intentional mind is represented by the six swords coming to the center of the Rosicrusian cross. The cross itself is a universal symbol of integration, synthesis and blessing, and so the Six of Swords represents the integrative mind that recognizes sources of inspiration that are sometimes unexplainable.

The astrological aspect that is found on this card is Mercury in Aquarius. Mercury is represented at the top of the card and is the planet that is associated with communication. Aquarius is the astrological sign that is most associated with originality, innovation and pioneering work, and is the sign located at the bottom of the card. Mercury in Aquarius indicates the ability to communicate new things in such an objective way that they can be received and heard. Objective communication is the ability to communicate in such a way that it is non-threatening and it allows people to consider new ideas, thoughts, beliefs or attitudes from perspectives that they had not previously considered. The Six of Swords represents the mind that can consider multiple things at once, which is represented by all the pinwheels and the criss-crossing in the background of this card.

When you pull this card, it indicates that in the next six weeks or the next six months, it's important for you to look at things as they are rather than as you want them to be. It is also important to communicate new ideas or decisions in such an objective way that they can be received and heard. This is the mind that's focused, creative, integrative, and willing to look at the whole. It can also indicate that the next six weeks or the next six months would be a useful time in which to extend communication to important Aquarius people in your life, anyone born January 21 to February 21, and in an objective and creative manner.

EVEN OF SWORDS

The Seven of Swords is that state of mind which produces futility, or the sense of helplessness, hopelessness, or "what's the use?" Basically, this state of mind is knowing mentally what you want, which is represented by the central sword, and then telling yourself all the reasons why it's not going to work, which is represented by the six swords coming in at the central sword. This is negative thinking, or the sabotaging mind, that sabotages what it is that you really want. It's the *yes-but* tape in the mind, telling yourself the reasons why things won't work.

The Seven of Swords is Sun and Moon in Aquarius. The two wavy lines at the bottom of the card are associated with Aquarius. The circle with the dot in the middle is the sign of the Sun, and the crescent moon symbolizes the Moon. Six ways that we sabotage what we want are revealed by the astrological symbols on the handles of the swords. The negative aspect of Saturn, or the *yes-but* aspect of Saturn, is telling ourselves that there is too much red tape or too many details. The other handle of the sword has the symbol of Mercury, the planet of communication on it. The negative self-talk of Mercury, negative communication to the self, is using such words as "I can't ......if only......someday I'll......wish I'd a......", all negative communication to the self about why this project or situation won't work. On the other handle of the sword is Jupiter; Jupiter is the planet of flexibility and expansion. The negative self-talk of Jupiter is that, "I'm not lucky......it's too constricted, too limiting." On the other handle of the sword is Mars; the positive aspect of Mars is energy, vitality, and assertion. The negative self-talk of Mars would be, "I don't have enough energy......I'm exhausted, burned out......it's dull, boring." On the other handle of the sword is the sign of Venus, which is associated with love. The negative self-talk of Venus is, "I really don't care......it doesn't mean anything to me anyway," is the sabotaging component of Venus. The final handle of the sword has double loops on it, which is associated with the Sun and the Moon. The negative aspects of the Sun and the Moon is that consciously and subconsciously you sabotage yourself out of doing what it is that you want to do.

The sabotaging mind or the *yes-but* tape will generate the experience of futility, or what's-the-use, or helplessness and hopelessness. Basically, it's important to remember that the Seven of Swords represents the mind that knows what it wants, which is symbolized by the central sword, and the other six swords represent the *yes-but* tape in the mind, or ways of telling ourselves all the reasons why things are not going to work.

When you pull this card, it indicates that in the next seven weeks or the next seven months, you are no longer willing to sabotage what it is that you want. The number 7 is associated with the Chariot, which is the generator and motivator of change, and 7 is the number of movement, so somehow, in the next seven weeks or the next seven months, you are wanting to move through negative thinking in the mind that sabotages what it is that you want. Also, during the next seven weeks or the next seven months there would be an opportunity to release sabotaging patterns that have surfaced either in the last seven months, or sabotaging patterns that go back to seven years ago, or sabotaging patterns that may have been implemented when you were seven years old. It might be interesting to see which of your parents had a tendency to sabotage what he or she wanted through negative thinking, because somehow, in the next seven weeks or the next seven months, you are no longer willing to be the lineage bearer or the legacy bearer of family futility patterns or sabotaging patterns held in the mind.

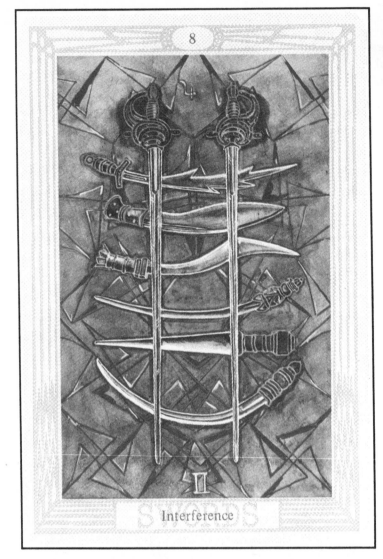

EIGHT OF SWORDS

The Eight of Swords is the doubting, non-trusting, over-analytical mind. Basically, it's the mind that is considering either two options, two issues, two situations, or two people, and then going back and forth on which would be the better option or the better choice.

Whenever you pull this card, it's a reminder that when you are in states of doubt or confusion or interference, that it is a time to wait, it is not a time to act. The Eight of Swords represents that somehow in the next eight weeks or the next eight months, there will be more clarity. The work to be done at this time is to trust and wait rather than to over-analyze for purposes of attempting to control situations, or for purposes of over-analyzing things to such a degree that it creates doubt, confusion and interference. This symbol can also represent that in the next eight weeks or the next eight months there will be more clarity and it's important that when there is not clarity, that one waits rather than acts, until that clarity reveals itself. The Eight of Swords also represents that you may be considering ways of how you can bring two issues, or situations, or people, together to create a greater whole rather than feeling that you need to make a choice between two issues, situations or people. The Eight of Swords may also indicate there could be choices surrounding Gemini people in your life, anyone born May 21 to June 21, and that if you are in states of doubt or confusion about Gemini people, that it is not a time to act or be decisive, but it is a time to wait. The Adjustment archetype in the Major Arcana section is available to be drawn on for support in balancing and weighing the choices that one is considering at this point in time. Also, during the next eight weeks or the next eight months would be a good time to release old analytical, non-trusting patterns in the mind that may go back to eight years ago, or may have been first imprinted when you were eight years old. It might be interesting to see which of your parents had a tendency to over-analyze to such a degree that doubt or interference was created, because somehow, in the next eight weeks or the next eight months, you are no longer willing to be the lineage bearer or the legacy bearer of family over-analytical patterns or family doubting patterns held in the mind.

The astrological aspect of this symbol is Jupiter in Gemini. Jupiter is the planet that requires that we grow and expand and weigh different possibilities or options, which is Gemini. During this time, it is important to consider different options and to wait on making decisions if you are experiencing doubt or confusion.

NINE OF SWORDS

The Nine of Swords represents mental self-cruelty or the tendency mentally to put oneself down. It's the self-critical mind or the self-judging mind. This symbol reflects the mind that actively wounds the self through thought, symbolized by the bleeding swords. The spirit weeps in the background, wondering why you are being so hard on yourself, which is represented by the white tears in the background. Swords in general are representative of varied ways of thinking. The astrological aspect on this card is Mars in Gemini. Mars is the planet of energy, vitality and assertion, so this is self-criticalness that has vitality and assertiveness to it. Gemini indicates a tendency of reworking things, going back and forth, particularly self-critical things. Mars is dynamic energy and power of mental degradation that is felt both dynamically and magnetically within the nature of the personality which is Gemini.

When you pull this card, in the next nine weeks or the next nine months, you are determined to release negative thinking and self-criticalness held in the mind. Nine is the number of completion, it's associated with the Hermit archetype. It indicates also that in the next nine weeks or the next nine months, you may release negative thinking or self-criticalness about what you've done or haven't done, or negative thinking about Gemini people. Gemini often represents two arenas of your life, whether it is personal or professional, or two issues in your life. The Nine of Swords also symbolizes that somehow in the next nine weeks or the next nine months, you are determined to release self-criticalness about two aspects of your life, or two aspects of your self, or two aspects about other people. It also indicates that in the next nine weeks or the next nine months, you may be releasing parts of the past where you have been very self-critical about your self, parts of the past that may have resurfaced in the last nine months, or go back to nine years ago, or go back to when you were nine years old. It might be interesting also to take a look at which of your parents may have been very self-critical or self-judging, because somehow, in the next nine weeks or the next nine months, you are wanting to release self-critical family patterns. The Hermit is the major archetype of completion and introspection and self-reflection, and is a source of energy that can be drawn for guidance and support as you work through self-criticalness in the mind in the next nine weeks or the next nine months.

EN
OF
SWORDS

The Ten of Swords symbolizes fear of ruin. This is a state of mental despair, or fear held in the mind to such a point that you have made a conscious decision that things are not going to work out in two arenas of your life, either in an emotional relationship, which is symbolized by the pierced heart, or about finances, which is symbolized by scales at the top of the card. The astrological aspect of this card is Sun in Gemini. Individuals who have Sun in Gemini are mentally gifted in synthesizing polarities, oppositions and paradox. Because they have this ability, they are able to look at all aspects of a situation, the positive aspects as well as the negative aspects, and in their facility to do this, sometimes they are able to see things which produce fear within their nature and especially in those issues concerning matters of the heart or finances, or practical implementation of creative ideas.

When you pull this card, it may indicate that in the next ten weeks or the next ten months you will want to resolve negative thinking that produces fear of ruin about your relationship with Gemini people in your life, anyone born May 21 to June 21; or in the next ten weeks or the next ten months, you may want to release fears of ruin surrounding financial situations or fears of ruin surrounding emotional relationships that are important to you at this point in time. Also, what you may be releasing could be old fears held in the mind or old memories that were imprinted about relationships or about finances that may go back to the last ten months or to ten years ago, or when you were ten years old. It might be interesting to take a look to see which of your parents had a lot of fear about finances, or fear about relationships not working out, because within the next ten weeks or the next ten months, you are determined to release old fears of ruin concerning finances and relationships that might have been imprinted through family conditioning. The number 10 is associated with an aspect of the Wheel of Fortune, so this is fear that is moving, or there is an attempt consciously in the mind to turn things in a more fortunate, positive direction in the next ten weeks and in the next ten months. The Wheel of Fortune card can be drawn upon for visual support in turning this situation into the direction of more positive results rather than fearful results. This symbol reminds us not to make statements such as "It's not going to work," or "I know it's not going to work," which is consciously deciding that things are not going to work. Somehow in the next ten weeks or the next ten months, you will release the fear that produces negative thinking that leads to conscious decisions about things not working.

ACE THROUGH TEN
OF
CUPS

Ace of Cups

ACE OF CUPS

The Ace of Cups is the open heart, the clear heart, the trusting heart, the spiritual heart. This is the Holy Grail sitting within the emotional nature, which is represented by the blue cup. It's the state of emotional integrity, which is represented by the double reflected rainbow, the capacity to express accurately feelings that are being experienced internally. The rainbow represents the reflection of emotional feelings from such a base of integrity that there is no dichotomy between what's being experienced inside and what's being reflected outside. The Ace of Cups symbolizes emotional balance required to nurture, comfort, support, and heal oneself in equal proportion to how one would nuture, support, comfort and heal others. This quality, represented by the ray of light coming into the cup, is the capacity to nurture oneself in equal proportion to what one gives out. This is love with wisdom. Love is represented by the cup, and wisdom by the blue grail. This is love that is constantly regenerating itself, symbolized by the handles of the cups on which are coiled regenerated snakes. It's the trusting heart, represented by the lotus blossom, trusting the natural organic unfoldment of its own development. The trusting heart does not push or use effort to make things happen, and the trusting heart does not resist or protect itself, or hold back. Love with wisdom is the capacity to trust without over-extending oneself emotionally or overprotecting oneself emotionally, which is represented by the organic unfoldment of the lotus blossom.

When you pull this card, it indicates that within the next year there is emotional integrity, equal balance in self-nuturance and the nurturance of others, and the implementation of trust can be experienced in your relationships. It's the reflecting of one's feelings accurately, particularly to water sign people in your life, any Pisces, born February 21 to March 21, any Scorpios, born October 21 to November 21, and any Cancer people, born June 21 to July 21; or that in the months of Pisces, Cancer and Scorpio, it is important to demonstrate love with wisdom, emotional integrity, and a trusting open-hearted nature. The Ace of Cups is a quality of the Magician, particularly the aspect of the Magician that is able to communicate feelings. The Magician is the archetype of communication, and is the number 1. The Ace of Cups is the aspect of being able to communicate feelings from a place of emotional integrity and from a place of trust rather that control.

TWO OF CUPS

Love

The Two of Cups is love. This represents the type of love that is nurturing, creative, inspirational, clear, and equally fulfilling. This is love that reflects strong communication, as symbolized by the red dolphins, in total expression to each other. It's love that is internally experienced as well as externally experienced, which is reflected by the double pink lotus blossoms, representing the concept of "as above – so below, as within – so without." The Two of Cups represents love that is equal and special, which is symbolized by the equally filled cups. This is love that is not symbionic. It is love that is fully expressed from an individual place, and love that is extended to another without self-abandonment or self-diminishment. It is the type of love where each of the individuals feels equal to the other and simultaneously very special to each other. We all have had the experience of what it is like to have an equal relationship and yet not feel special, which is often the colleagial or professional relationship, and we've often had the experience of knowing what it is like to be special but not equal. The Two of Cups represents both equal and special love. It is a creative love, which is represented by the green sea. It's an inspirational and spiritual love which is represented by the yellow reflection on the water, and it's love that's clear and focused, which is represented by the blue sky. The astrological aspect of this card is Venus in Cancer. Venus is the planet of love, beauty and creative power; Cancer is the astrological symbol of nurturing, comforting, supporting, and healing. The sign of Cancer is associated with family and the home, so this is also love that is comforting, supporting, healing. It is also love that is very much expressed within the family and the home, and in all other areas of our life.

Whenever you pull this card, it indicates that within the next two weeks or the next two months, there will be an experience of emotional balance and emotional fulfillment with capacity to give love as well as to receive love in equal proportion. It also indicates that in the next two weeks or the next two months would be a good time to extend and receive love from Cancer people in your life, anyone born June 21 to July 21; or it would be a good time to extend and receive love from important family members or extended family members. This can also indicate a love for two people, two situations, two gifts, talents, resources that you have, and that somehow those two loves in your life whatever they may be, are equally balanced and fulfilling in the next two weeks or the next two months.

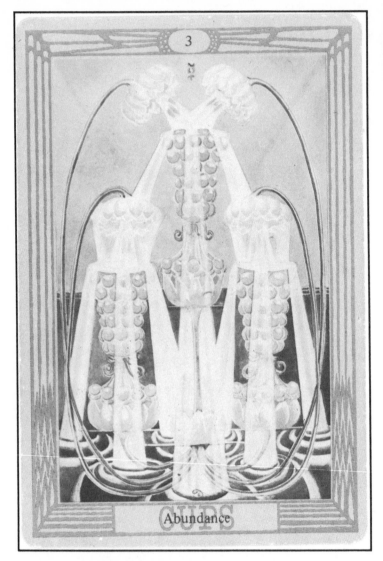

HREE OF CUPS

The Three of Cups is abundance. This is the abundant communicating heart. The astrological aspect of the Three of Cups is Mercury in Cancer. Mercury is the symbol of communication at the top of the card. Cancer, the astrological symbol located at the bottom of the card, is associated with nurturement. Mercury in Cancer is the ability to communicate the abundance of feelings that one has, especially the nurturing, positive, lighted feelings, which is represented by the golden lotus blossoms whose pollen has totally changed into light and fills the pomegranate cups. The pomegranates are associated with the riches that we have experienced emotionally. Pomegranates were the rare fruits that were often given to visiting royalty in Greece and Egypt, so the ability to communicate the riches that one has received emotionally from others is represented by the pomegranate cups. Communication is represented by Mercury on the card, but it is communication that is coming from deep within, which is symbolized by the golden lotus blossoms. The Three of Cups also represents the abundance of feelings that one may have for three very important people in our lives, and particularly communicating the abundance of feelings that you may have for one person more than the other two, which is represented by the elevated cup above the other two cups.

When you pull this card, it indicates that in the next three weeks or the next three months would be a good time to communicate the abundance of feelings that you have for three very important people in your life; or it can indicate that the next three weeks or the next three months is a good time to utilize your communication gifts in ways that nurture, comfort, and motivate people in such a way that it generates tangible abundance for you. It could also indicate that the next three weeks or the next three months would be a good time to communicate the abundance of feelings that you have for Cancer people in your life or for family members or extended family which is represented by the Cancer symbol at the bottom of the card.

 OUR OF CUPS

The Four of Cups is emotional luxury and fulfillment. This symbol represents the experience of feeling emotionally fulfilled and satisfied internally, which are the cups filled from deep within, radiating out; and feeling equally satisfied about external situations, which are the cups reflecting outwardly. What we have represented here is the two-way flow of internal and external fulfillment and satisfaction that is being experienced emotionally. The astrological symbol associated with this card is Moon, the crescent moon at the top of the card, in Cancer, the astrological symbol at the bottom of the card. Moon in Cancer is the aspect of feeling very nurtured (Cancer) from deep within (the Moon).

Whenever you pull this card, it is an indication that in the next four weeks or the next four months, you are determined to experience emotional luxury internally and externally. You are no longer willing to support the dichotomy of feeling internally full and externally empty, or feeling externally full and internally empty. True emotional luxury is the experience of feeling internally satisfied and fulfilled as well as feeling emotionally fulfilled externally also. It also indicates that in the next four weeks or in the next four months, you could work well with luxury items, such as jewelry, antiques, computers, counseling, fashion design or anything that would be considered a luxury. The Four of Cups can symbolize that in the next four weeks or the next four months that there is an experience of internal and external emotional satisfaction; also, luxury can be experienced in your life in the next four weeks or in the next four months through Cancer people, family members or extended family members.

Disappointment

IVE
OF
CUPS

The Five of Cups is emotional disappointment. Disappointment makes you feel fragile, breakable and vulnerable, like the glass cups represented on this symbol. Disappointment is the state where you experience emotional depression, like the murky seas, and anger, like the red sky. Disappointment takes us off balance, which is symbolized by the askewed star, and makes us feel uprooted, like the lily pads with the falling lotus blossoms. Yet disappointment can be a transformative agent, the roots of the lily pad make the shape of a butterfly, which is a universal symbol for transformation. The astrological aspect of this card is Mars in Scorpio. Mars is the planet that is associated with energy, vitality and assertion. Like Mars, this is disappointment that is deep and vital; this is disappointment that goes to a very deep level, like Scorpio. Scorpio is associated with the depths. This is not a superficial disappointment. It can be disappointment that has been experienced within the last five months, or disappointment that has been experienced within the last five years or goes back, specifically, to five years ago, or disappointment that can go back as early as when you were was five years old. It might be interesting to take a look at which of your parents was severely disappointed, because somehow in the next five weeks or the next five months, you are no longer willing to be the lineage bearer, the legacy bearer of family disappointment patterns.

When you pull this card, it indicates that in the next five weeks or the next five months, you may want to release old disappointments connected with Scorpio people or disappointments connected with family members, or extended family members. Also, in the next five weeks or the next five months, you are no longer willing to hold onto past disappointments and will make a conscious intention to let go of them. The Hierophant can be drawn upon for support in working through this disappointment, since the Hierophant is the principle symbol of faith and family and has the ability to release old disappointments tied with the past.

SIX OF CUPS

Pleasure

The Six of Cups is pleasure. This card represents emotional pleasure that is healing, like the copper cups, and revitalizing, like the orange lotus blossoms, and renewing and regenerating, like the snakes coiled within the cups. This is pleasure that is very deeply nurturing, which is symbolized by the astrological aspect of Sun in Scorpio. Scorpio is the astrological sign that experiences life at very deep levels.

When you pull this card, it indicates that within the next six weeks or the next six months, there is an emotional determination to bring pleasure into your life that is renewing, revitalizing and regenerating. This pleasure could be experienced through Scorpio people in your life, anyone born October 21 to November 21; or in the month of Scorpio you could experience a time of regeneration and renewal that is emotionally energizing and pleasureful. Out of the experience of pleasure, you are regenerated and renewed to such an extent that pleasure and the sense of pleasure is extended to others in the next six weeks or in the next six months.

SEVEN OF CUPS

The Seven of Cups is debauch, or emotional indulgence. This card represents the state of emotional depression and moods. The Seven of Cups often is a picture of our emotional addictions or indulgences. Whenever we are depressed, it reflects what it is that we will reach for to make ourselves feel better, whether it's over-eating, over-shopping, over-drinking, smoking, drug usage, or sexual promiscuity. This symbol reflects a tendency to indulge in moods or wallow in negative emotional reactions and responses, or emotional memories of the past. Debauch is a tendency of feeling sorry for yourself or indulging in being a martyr or a victim. The Seven of Cups represents a destructive way of coping with depression or issues that one does not want to face by indulging in patterns that involve excessive behavior.

Whenever you pull this card it indicates that in the next seven weeks or in the next seven months, that you are willing to move through indulgence or addictive patterns. The number 7 is associated with the Charioteer, which is the principle of change and movement, so that in the next seven weeks or the next seven months, there is support for movement in those areas where you are experiencing depression and debauch patterns. The astrological aspect that is associated with this symbol is Venus in Scorpio. Venus is the planet of love, and Scorpio is the astrological symbol of transformation and in-depth exploration. Venus in Scorpio reflects that somehow, in the next seven weeks or in the next seven months, you are willing to move through indulgence patterns that have affected you emotionally in very deep and transformative ways. The Seven of Cups also indicates that in the next seven weeks or the next seven months, you may not be willing to any longer tolerate the indulgence or debauch patterns of others; or that in the next seven weeks or the next seven months, you are wanting to move through depressive or indulgent dynamics that you experience with Scorpio people in your life, anyone born October 21 to November 21. The Seven of Cups also indicates that you may be wanting to release moods or depressive memories that are associated with either the last seven months or seven years ago or when you were seven years old. Or, this symbol may reflect that in the next seven weeks or the next seven months, you are no longer willing to be the lineage bearer or legacy bearer of family debauch or indulgence patterns of any kind.

EIGHT OF CUPS

Indolence

The Eight of Cups is indolence, or emotional inertia as a result of over-giving patterns. This symbol represents emotional stagnation and inertia as a result of over-extending yourself and not honoring your own limits and boundaries, or being able to set limits and boundaries. The Eight of Cups represents the emotional state of feeling tired, drained, depleted, and emotionally ripped off, as a result of filling others' needs and wants to the brim, which is symbolized by the lighted holes in the sea that are filled up with over-extended energy . This symbol reflects the tendency to over-give or randomly over-extend oneself. It symbolizes a need to honor your own limits and boundaries, especially in areas where one is emotionally involved. The astrological aspect of this symbol is Saturn in Pisces. The planet Saturn reminds us that we must establish structures or discipline in our life, and Pisces is the astrological symbol of emotional fluidity. Saturn in Pisces reminds us that we need to know what our limits and boundaries are emotionally, otherwise, we will totally over-extend ourselves emotionally and experience the results of depletion, exhaustion and emotional unfulfillment.

Whenever you pull the Eight of Cups, it indicates that personally and professionally, you have over-extended your energies to the point of emotional exhaustion and depletion, or burn-out. The next eight weeks or the next eight months would be a good time to honor your limits and boundaries and to break old patterns of over-extension in any arena of your life. The next eight weeks or the next eight months may also be a time when it is important for you to set emotional limits and boundaries with important Pisces people in your life, anyone born February 21 to March 21; or that this may be a reminder that the month of Pisces is a time to honor your own limits and boundaries and not to over-extend yourself emotionally in personal and professional aspects of your life. The

Adjustment card is the Major Arcana card which can assist you in the next eight weeks or the next eight months in breaking old patterns of over-extension that lead to indolence, inertia or stagnation. The Eight of Cups also reflects that in the next eight weeks or the next eight months, that you may want to break old over-extension patterns that may have resurfaced in the last eight months or may go back to eight years ago, or may even go back to when you were eight years old. It might be interesting to see which of your parents had emotional patterns of over-giving or over-extending to such a point that it led to emotional exhaustion or depletion, because somehow in the next eight weeks or the next eight months, you are no longer willing to be the lineage bearer or the legacy bearer of family indolence patterns or over-extension patterns.

NINE OF CUPS

The Nine of Cups is happiness. The pewter cups reflect tangible happiness that is associated with either health, finances, work, creativity or relationships. This is happiness that is fulfilling internally as well as externally. Internal happiness is represented by the three vertical cups representing happiness of body, mind, and spirit ; the horizontal three cups represent happiness experienced in body, mind, and spirit externally. The astrological aspect of this card is Jupiter in Pisces. Jupiter is the planet of opportunity, growth and luck. Pisces is the astrological symbol of fluidity and fullness, and so the Nine of Cups represents happiness that is expansive like Jupiter and fluid and abundant like Pisces. This is total happiness that is internally being experienced, represented by the lotus blossoms, and externally expressed, as symbolized by the pewter cups.

When you pull the Nine of Cups, it is an indication that you are able, in the next nine weeks or the next nine months, to experience emotional expansion that comes from the feeling of fulfillment in completion, internally and externally. There's an ability to integrate and balance feelings in deep and expansive ways for your own emotional happiness and well-being.

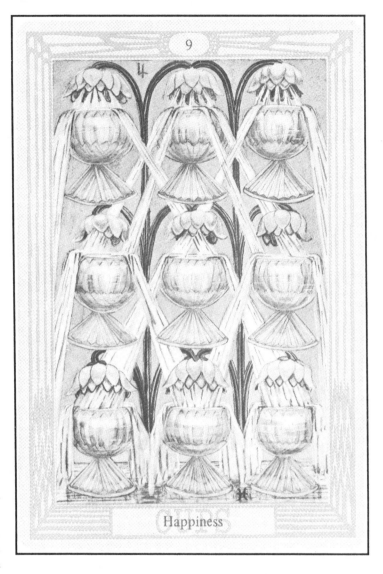

Happiness

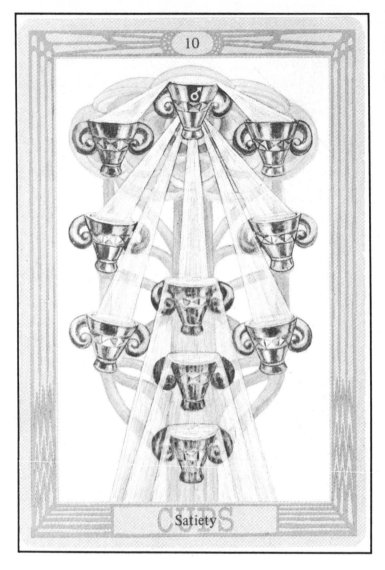

10

Satiety

EN
OF
CUPS

The Ten of Cups is satiety or emotional contentment and satisfaction. This is the state of emotional contentment that comes from deep within and radiates out in all aspects of your life, which is represented by the ten cups on the Cabala or Tree of Life. This is satisfaction or contentment that is coming from within the cups and radiating out. The Ten of Cups is different from the Nine of Cups in the extent that Nine of Cups is happiness that can be tangibly pointed to in the external reality. The Ten of Cups is deep emotional contentment and satisfaction that comes from within and externally radiates the quality of contentment and satisfaction. The astrological aspect of this is Mars in Pisces. Mars is the planet of energy and vitality, so this is satisfaction and contentment that has enormous vitality and expressiveness. It comes from within and radiaties out in a very fluid and expansive way, which is symbolized by the astrological sign of Pisces. Basically, the Ten of Cups represents an energy and enthusiasm that is being experienced at very deep levels within and radiates out in all aspects of your life.

When you pull this card, it can indicate that in the next ten weeks or the next ten months, there is an experience of emotional contentment and satisfaction that comes from deep within and radiates out in all aspects of your life. The Ten of Cups could also indicate that in the next ten weeks or the next ten months, you will have a sense of deep energy and vitality, like Mars, that's very fluid, like Pisces, which can be expressed outwardly in all aspects of your life; or it could indicate, also, that in the next ten weeks or the next ten months, there is an experience of emotional contentment and satisfaction with Pisces people in your life, or that contentment and satisfaction could be experienced in the Pisces month of February 21 to March 21.

ACE THROUGH TEN
OF
WANDS

Ace of Wands

ACE OF WANDS

The Ace of Wands is a symbol of spiritual self-realization, awakening, and is associated with the principle of truth and authenticity. The Ace of Wands is the torch of fire, a symbol of the uncontainable life-force that's within. The lightning bolts are a symbol of awakening to the spiritual truth and authenticity of who you are.

Whenever you pull this card, it is an indication that you've awakened to the uncontainable and irrepressible inherent Being within. It is a reminder that in the next year, it will be very difficult to edit, rehearse or hold back any parts of who you are. The Ace of any suit stands for the time frame of a year. During the fire sign months of Leo, Aries, Sagittarius, or with fire sign people of Leo, Aries, Sagittarius, it is important that you stay in your truth and authenticity. This symbol represents an unwillingness to abandon yourself and an unwillingness to edit, rehearse or hold back your basic nature. This is a representation of intuition that is completely honored and trusted. The Ace of Wands is representative of awakening, or seeing aspects of the self so clearly that there is a commitment to burn out any negativity, blocks, obstacles, or obstructions that might prevent you from actualizing your full potential within the fire sign months, or with fire sign people or in the next twelve months.

When you pull this card, it represents that the next twelve months is an important time to stay in your authenticity and truth and not abandon yourself. It is also a time to come from a place of full energy, vitality and spontaneity in the fire sign months of Leo, Aries and Sagittarius, or to be in your full spontaneity and vitality with fire sign people.

TWO OF WANDS

The Two of Wands is a symbol of the state of dominion, balance, and integration. This symbol represents optimum balance of energy or the sense of sovereignty or being very comfortable with your domain, which is the root word of dominion, the sense of experiencing harmony and balance within your domain. This symbol illustrates the Tibetan *dorjes* which are sacred power objects that have been unified. This is essentially a symbol of coming into your own power from deep within in a very balanced way, which is the principle of dominion. The symbol of power is also represented by the horses on the *dorjes* caps. The symbol of renewal, regeneration and healing that comes from states of balance is represented by the serpents on the arrowheads of the *dorjes*. The astrological aspect of this card is Mars in Aries. Mars is the planet of vitality, energy and assertion; Aries is the astrological symbol of exploration and pioneering.

When you pull this card it indicates that in the next two weeks or in the next two months, that you will have the energy, like Mars, to move in new directions, like Aries, from a place of integration, balance and harmony, or the feeling of being on top of things. Basically this is a symbol which indicates that you have the energy to move in new directions because you have attained a certain state of balance and harmony or sovereignty within.

Dominion

THREE OF WANDS

The Three of Wands is symbolized by the quality of virtue or integrity. Integrity is the union of mind, heart and action working in concert with each other. This principle is represented by the unity of the three lotus blossoms which represent mind, heart and action that is unified, consistent and congruent. The astrological aspect that is associated with this symbol is Sun in Aries. It is radiant dynamic energy, which is the Sun, to move in new directions, which is Aries, but from a place of integrity or virtue, making sure that mind, heart and action are all conjoined and wanting to move in that new direction. This symbol reminds us that one should not move in new directions until there is an alignment of mind, heart and action, and when there is not that alignment of mind, heart and action to move in the same direction, it is a time to wait until there is the alignment, rather than to act.

When you pull this card it indicates that in the next three weeks or the next three months, it is important to operate from a place of integrity as you move forward in new directions; or it is important to operate from a place of making sure that your mind, heart and actions are clear in how you want to handle your relationships with Aries people, anyone born March 21 to April 21. In the state of integrity, you are able to demonstrate natural clarity which is symbolized by the crystalline structure in back of the wands, and are able to allow things to naturally unfold, which is symbolized by the fire flames in the background. The Three of Wands also indicates that during the month of Aries, or with Aries people (March 21 to April 21), it is important to operate from a place of virtue or integrity and to make sure that mind, heart and action are in alignment with important choices that you are making in the next three weeks or in the next three months.

FOUR OF WANDS

Completion

The Four of Wands is completion. Four of Wands reminds us that before we can energetically move forward in new directions that have heart and meaning, it is important to consummate or complete that which we have set in motion. This symbol also represents the principle of having achieved something, which is also associated with completion. The astrological signs that are represented here are Venus in Aries. The sign of Venus is at the top of the card, and the sign of Aries is at the bottom of the card. Venus in Aries is also duplicated on the wheel. Venus is represented by the doves on the wheel, and Aries is represented by the rams on the wheel. The wheel itself represents completion and new beginnings, as portrayed by Eastern mandalas and Western medicine wheels, which represent wholeness and individuation.

Whenever you pull this symbol it both represents simultaneously something being completed as well as initiated. The Four of Wands is visually a reminder of an emotional desire, Venus, to move in new directions, Aries, but from a sense of feeling that there has been a completion or consummation of projects or relationships or issues, before one ventures forward. When you pull this card it indicates that in the next four weeks or the next four months would be a good time to move in new directions and simultaneously to complete things; or to move only in new directions as a result of feeling that you are complete with certain issues, projects or important relationships. This symbol can also indicate that in the next four weeks or in the next four months, there may be something that you want to initiate or complete with important Aries people in your life, anyone born March 21 to April 21. If there are no important Aries people in your life, then the month of Aries may be a time where certain things can be achieved, completed and consummated, while simultaneously initiating new things into certain aspects of your life. The Four of Wands basically reflects to us that some aspect of the self is in the process of completion and is whole, while another aspect of the self desires to experience something new, which is represented by Venus in Aries. Basically, this symbol represents the ability to look at oneself as being whole in external situations during the next four weeks and in the next four months.

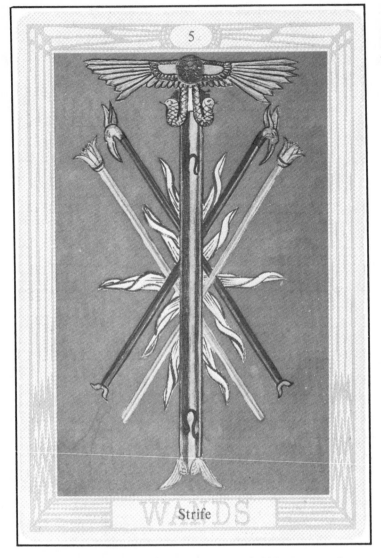

Strife

FIVE OF WANDS

The Five of Wands is a symbol of the state of strife, anxiety or frustration. Anxiety is an energetic experience caused by holding back. Basically, it is the state of frustration. It is the experience of having abundant energy but not knowing what to do with that energy, or it's a lot of energy that's being contained or held back, which will produce anxiety or the state of strife. The astrological aspect that's represented on this symbol is Saturn in Leo. Saturn is the planet of discipline, of knowing what your limits and boundaries are and being able to set limits and boundaries. Saturn is the planet that reminds us to do things step-by-step. Leo is the astrological sign of creative power that does not want to be limited, restricted or restrained, and desires full expression.

When you pull this card, it can reflect the state of feeling limited, restricted or restrained in your creative endeavors. It can also reflect the state of anxiety or strife that you might be experiencing with Leo people in your life, anyone born July 21 to August 21. A sense of feeling limited, restricted, restrained by Leo people, or a sense of limiting, restricting and restaining your own creative ability, is reflected by this aspect of Saturn in Leo. Strife or anxiety is that state where energy is stuck or unmoving, which is represented by the leaded or greyed-over coloration of this symbol. Any holding back or self limitation will move you into that state in alchemy which was known as *leaded consciousness*. Leaded consciousness is symbolically represented by the greyed-over areas of this symbol. The lotus blossoms are grey, which means that in states of anxiety you have difficulty opening or unfolding. In states of anxiety or strife you have difficulty accessing inherent wisdom, the Ibis heads, or in moving in new directions to regenerate yourself. In states of anxiety or frustration or strife, you don't see things clearly, which is represented by the winged Eye of Horus at the top of the card which is greyed-over, and are unable to renew and regenerate yourself like the snakes coming off the winged Eye of Horus. Yet the entire background of the card is yellow, which symbolizes energy that wants to be used but is being contained or limited, which creates the response or experience of strife.

When you pull this card it indicates that in the next five weeks or the next five months, there is an opportunity to release anxiety or frustration that's being experienced, either in the month of Leo or with Leo people or with your own creativity, all of which is symbolized by the sign of Leo. In the next five weeks or the next five months would be a good time to move towards creative endeavors where you feel that you can express yourself fully, instead of binding or restricting yourself in any way. The Five of Wands reflects that in the next five weeks or in the next five months, you could release old anxiety patterns or frustrations that have surfaced in the last five months, or that go back to the last five years, or when you were five years old. Somehow in the next five weeks or in the next five months, you are determined to release anxiety patterns or frustration patterns that have been conditioned within your own family. It might be interesting to see which of your parents had a tendency to hold back, or felt limited in his or her own work and creativity to such a degree that it created frustration and strife. This symbol reminds you that in the next five weeks or in the next five months, you are no longer willing to be the lineage bearer of family anxiety patterns. The aspect of family here is represented by the number 5, which is associated with the Hierophant, which is the symbol of the archetypal family and the spiritual learning and teaching that is found in every family. The Hierophant archetype would be a good card that would lend additional support to you in the next five weeks or the next five months as you release old anxiety patterns.

SIX OF WANDS

The Six of Wands represents the quality of victory. This is the experience of a deep victory or win that touches you at an intuitive and spiritual level. The astrological aspect of this symbol is Jupiter in Leo. Victory allows us to feel expansive and fluid like Jupiter, and highly creative, like Leo. Any victory requires creativity and flexibility in order for it to be achieved, which is another aspect of Jupiter in Leo. The ultimate victory or spiritual victory is the victory which provides a win-win situation rather than a win-lose situation, which is pictured by the lotus blossom. Victory that is a win-win allows for mutual unfolding and opening; and allows for new energy and revitalization, which is represented by the Ibis heads or the Phoenix heads. Victory allows for clarity of vision and creative expression which is symbolized by the winged Eye of Horus with the regenerative serpentine snakes. A spiritual victory is experienced at all four levels of consciousness, symbolized by the four diamonds which represent a victory that has been achieved mentally, emotionally, spiritually and physically.

When you pull this card, it indicates that in the next six weeks or the next six months, there is an opportunity to experience a victory either with Leo people in your life, anyone born July 21 to August 21, or a victory in your own creative expression. Regardless, the next six weeks or the next six months is a time where you can experience a win-win situation in areas of your life that are important. The Six of Wands represents that there could be opportunities or expansiveness in creative arenas of your life in the next six weeks or the next six months that could give you the experience of revitalization, expansion, and break-through.

SEVEN OF WANDS

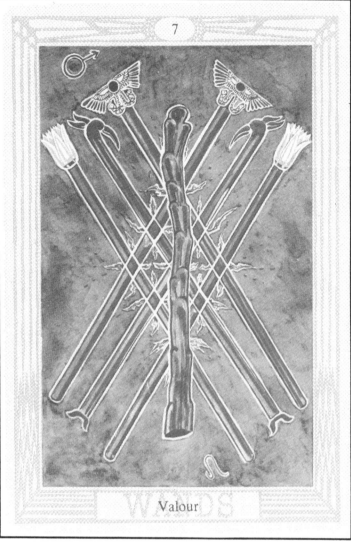

Valour

The Seven of Wands represents the quality of valour. Valour is the courage to stay by what you value, not to compromise or to settle for less. The central niched wand on this card represents a reminder to trust your experience. If you have the courage to stay by what you value, things will unfold like the lotus blossoms, renew and regenerate themselves or allow you to move in new directions that you value, which is represented by the Ibis or Phoenix heads; and you are able to see things more clearly, and able to honor your vision and creativity, which is represented by the Eye of Horus, the winged Eye of Horus staff. The astrological symbol of this card is Mars in Leo. Mars is the planet of energy and vitality that can support your creative expression, which is Leo.

Whenever you pull this card it indicates that in the next seven weeks or the next seven months, it's important for you to have the courage to stay by what you value, especially in the month of Leo or with Leo people in your life, anyone born July 21 to August 21. In the next seven weeks or the next seven months, it's important for you to stay by what you value as far as your creative expression or work or career is concerned, and not to compromise or to settle for less. It is a time to trust your intuition and past experiences.

EIGHT OF WANDS

The Eight of Wands symbolizes the quality of swiftness. This symbol represents direct communication and swift action. It's a reminder that any block or obstacle that you may be experiencing internally or externally, which is represented by the square, can be transformed into the electrified, energized diamond, if you will communicate directly, which is represented by Mercury in Sagittarius. Mercury is the planet of communication, Sagittarius is the astrological sign that is associated with directness and swiftness. The Eight of Wands reminds you that you can transform any situation, problem or obstacle and resolve it, by taking swift action and communicating directly. The opposite of this symbol is procrastination and covert communication.

When you pull this card, it is a reminder that in the next eight weeks or in the next eight months, it's important to take swift action and communicate directly in order to eliminate patterns of procrastination or covert communication. The perfectly seen rainbow reminds you that whatever you have initiated, you must complete in your communication and in your actions within the next eight weeks or the next eight months. The Eight of Wands indicates that the next eight weeks or the next eight months would be a good time to take swift action and to communicate directly to important Sagittarius people in your life, anyone born November 21 to December 21. Regardless, the next eight weeks or the next eight months is an important time to communicate directly, as things come up, and to take swift action, as things present themselves.

NINE OF WANDS

The Nine of Wands is strength. This is spiritual and inituitive strength of vision. Astrologically, this card is Sun and Moon in Sagittarius which symbolizes conscious and subconscious strength. The Nine of Wands indicates strength of vision, perception and intuition. It reflects strength on every level of consciousness, which is represented by the four intercepting arrows – mental strength, emotional strength, spiritual strength and physical strength. This is a symbol of the unlimited strength that comes from deep within.

Whenever you pull this card, it indicates that in the next nine weeks or the next nine months, there is unlimited strength to call upon to manifest those visions, insights and perceptions that are important to you. It is also strength that is accessible to handle situations with important Sagittarius people in your life, anyone born November 21 to December 21. In the next nine weeks or the next nine months you have deep internal resources to resolve issues that you might have with Sagittarius people. The Nine of Wands reflects that the next nine weeks or the next nine months is a good time to implement your strength in what it is that you see can work more effectively in both personal and professional arenas of your life.

EN OF WANDS

The Ten of Wands is oppression. On this card the two Tibetan *dorjes*, or the sacred spiritual power objects, are dulled or greyed-over, to symbolize the state of oppressing oneself, either through holding back, editing, or rehearsing oneself or not fully expressing oneself – mentally, emotionally, spiritually or physically. The astrological aspect on this card is Saturn in Sagittarius. Saturn is the planet of discipline and knowing one's limits and boundaries, as well as being able to set limits and boundaries. There may be a tendency to limit oneself or one's vision, which is represented by the astrological sign of Sagittarius.

When you pull this card, it indicates that in the next ten weeks or the next ten months, it's important for you to release self-oppression patterns such as holding yourself back, or restricting yourself in any way. It is also a reminder that in the next ten weeks or the next ten months is an appropriate time to begin to remove yourself from oppressive situations, where you feel that you hold back or are not fully able to express all of who you are. The Ten of Wands could indicate that the next ten weeks or the next ten months is a good time to release oppressive patterns that you've developed with Sagittarius people in your life, anyone born November 21 to December 21. Basically, the Ten of Wands is that state of consciousness where you hold back your power.

ACE THROUGH TEN
OF
DISKS

Ace of Disks

The Ace of Disks is success that is experienced both internally and externally. Internal success is represented by the four sets of angel wings, which represent the four levels of success in consciousness – mental, emotional, spiritual and physical. External success is represented by the coins within the coins and the crystals within the crystals in the center of this symbol. This card represents success that is manifested internally as well as externally.

When you pull this card, it is an indication that you are no longer willing to support the dichotomy of experiencing internal success and not external success, or the other dichotomy of where you experience external success but not internal success. When you pull this card, it is an indication that there is the sense of success that has manifested deep inside as well as externally. This symbol is the highest of the manifestation cards, it is the capacity to manifest or produce what you want in both internal and external worlds.

The Ace of Disks represents the opportunity to experience internal and external success that's manifested equally within a year's time. It also indicates that this experience could manifest in the earth sign months of Capricorn, Virgo and Taurus, or that there may well be an experience of internal and external success with Capricorn, Taurus and Virgo people in your life. The Ace of Disks symbolizes success that comes from being organized and centered internally and externally. When you draw this card, it's an indication that this gift of practical organization and manifestation is able to be used and drawn upon for the next twelve months.

TWO OF DISKS

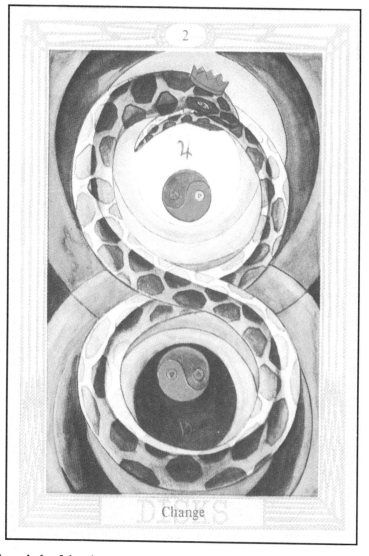

The Two of Disks represents change. The oriental Uroboros snake that eats its own tail reminds us that change is the only constant and is cyclic. For purposes of rebalancing that which is out of balance, the serpent is making the number 8, which is the number for balance and adjustment. Change is for the purpose of expanding our awareness, which is symbolized by the crown on the snake's head. Change is also for the purpose of revealing to us that which is knowable, and that which is unfamiliar, which is represented by the black and white serpent. The black and white serpent is the oriental representation of the *yin-yang* symbol, which is associated with the principle of unifying opposites. The Two of Disks represents tangible changes that can be pointed to in the external reality which is reflected by the *yin/yang* symbols that are horizontally on their sides. The vertical *yin/yang* symbol indicates internal change, whereas the horizontal *yin/yang* symbol indicates external change. The change that is represented here is also elemental, because within the *yin-yang* symbols, the old alchemical symbols of the elements of earth, fire, water and air are drawn in their triangular shapes. The astrological aspect of this card is Jupiter in Capricorn. This is expansive, positive, opportunistic change (Jupiter) that is also stable, solid and secure, which is Capricorn.

When you pull this card, it indicates that in the next two weeks or the next two months, there is an opportunity to make external changes that are both expansive and stable in your life. It is an opportunity to make changes that can rebalance your life experience. The Two of Disks indicates that in the next two weeks or the next two months is a good time to make expansive and more balancing changes in your relationships with Capricorn people, anyone born December 21 to January 21.

THREE OF DISKS

The Three of Disks is the capacity to give things "the works." It represents persistence, tenacity, and getting clear on your priorities and commitments. This symbol reflects the power of focus, priority and commitments, which is represented by the pyramid. The three red wheels symbolize the alignment of mind, heart and action. Clarity of what it is that you want to give your energy or the *works* to, and what it is that you don't want to give your energy to, is symbolized by the blue light surrounding the pyramid. The lighted pyramid represents the power of intention and the clarity of priorities and commitments which can break through any sense of confusion or obstruction, represented by all the grey waves in the background.

The astrological aspect of this card is Mars in Capricorn. Mars is the planet of energy, vitality and assertion. The Three of Disks is the assertion of mind, heart and action, moving in the same direction. This kind of focus and intention allows things to be made tangible and secure, which is represented by the astrological sign of Capricorn.

When you pull this card, it indicates the next three weeks or the next three months is the best time to get clear on your priorities and commitments, and to determine what it is that you want to give the works to, and what it is that you don't want to give the works to. It's also the best time to clarify or reassess your relationships with Capricorn people, anyone born December 21 to January 21. The next three weeks or the next three months is also a time where one's priorities or commitments may be so clear that you are able to tenaciously stick with or see through those endeavors that you want to make stable, solid and tangible in your life.

FOUR OF DISKS

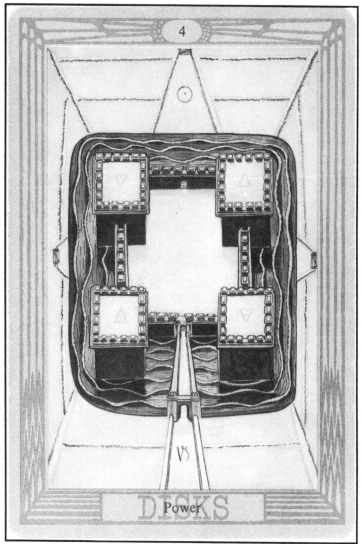

The Four of Disks is power, vitality, forcefulness. Represented on this card is a castle, with a moat around it, which is a symbol of knowing what ones limits and boundaries are, or being very able to take care of ones own castle or domain, which is the true meaning of power. Power is the ability to empower one-self and to empower others.

The astrological aspect of this card is Sun in Capricorn. The Sun in astrology is a symbol of your inherent dynamism or power. Capricorn is the astrological sign of being able to implement or apply your full power in the world in a practical and tangible way.

When you pull this card, it indicates that in the next four weeks or the next four months, it's very important for you to know what your limits and boundaries are and to be very comfortable in setting limits and boundaries. It also may indicate that in the next four weeks or the next four months, that any issues that came up during the month of Capricorn or with Capricorn people can be resolved if you are willing to honor your own domain, your own limits and boundaries, your own inner and outer castle, or that which you have created for yourself.

The Four of Disks reminds us of inner and outer power that is manifested through the four towers, which represent the four levels of consciousness or the four elements. The towers on the castle symbolize the four elements. The element of air is associated with mental power, the element of water is associated with emotional fluidity and power, the element of fire is associated with spiritual energy, life-force and vitality, and the element of earth is representative of our physical health and well-being. Those four elements and those four levels of consciousness are represented by the four towers, and the four alchemy symbols on top of each tower are those for earth, fire, water and air.

Worry

IVE OF DISKS

The Five of Disks is worry, physical concern and rumination. This is worry about external things involving health, finances, work, creativity or relationships. Astrologically, the aspect represented here is Mercury in Taurus, which could also reflect worry about communication, which is Mercury, and worry about how that communication is being received or coming across, which is Taurus. It could also be worry about your own productivity and ability to implement or apply your communication effectively.

Whenever you pull this card, it indicates that in the next five weeks or the next five months, there is an opportunity to release worry about health, finances, work, creativity, relationships, or worry about communication. Or you may release old worry patterns that may go back to five months ago or five years ago or when you were five years old. Worry is an interesting state of consciousness because it takes us to the future and it takes us to the past, and has us totally avoiding the present. One way to collapse worry is to stay in the present and handle things as they come up, and not get pulled into the *what-ifs* of tomorrow, or the *if-onlys* of yesterday. This could also be worry about Taurus people in your life, anyone born April 21 to May 21, and that somehow in the next five weeks or the next five months, there is an opportunity to release worry patterns with Taurus people, or somehow to release worry surrounding communication that affects Taurus people in your life. It's important in the next five weeks or the next five months, to see which of your parents carried worry within his or her nature, because somehow in the next five weeks or the next five months, you are no longer willing to be the lineage bearer or the legacy bearer of family worry patterns, and especially worry about health, finances, work, creativity or relationships. The Hierophant is the major archetype that has moved through worry, and can be drawn upon in the next five weeks or the next five months to help you with old worry patterns that have been imprinted from the past; or you can release worry about events or situations that may have surfaced in the last five months, or five years ago, or when you were five years old. You can release worry concerning external situations or Taurus people in your life in the next five weeks or the next five months. Worry is the state of preoccupation about future or past events, which has us avoiding or handling present issues. In the next five weeks or the next five months, you can collapse worry by staying present and not getting pulled into future concerns or past experiences.

SIX OF DISKS

Success

The Six of Disks is success, which is a symbol of physical attainment and accomplishment. The astrological aspect on this card is Moon in Taurus. The symbol of accomplishment or productivity is Taurus, and deep inner satisfaction is represented by the Moon. Or, there is a deep desire at a subconscious level, the Moon, to have some very tangible, productive results, which is Taurus. This card contains the formula of success which is represented by the six planets with the planetary astrological symbols within them. Saturn represents that success is achieved through discipline and step-by-step procedures; Jupiter reminds us that success is achieved by being open and flexible to options that we may not have entertained and to opportunities that present themselves; Venus reminds us that success is attainable as a result of following what has heart and meaning in our lives; the Moon reflects that success is attainable if we will stay in our authenticity and truth; Mercury, the planet of communication, reminds us that success is attainable if we will organize our communication so that context and timing are all aligned; and Mars reminds us that success is attainable if we will put consistent energy into personal and professional issues, rather than to expend marathon energy or inconsistent energy into our life situations.

The Six of Disks represents success that comes from deep within and manifests out. It is the sense of success experienced internally, which is pictured by both the Western and Eastern spiritual symbols that have been cojoined – here we have the Eastern lotus blossom that is superimposed on the Western cross. Both symbols remind us that all outer success is a picture of what we can manifest and create as a result of being motivated from deep within. These two symbols also indicate that success comes from a deep inner ability to integrate and synthesize our experience, which is symbolized by the cross, and to have the ability to open and unfold which allows for success, and which is symbolized by the lotus blossom.

When you pull this card, it indicates that in the next six weeks or the next six months, you can manifest success by following the six-step formula of success that is represented by the planets on this symbol. It also indicates that in the next six weeks or the next six months, there is an experience of being successful in producing something that has a deep internal motivation or inspiration for you.

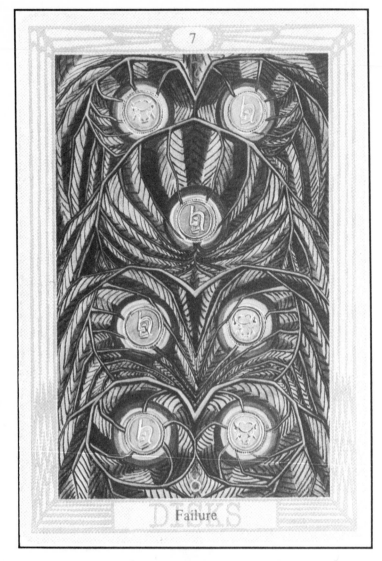

SEVEN OF DISKS

The Seven of Disks is a picture of fear of failure, or fear of success. The astrological aspect of this symbol is Saturn in Taurus. The whole function of fear is to constrict energy or to distort energy, which is symbolized by the astrological planet of Saturn, that often people experience as the feeling of limitation or restriction. Taurus is the astrological sign of productivity and achievement. This aspect is often experienced as feeling that your productivity or achievement is limited, or it can produce a sense of failing, or induce fears of success or fear of failing. This same astrological aspect is duplicated in the coins. Taurus is symbolized by the bull in the coins, and the helmeted figure is a symbol of Saturn, representing that sense of limitation on your consciousness or awareness, which is represented by the helmet.

When you pull this card, it indicates that in the next seven weeks or the next seven months, you have an opportunity to move through old fears of failure that may have surfaced in the last seven months or that go back to seven years ago or to the last seven years, or that go as far back as when you were seven years old. It's fear about finances, health, work, creativity, relationships; it's fear about something external failing, or fear that something external might succeed, or fear of handling success. It could also be fear of failure surrounding Taurus people in your life, anyone born April 21 to May 21. The number 7 is associated with the Chariot. The Chariot is the major archetype of change, transformation and movement. The Chariot can be used as a meditation symbol to help you move through old fears of failing. The next seven weeks or the next seven months is an opportunity to move through fears of failure or fears of success, or to release old memories of failure or of having failed.

EIGHT OF DISKS

The Eight of Disks is prudence, wisdom, or the Harvest Tree. This symbol represents the Harvest Tree that manifests as a result of utilizing prudence and wisdom. The astrological aspect represented on this card is Sun in Virgo. Virgo, the astrological sign, reminds us that harvest can be generated by attending to details, or utilizing our organizational skills. Harvest follows order, it does not follow chaos, and harvest follows trust, it does not follow control. Prudence and wisdom are those qualities of not pushing to make things happen, or resisting or holding back. Here the coins have exploded into flowers and they are perfectly protected by leaves that embrace each bloom.

When you pull this card, it indicates that in the next eight weeks or the next eight months, you can experience harvest as a result of utilizing prudence and wisdom, and as a result of organizing, systematizing, or attending to details. It also indicates that in the next eight weeks or the next eight months, there might be harvestful opportunities through Virgo people, or that by utilizing prudence and wisdom with relationships with Virgo people, anyone born August 21 to September 21, the results can be a harvest in those relationships. The Eight of Disks reminds us of that state of consciousness that is prudent and wise, of that state of consciousness that does not move to extremes or over-extends itself externally. It is operating from a place of centeredness and integration, or from a place of order rather than chaos.

NINE OF DISKS

The Nine of Disks is hitting the mark, hitting the bulls-eye. This symbol represents physical profit, benefit, and gain, in all arenas of our life – mentally, emotionally, spiritually, physically, and financially. The astrological aspect is Venus in Virgo. Venus is the planet of love, beauty and creative power; Virgo is the astrological sign associated with balance, order, and organization. The Nine of Disks reminds us that if we follow what has heart and meaning for us, which is the meaning of Venus, and that if we organize and systematize things, which is Virgo, the results are gain – tangible gain, giving one the feeling of having hit the mark, or the bulls-eye, which is represented on this card. Gain comes as a result of unifying our wisdom, the blue circle, with our love nature, which is the pink circle, in a creative way, which is the green circle that is at the center of this card. Creative love and wisdom facilitates tangible gain in all arenas of our life. This card also indicates, by the coins, that gain comes as a result of utilizing our dynamic energy, symbolized by the three male figures in the top three coins which hold the symbols of Saturn, Mars and Jupiter. Saturn, the helmeted warrior, reminds us that gain will come as a result of knowing what our limits and boundaries are and by doing things step-by-step; Mars, the male figure that is the page with the feathered cap, reminds us that through our energy, vitality and assertion, we can manifest gain; Jupiter, which represents the king, reminds us that gain can come as a result of being flexible and by being open to opportunity that can expand our leadership. The bottom three coins illustrate the types of feminine power that can bring gain. The first feminine power, represented by Mercury, which is on the coin with the woman with the queen's hat, reveals the power of communication and leadership skills that can bring gain; the second feminine power of Venus is hidden within the youthful feminine figure without a headdress, which indicates that gain can come as a result of following what has heart and meaning; and the third feminine power, reflected by the wise woman within the moon on the coin, illustrates that gain can come as a result of trusting our own truth and authenticity, the power of the Moon. The Moon represents the power of the feminine and allows us to experience gain in the outer world as well as in the internal worlds.

When you pull this card, it indicates that in the next nine weeks or the next nine months, there is tangible external gain as a result of organizing things, which is Virgo, and in following what has heart and meaning, which is Venus. This is tangible gain experienced as a result of being dynamically assertive and of being magnetically open to following what has heart and meaning.

TEN
OF
DISKS

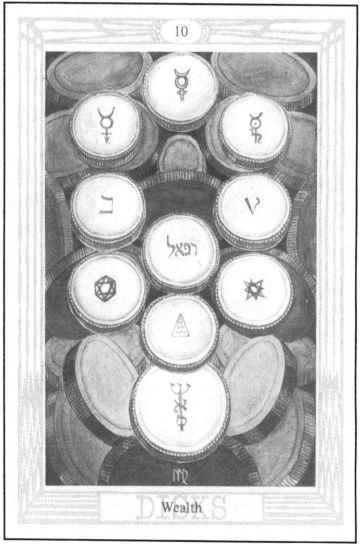

Wealth

The Ten of Disks is wealth, or riches, abundance, prosperity. The astrological aspect that's represented on this card is Mercury in Virgo. It is through your communication skills, which is Mercury, and through your organizational skills, Virgo, that you can manifest abundance or prosperity in a tangible way. This card also symbolizes that by using your communication gifts (the three Mercury signs on the top three coins), your healing gifts (the healing caduseus on the bottom coin) and your inspirational gifts (the coins which hold stars within them), you are able to manifest abundance, which is represented by the Hebrew symbols for abundance in the middle three coins. This is wealth on every level of consciousness, mental, emotional, spiritual, financial and physical wealth, which is made tangible in the external reality. By utilizing communication, healing and inspirational gifts, we can manifest abundance in a tangible way. The coins and the slices from trees represent the abundance found on earth, which is disks.

When you pull this card, it indicates that in the next ten weeks or the next ten months, that you can manifest abundance by communicating, by organizing or systematizing things in your life. The results are a better alignment with the principle of prosperity and abundance. It also indicates that in the next ten weeks or the next ten months, by communicating to Virgo people in your life, anyone born August 21 to September 21, that the results could be healing, inspirational and enriching.

PORTALS OF
INITIATION AND GROWTH
AS REVEALED BY
THE MINOR ARCANA

INTRODUCTION

In the entire Book of Thoth, or the Book of Wisdom, we find only thirteen challenges or tests pictured. From an Egyptian point of view there were only thirteen Bardo states, or challenges, or negative states that one could experience. Six of those were in the mind, three were emotional reactions to thoughts in the mind, two affected the energy or vision or how one saw things, and two then ultimately affected one's outer reality in health, finances, work, creativity and relationships. In Jungian psychology these thirteen tests or challenges would be referred to as *the aspects of the Shadow*, or those parts of ourselves that are negative, or fearful, and are difficult to own or claim in any way. In Shamanistic terms, perhaps these Bardo states might be found in the "Journey to the Underworld", where it is important to claim one's power animals or to empower oneself. The positive function of any test or challenge is to exercise our gifts, talents, and resources, to face that which is difficult from a place of empowerment rather than constriction.

The number 13 is interesting, because in the Major Arcana, it is associated with the Roman Numeral XIII, which is the Death/Rebirth card. In the Minor Arcana, there are thirteen ways in which one, through tests and challenges, can change or transform, like the Death/Rebirth symbol. It is important as you go through the Bardo states, or the Shadow aspects of who you are, that you remember, recognize, and reclaim the beauty of who you are by using the twenty-seven gifts, talents and resources that can transform these states.

In the Minor Arcana, we can take a look at these forty symbols as the archetypal motif of the "Beauty and the Beast" that's within. There are thirteen Beasts that we might confront, move through or attempt to tame in our consciousness, yet there are twenty-seven gifts, talents and jewels in the consciousness that are much greater than the thorns in consciousness.

POSITIVE AND NEGATIVE STATES OF MIND

**Six Beasts
or Bardo States
of the Mind**

1) **The Three of Swords** is *sorrow*. Swords always are a picture of what's happening in the mind. There is a tendency to rework past sorrows in the mind, and particularly past sorrows or wounds that have a negative connotation. The first triangle that we experience is the family – father, mother, child. So, this could be a sorrow or a wound that goes back to childhood, perhaps around three years old, that is still being reworked in the mind; or it could represent unfinished family business tied with the past. How we handled the first triangle of father–mother–child is how we'll handle subsequent triangles of friend–co-worker–friend, or friend–lover–friend, or friend–lover–mate, or whatever combination of triangles that we experience in life. Until that initial family patterning is broken, we do not free ourselves from this tendency in the mind, and it is only in the mind that we have this tendency to rework the old wounds of the past or the old sorrows of the past.

Two swords are bent upon this card, which indicates that reworking old wounds in the mind has the tendency to distort. This is the astrological aspect of Saturn in Libra. Saturn is the planet which reminds us to do things step by step, not to take any shortcuts, and not to go too fast. And Libra is the Zodiac symbol of balance and realignment. Saturn in Libra reminds us that if we handle things step by step, that we can bring things into balance. This aspect reminds us not to rework the past in the mind. Reworking the negative parts of the past in the mind can take us off balance and make us feel limited, restricted, restrained in the present. This is not a superficial sorrow that is being reworked in the mind. Here we have the lotus blossom being pierced to the center, with petals falling out. This indicates an active mind that is actively reworking past events in a wounding and detrimental way.

Whenever you pull this card it can also indicate that you're determined in the next three weeks or in the next three months to release old tapes in the mind which rework old sorrows tied with the past, old sorrows that could go back to any time in the last three months, three years, or could go back to when you were three years old. It could also be sorrow connected with Libra people in your life, anyone born September 21 – October 21. It is an earnest effort somehow to reprogram the mind not to rework the old sorrows tied with the past. This is often the-digging-up-the-old-bones-syndrome when you pull this card; it reminds you that you have a conscious choice, somehow, in the next three weeks or the next three months to release sorrow in the mind.

2) If you continue to rework sorrow in the mind, then the next beast in the mind, or the next Bardo state in the mind that you will face is the **Five of Swords**, which is *fear of defeat*. The astrological aspect of this is Venus in Aquarius. This card can reveal fear about two things: fear about new relationships, or fear about moving in new directions that are emotionally important to oneself. Here we have an old wound, depicted by a bloody handkerchief, an old wound that has been reopened. When we reopen old wounds, which we do with the Three of Swords, it will bring up fear. This is fear of defeat, based on past memory. The whole function of fear is to constrict. Here is a picture of an old wound being reopened. The Pisces fish on one of the Sword's handles indicates that it is an old wound or old fear tied with the past. Pisces, the Piscean age, is associated with the past. When we are in states of fear of defeat about things that are emotionally important to us, it constricts and distorts, allowing nothing to be renewed or regenerated (pictured by the sleeping snake on one handle of the sword). We cannot move forward, which is Aries the Ram on the other handle of the sword, and literally we feel that we are not in balance, or that we are askew, which is the upside-down crown on one of the sword's handles. And yet, the spirit of who we are, the white light in the background, is attempting to move through fears of defeat, particularly, fears about moving forward in new directions or moving forward in new relationships.

3) If we stay in fears of defeat long enough in the mind, which we started by reworking the negative parts of the past (Three of Swords), we will then move into the **Seven of Swords**, which is *futility*, and *the sabotaging mind*.

Basically, here is a portraiture of what it is that we truly want, which is the central sword. The other six swords, coming at the central sword, is what one could call the *Yes/But* tape, or a tendency in the mind to sabotage what it is that we want. The Seven of Swords has Sun and Moon in Aquarius (the Sun sign is the circle with the dot at the bottom of the card, and the moon is at the tip of the sword). The Sun and the Moon in Aquarius is the innovative, pioneering, and creative mind. It is wanting to literally manifest something new. The other six swords are all the reasons why we tell ourselves we can't do this. This is the sabotaging mind or the *Yes/But* tape.

Saturn is pictured on the sword that has a little fancy "h" on it. The negative aspects of Saturn are the attitudes like *I don't have enough time...There are too many details to attend to...It would require too much discipline*, and so forth.

The next handle has the symbol of Mercury on it. Mercury is the planet of communication; negative aspects of Mercury are negative self-talk, statements using terms such as *I can't*, or *It won't work*, or *If only...Wish I had a...Someday I'll*...as ways of sabotaging the initial intention to go for what it is that one wants.

Jupiter is on the next handle, the one with the fancy "4", which indicates the negative aspect of Jupiter. Jupiter is the planet of luck and opportunity and growth. The sabotaging part of Jupiter would be to promise more that you can give, or to believe that *I'm unlucky*, or *Opportunities never come my way*.

Mars, which is the circle with the arrow on it, is associated with energy and vitality. The negative aspect of Mars would be saying things like *I don't have enough energy...I'm exhausted...I'm burnt out...I just can't do it.*

Then we have Venus, the planet of love and beauty and creative power. Venus is pictured as a circle with a little cross on it. The negative aspect of Venus would be *I don't care...It doesn't mean anything to me.* This is negative self-talk that creates futility or, *what's the use, it's not going to work anyway.*

Then the last sword, the one moving inward on the major sword and showing double rings, represents the Sun/Moon. Negative usage of Sun and Moon occurs when one talks oneself completely out of a project, not only consciously, which is the Sun, but also subconsciously, which is the Moon.

Futility is the state that we experience when we sabotage what we want by listening to the *Yes/But* tapes in the mind.

4) If we stay in states of sabotaging what we want long enough, then we will move into the next Bardo state in the mind, or the next beast in the mind, the **Eight of Swords**, which is called *interference*. Interference in the mind is created by the doubting mind, the confused mind, or the over-analytical mind. The opposite of the over-analytical mind is the trusting mind, so a tendency to over-analyze in the mind is also a need to control. The controlling mind needs to figure things out, compartmentalize things and has difficulty with being surprised. If we stay in states of sorrow, fear of defeat, and futility long enough, then what we will try to do is to control the situation by over-analyzing it, which will ultimately create doubt and confusion. Whenever we pull this card, it is an indication that we are in a state of doubt and confusion. That is not a time to act, it is a time to wait. It could represent doubt and confusion about two choices (the central swords), or two issues, places, people, or situations. There is a tendency in the mind to go back and forth as to which would be the better choice, or how to bring two or more things together to create a greater whole.

5) If we stay in states of over-analyticalness to such a point that it creates doubt and confusion or interference, then we will move into the next Bardo state in the mind, which is the **Nine of Swords**, which is *self-cruelty*. This is a tendency in the mind to wound the self through thought. The spirit, or essence of who we are, is weeping in the background wondering why we are being so hard on ourselves. This is self-criticalness, the inner-judge. It's literally being very hard on ourselves mentally. It's negative self-talk.

6) If we stay with our inner critic long enough, we will move into the final beast or Bardo state in the mind, which is the **Ten of Swords**, which is *fear of ruin*. What's important about this particular symbol is that this is the point where we make a mental decision, and believe in the mind that things are not going to work. We have made a conscious choice in the mind that things are not going to work, particularly in two arenas in our lives: in areas of finances, which are the scales at the top of the card; and also in areas of relationship, which is the pierced heart in the middle of the card; or it could be fear of ruin about two things that are equally important to us. This

is Sun in Gemini, and the two issues here could be relationships or finances, or it could be personal and professional, or it could be issues related to Gemini people in our lives, anyone born May 21 – June 21.

There are six challenges in the mind for us to watch: the tendency to rework old wounds in the past (the Three of Swords); the tendency to experience fear of defeat about moving in new directions or about new important relationships (the Five of Swords); the tendency to sabotage what we want, creating futility (the Seven of Swords); by staying in futility long enough, the tendency to over-analyze things (the Eight of Swords) to such a point that it creates doubt and confusion; by over-analyzing to the point of self-doubt, the tendency of self-judgment, self-criticalness, self-cruelty (Nine of Swords), wounding the self through thought; with the ultimate result being (the Ten of Swords) where we actually not only experience fear of ruin, but we are convinced in the mind that things are not going to possibly work for us.

Four Positive Mental States To Counter Negative Thinking

1) Even though we have these six Bardo states in the mind, there are four positive ways in the mind that we can counter these problematic tapes. The mind is most easily reprogramed through creative visualization and affirmation, and through utilizing the **Ace of Swords** which is *clarity*, the mind that has no doubt, the mind that has come out of the clouds of doubt and confusion totally into the light. The Ace of Swords is the inspired, innovative, creative and expanded mind. The green sword going into the crown is a symbol of expansion, the halo effect. There is no culture in the world that does not make head-dresses or does not have crowns, which is an acknowledgment of expanded awareness or the inspired mind. This is the mind that utilizes wisdom (the blue in the background). The Ace of Swords is a resource that we have in the mind that can transform any of the mental negative states or Bardo states. It's an unlimited resource of clarity, decisiveness, inspiration and creativity that's always available in the mind.

2) The other quality in the mind that we can utilize as a portal for growth, or as a gift, talent and resource, that can transform any of the Bardo states in the mind, is the **Two of Swords**, which is peace. The Two of Swords is peace of the mind, or the meditative mind. It's the mind that has resolved conflict. It's represented by two swords coming together, piercing the blue lotus blossom of wisdom. The astrological symbol that is associated with the Two of Swords is Moon in Libra, which is peace that is experienced at a deep subconscious level (the Moon), and peace that gives one the experience of balance, harmony and objectivity, which is Libra. It's the meditative mind, the reflective mind, the mind that has totally resolved conflict. The Two of Swords pictures to us that quality of mind that is our inner guidance, or the meditative mind where resolution, or peace of mind, can be experienced.

3) Besides the Ace of Swords and the Two of Swords, we have the **Four of Swords** which is *truce*. Truce is different from the Two of Swords (peace). Truce is peace in action. The Four of Swords is actually applying the concept of peace externally, through negotiation, through peace-making with family members, colleagues, deep emotional relationships, or within communities, or within cultures, or globally. This is Jupiter in Libra, which reminds us that truce-making of any kind requires openness and flexibility of mind (Jupiter), and negotiating requires that we stay in balance and not get in any kind of extreme position (Libra).

What we have here is a picture of four swords coming to the center of a four-petaled lotus blossom. Truce is the capacity to mentally, emotionally, spiritually, and physically resolve things at the core of who we are (the four petaled lotus blossom). Once a truce has been reached, we can move out of conflict, doubt, and confusion (all the webbing in the background of the card).

4) Another resource in the mind that can transform any of the problematic states that we might be experiencing in the mind is the **Six of Swords** which is called *science*, or *science of mind*. This is the objective mind, the fair-witnessing mind, the observing mind. It's the mind that's willing to look at things as they are rather than as we want them to be. The circle, the crystalline sphere on the symbol reminds us to look at things wholistically. When we look at the whole of things we are able to stay objective and also to look at things creatively (the diamond on the card). The astrological aspect of this symbol is Mercury in Aquarius. Mercury is the planet of communication; Aquarius is the zodiac sign associated with creativity, innovation and that which is new or ahead of its time. The Six of Swords reminds us that the objective mind is the mind that is able to communicate (Mercury) new things (Aquarius) in such an objective way that it can be received and heard. This is *science of mind*, it's the objective mind, the fair-witnessing mind, the observing mind. More importantly, it is the mind that is willing to look at things as they are rather than as we want them to be.

Everything on this card comes to the center of the Rosicrucian Cross, which is the cross that is symbolized on the back of each of the cards in the entire deck. This symbol reminds us that objectivity will always allow us to experience the emotional center of who we are (the rose within the cross), and that the objective of mind allows us to have the experience of unifying the internal experience with the external experience, which is the cross-cultural meaning of the cross. The cross is the synthesis of inner experience (the vertical line of the cross) combined with outer experience (the horizontal line of the cross).

On the mental level of consciousness there are four ways that we can totally transform any mental challenge or problematic state on the mental realm of consciousness: we can access clarity and creativity with the Ace of Swords; we are able to ask for inner guidance and access the meditative mind (the Two of Swords); which then allows us to freely negotiate or be open to negotiation in getting our needs met (Four of Swords); and finally, the Six of Swords reminds us of the fair-witnessing mind that can communicate things in such an objective way that they can be received and heard.

POSITIVE AND NEGATIVE STATES OF THE HEART

The emotional level of consciousness is represented by Cups and there are three Bardo states or tests or challenges that we experience emotionally as reactive patterns to the six mental challenges in the mind.

1) **The Five of Cups** is *disappointment*. This is a reactive pattern or response to either sorrow in the mind, fear of defeat, futility, doubt or interference, cruelty or ruin created through negative thinking in the mind. It's a natural response to negative mental thoughts. The Five of Cups is a picture of disappointment. The astrological aspect is Mars in Scorpio. This is not a superficial disappointment, it's a very deep disappointment and a very strong reaction because of the Mars in

Scorpio aspect. Mars is the planet of action, energy and assertion. Scorpio is the Zodiac sign of death and transformation. Disappointment makes us feel fragile and breakable, like the glass cups. Disappointment takes us off-balance, like the askewed star. Disappointment makes us feel uprooted (the lily pads with the blossoms falling off their lily pads). And yet, disappointment can be a transformative experience, symbolized by the roots of the lily pads making the shape of a butterfly. Disappointment often brings up anger, which is reflected by the red sky; it often makes us feel depressed, which is symbolized by the murky seas. The important thing is how we handle disappointment. The I-Ching says: "The event is not so important, but rather my response to the event is what matters."

2) If we stay in disappointment and have difficulty handling it, then the next emotional Bardo state or challenge that we might face if we dwell and indulge in disappointment would be the **Seven of Cups**, which is *debauch*. This is emotional depression, it's also emotional indulgence. Another word for debauch is indulgence, whether it is indulgences with the past, or indulgences in moods. Whenever we are depressed or feel sorry for ourselves we might reach for something or do something to make ourselves feel better, which might be over-working, over-shopping, over-eating, drinking, smoking, or indulging in sexual activities. When we're disappointed (Five of Cups), we move into debauch or indulgence patterns, which are a way of reaching for something or doing something in that moment that will make us feel better, but ultimately is a destructive relief rather than a constructive resolution. Another word besides indulgence might be addiction. What we find ourselves reaching for to make ourselves feel better temporarily that is not constructive is mirrored to us in the Seven of Cups.

3) If we stay in indulgence or debauch patterns (Seven of Cups) long enough, another reactive pattern that we might move into on the emotional level is the **Eight of Cups**, which is *indolence* or *inertia*, which is caused by over-giving or over-extending ourselves. It's filling up other people's needs and wants to the brim (all the circles in the sea have been filled up with our own energy and vitality) to the extent that we have just enough energy for the left and the right sides of the body (the four cups), or barely enough energy – mentally, emotionally, spiritually and physically – which are the lotus blossoms filling just the four cups, or filling the two sides of the body. The rest of the cups are empty, chipped, and the handles are ripped off, the symbol of feeling emotionally drained, tired or ripped off. The Eight of Cups reminds us that it is important in its astrological aspect of Saturn in Pisces to know what our limits and boundaries are and to be able to set limits and boundaries. It reminds us that we are in a place of over-giving, over-compensating, over-extending ourselves, and what we actually need, like Saturn, is to know what our limits and boundaries are and to set limits and boundaries, particularly in those arenas of our lives where we have emotional investment, which is Pisces.

Even though there are three challenges or states in the heart, we can transform those three problematic states in the heart, disappointment, debauch and indolence or over-extension, through the seven gifts or talents that we all emotionally have.

1) **The Ace of Cups** is *love with wisdom*. It's the Holy Grail. It pictures to us three ways in which we can transform disappointment, debauch patterns, or indolence: one, through reflecting ourselves accurately (the double rainbow on the

Three Beasts or Bardo States of the Heart

Seven Positive Emotional States

symbol); two, by not pushing, not holding back, but trusting (the perfectly balanced unfolding lotus blossom); and three, by nurturing ourselves in equal proportion to how we nurture others (the light moving into the Holy Grail).

2) **The Two of Cups**, which is *love*, shows us that we won't be disappointed, move into debauch patterns or over-extension patterns if we become very clear about what we need and want emotionally and what we don't need and want. Here we have two red dolphins facing each other filling each other's cups equally. The Two of Cups mirrors to us relationships that are both equal and special. Most of us know what it is like to have equal and not special relationships, such as relationships with co-workers or colleagues, equal but not special. We also know what it is like to have relationships that are special but not equal. The Two of Cups symbolizes relationships that are equally and mutually fulfilling, where one is not giving more than the other, where the result is creative love (the green sea), a deep spiritual connection (the yellow sea), and a mental stimulus (the blue sky). It's love that is nurturing (Venus in Cancer), comforting and supportive to each other equally.

3) **The Three of Cups** is *abundance* and the astrological aspect of this is Mercury in Cancer. Another way that we can transform disappointment, debauch and indolence emotionally is by communicating, which is Mercury, the abundance of feelings that we have (Cancer), and especially those nurturing feelings to three very important people in our lives, which is pictured by the three pomegranate cups that are equally filled with the gold lotus blossoms.

4) If we are willing to communicate the abundance of feelings that we have, then we move into another emotional state which is pictured to us by the **Four of Cups**, which is Moon in Cancer, the feeling of luxury that is not only experienced emotionally within (the ray of light going into the inner cups), but also externally. This is a card which indicates that we are no longer willing to support a dichotomy of being emotionally filled inside but not emotionally filled outside, or the other dichotomy of feeling externally full but internally empty. True emotional luxury is the sense of fulfillment internally and externally without any disparity or dichotomy. And so, one way that we can transform disappointment, and debauch and indolence emotionally is by making sure that we place ourselves in situations where we are both internally and externally emotionally fulfilled, which is the meaning of true luxury.

5) Having that experience of internal and external fulfillment then moves us into an emotional state which can also transform disappointment, debauch and indolence. This is being clear about what gives us *pleasure*, which is pictured by the **Six of Cups**. This is pleasure, fun and play that's healing (the copper cups), and revitalizing (the orange lotus blossoms), and renewing and regenerating itself (the snakes wrapped in the cups). It's an incredible ability to experience pleasure at the depths, not superficial pleasure, deep pleasure. This card or symbol is a reminder to us to really get in touch with what gives us pleasure and to have the capacity to bring fun, play and pleasure into our lives, regardless of what we might be facing emotionally.

6) **The Nine of Cups** is Jupiter in Pisces, and it is called *happiness*. Here we have nine pewter cups filled with lotus blossoms; this is complete happiness. This is tangible happiness (the pewter cups); it is happiness that one can definitively point to, not abstract happiness. It's happiness where we can tell the reasons why we are happy and are able to acknowledge people, places, interests, things that make

us happy. Tangible happiness that is experienced externally is pictured to us by the Nine of Cups.

7) **The Ten of Cups** is *satisfaction* or *contentment* that comes from deep within and radiates out in all aspects of our lives. Here we have ten cups, the Tree of Life, the Kabala, indicating that all the stations of our life, or all aspects of our life, are internally giving us emotional contentment and satisfaction (cups). The astrological aspect is Mars in Pisces, which is a lot of energy that's coming from deep within that's very fluid, like Pisces, and that's radiating out. It's satisfaction and contentment that comes from deep within.

We have explored the mental tests and challenges in consciousness and the emotional tests and challenges in consciousness, and now we are going to go into the challenges in consciousness that affect our energy, or our life-force or our spirituality, our intuition, and our vision and insight, which is represented to us by the Suit of Wands.

POSITIVE AND NEGATIVE INTUITIVE STATES

1) One of the two problematic states of consciousness that effect our energy is the **Five of Wands**, *strife*. Another word for strife is *anxiety* or *frustration*. Anxiety is created by holding back energy or not taking action on energy. It is a state of feeling extremely anxious because our energy, that wants to be used, is not being directed. Anxiety is like sitting in a chair, but energetically going 100 miles an hour. The astrological aspect of this is Saturn in Leo. Saturn is the planet of knowing what one's limits and boundaries are, and it's a reminder not to limit, restrict or hold our energy back, but to handle things step-by-step. Saturn in Leo is creative energy that is feeling limited or bound or held back in some way. Leo is the planet of creative power, and any kind of holding back will make us feel leaded, or dull, which is symbolized by the Eye of Horus staff being in colors of lead, the lotus blossoms being grey and dulled, and the Ibis heads or the Phoenix heads dulled in color. When we are in states of anxiety, frustration or strife, there is tendency of not doing, which is pictured by all the grey or the lead on the card. It is the feeling of being dulled in some way or limited, not creative, yet experiencing energy that is very active and wanting to be used. Anxiety is an energetic resource which shows us that if we spend a long time in the negative states of the mind, we will have emotional reactions which affect our essence, vision, and intuition. The Five of Wands reflects to us our anxiety, or creative power that is restricted, limited or held back in some way.

2) If we stay in states of anxiety for long periods of time, it will lead to the next challenging state that we experience internally, energetically and spiritually, which is **Ten of Wands**, *oppression*. The ways that we oppress ourselves are by editing, rehearsing or holding back who we are. The Ten of Wands is self-imposed oppression, or conscious choices that we make to stay in oppressive situations long past appropriateness. The astrological aspect that is represented here is Saturn in Sagittarius. It's limiting our vision. Saturn is reminding us to do things step-by-step and for some people, when they do things step-by-step, it makes them feel limited, bound or restricted. Sagittarius, is the sign of unrestricted visions, dreams or perception. Sagittarius, the visionary aspect of self, asks us not to hold ourselves

Two Beasts or Bardo States Which Affect Our Energy or Vitality

back through editing, rehearsing, not being all of who we are, or of staying in oppressive situations much longer than we need to.

Both anxiety and oppression are results of not taking action or feeling incapacitated to take action.

Eight Ways to Positively Maintain Energy and Vitality

At the core of who we are, or the spiritual essence of who we are – or by trusting our intuition – there are eight ways in which we can transform self-imposed or externally imposed strife or oppression, ways in which we can maintain life force and connection to the authentic aspects of who we are.

1) **The Ace of Wands** is the tonic for both anxiety and oppression and it is *truth* and *authenticity*. It's the state where we make the conscious decision not to abandon ourselves in any way. Often anxiety and oppression are announcements of self-abandonment or abandoning ourselves for someone else's love and acceptance, or for keeping peace, balance and harmony. The Ace of Wands is that state of consciousness where we absolutely refuse to abandon who we are and where we stay in the truth of who we are.

2) **The Two of Wands** is *dominion*. Dominion comes from the root word *domain*. By placing ourselves in situations that are balanced, integrated and harmonious, we allow ourselves to move through states of anxiety and oppression. Often, anxiety and oppression remind us that we are out of balance in some arena of our life. The Two of Wands allows us to be clear about what would bring peace, balance and dominion into arenas of our lives that would resolve anxiety and strife.

3) **The Three of Wands** is *virtue*. Another word for virtue is integrity. Here we have three wands that are clustered together in a bouquet, which is a reminder to us that integrity has three ingredients and if these ingredients of integrity are honored, we will experience less anxiety and oppression in our lives. The three ingredients of integrity are making sure that mind, heart and action are all in alignment with the direction in which we want to move. When our mind, heart and action are in alignment, then we are able to be consistent, congruent. The Three of Wands reminds us to wait – not act – if mind, heart and action are not in alignment.

4) **The Four of Wands**, *completion*, reminds us that often anxiety and oppression come up as we are wanting to complete things or to initiate things. It is also the desire to move in new directions from a place of wholeness and completion. Venus in Aries is the desire to initiate new things from a sense of completion. This astrological aspect reminds us that anxiety and oppression are alleviated if we are willing to move in new directions by making sure things are wholly complete before we move in those directions.

5) **The Six of Wands** is *victory*. We can become victorious over anxiety and oppression if we are open and flexible in handling situations in creative ways. Victory is like Jupiter in Leo. Victory requires the flexibility of Jupiter and the creativity of Leo. The combination of flexibility and creativity allows us to create win/win situations in our life rather than win/lose situations. The ultimate victory is where everyone experiences a win/win.

6) **Seven of Wands**, *valour*, is experiencing internal openness, creativity and win/win situations, allowing us to use another gift on the spiritual level of consciousness that will combat anxiety and oppression. Valour comes from the root

word *to value*. Valour is the courage to stay by what you value, not compromise or settle for less. It's the courage to trust your experience, which is symbolized by the large notched wands. The astrological aspect is Mars in Leo. Mars is the planet of energy and assertion; Leo is the sign of creative power. Valour requires energy to stay by what is creatively important. Having the courage to stay by what we value, allows things to unfold (the lotus blossoms), permits us to move in new directions (the Ibis heads), and to see things more clearly (the winged Eyes of Horus).

7) **The Eight of Wands**, *swiftness*, is another formula that will help us alleviate strife and oppression. The Eight of Wands is asking us not to procrastinate or be covert and manipulative in our communication. This is direct communication and swift action, which is reflected by the astrological aspect of Mercury in Sagittarius. The Eight of Wands is handling things as they come up. By taking swift action, and communicating directly, we are able to alleviate anxiety and oppression. Often anxiety and oppression are created by procrastinating or by not being direct in our communication.

8) **The Nine of Wands**, *strength*, is a reminder that regardless of whether we are experiencing anxiety or oppression, that at the core of who we are, we have unlimited resources of inner strength waiting to be utilized. The Nine of Wands mirrors to us strength that wants to be accessed on every level of consciousness. The intertwined arrows represent the mental, emotional, spiritual, and physical strength that is inherently available to us all.

POSITIVE AND NEGATIVE REALITY STATES

The physical level of consciousness is pictured to us by Disks. Disks is the external suit, which represents health, finances, work, creativity and relationships. Up to this point, the challenges that we have experienced have been internal challenges: six internal challenges of the mind, three internal challenges of the heart, two internal challenges energetically or spiritually. When we have spent our time exploring eleven problematic states of consciousness internally, then those internal problematic states will begin to reveal themselves externally.

1) **The Five of Disks** is *worry*. The astrological aspect of this symbol is Mercury in Taurus. Mercury is the planet of communication and Taurus is the sign most associated with application. This symbol represents possible worry about communication and how it's being received or misused or misunderstood. Worry is an interesting state of consciousness because it takes us to the future or it takes us to the past, and it has us totally avoiding the present. It is a very problematic state of consciousness because we definitely are not in the present when we are worrying. We are caught in the *what ifs?* of tomorrow and the *if onlys...* of yesterday, and as a result, totally avoiding the present. Avoid means to create *a void*. Nothing gets handled in the present because we avoid situations that are not present. The Five of Disks reflects back to us that state where we are either worried about something that concerns us in the future or we are worried about past activities or deeds. We can collapse worry by attending to the present needs and situation.

2) **The Seven of Disks** is *fear of failure or success*. The astrological aspect of this symbol is Saturn in Taurus. It's the feeling of being limited, restricted

Physical Beasts and Bardo States: Worry and Fears of Failure and Success

(Saturn) in our productivity and our actions (Taurus). This same astrological aspect is duplicated once again on the coins. The bulls on the coins represent Taurus, external productivity. Saturn is represented by the helmeted warrior on the coins. This is fear of failing, or fear of success. The function of fear is to constrict and distort our perceptions, our behaviors, and our realities. This is the experience of old fears that we will fail, like we have in the past, or fear that we will fail in the future. It is also fear of success – fear that we don't deserve or can't handle that which we have wanted and can achieve. It is amazing to watch the creative energy that can be used to sabotage our own success or actualize a negative, self-fulfilling prophecy.

Whenever we pull the *worry* card or the *failure* card, the Five of Disks or the Seven of Disks, it is an indication that we have been through all the other eleven Bardo states. Both of these symbols reflect to us that it is an important time for us to make a choice to redirect our energy and move into the areas of consciousness where we can use and access our talents and resources. These cards signal and warn that whatever we have been thinking about in our minds, the six Bardo states of the mind, or whatever we have been reacting to in the heart, or in whatever ways we have been sabotaging our energy (Wands) it is about to manifest itself in the outer reality if these states are not addressed. The Five of Disks and the Seven of Disks indicate that what we've been fearing, or what we have been experiencing in our Bardo states could manifest tangibly in the external world in areas of health, finances, creativity, and relationships if we don't begin to redirect our focus and energy.

Eight Ways To Transform Our External Reality

There are eight ways that we can transform worry and fear of failure. These are formulas in which we can transform or direct negative or problematic states so that we do not manifest what we fear or worry about; instead, we can begin to redirect the problematic states creatively, remembering and using our gifts, talents and resources.

1) **Ace of Disks** is *success*. This is internal and external success. The internal success is represented by the angel wings, symbolizing mental, emotional, spiritual, and physical success. Outwardly, we have external success, which is pictured by the coins within the coins and the crystals within the crystals. The Ace of Disks is the experience of fulfillment that is witnessed in external reality and is also experienced internally. There is no dichotomy of feeling externally full and internally empty, or of feeling internally fulfilled and externally unsatisfied.

2) **The Two of Disks** is *change*. This reminds us that we can change worry and fear of failure by being open to new opportunities. The astrological aspect of this symbol is Jupiter in Capricorn. By being flexible like Jupiter, and creating stability and security and solidity in our lives, like Capricorn, we can create expansive, stable change. Change has three functions: it allows us to bring back into balance what's out of balance; it reminds us that we have an opportunity to break patterns that bind, limit, restrict or hold us back; and it is an opportunity in which to grow and become even more of who we are. Pictured on this symbol is the Uroborous snake. The Uroborous snake is an Oriental serpent which eats its own tail. The Uroborous snake reminds us of Oriental philosophy which states that change is the only constant, and that change is cyclic. The Uroborous snake making

the number eight is reminding us that change is for the purpose of bringing back what is out of balance back into balance.

3) **The Three of Disks**, *works*, is a reminder that worry and fear of failing can be relieved and resolved if we are clear on our priorities and our commitments. It is giving every situation "the works" or all that we have. Another description for *works* is being clear on knowing what are our priorities and commitments. It is knowing what is our focus, intention, and commitment and in those arenas of our lives where we are willing, like the three red wheels, to give all of our mind, heart and action to a concentrated focus or purpose, which is symbolized by the pyramid.

4) **The Four of Disks**, *power*, reminds us that worry and fear of failing cannot occur if we are willing to empower ourselves and to empower others. True power is knowing what our limits and boundaries are, like the castle with the moat, and being comfortable in setting limits and boundaries in situations where they are needed.

5) **The Six of Disks** is *success*, the second success card in this suit, and on this card we have the formula for success. Things will be successful in our lives personally and professionally if we follow the formula of the six planets that are represented on this symbol. Things can be successful if we'll handle things step-by-step, which is the lesson of Saturn; things will be successful if we're open and flexible and resilient to new opportunities, which is the lesson of Jupiter; things will be successful in our lives if we follow what has heart and meaning, which is the lesson of Venus; things will be successful in our lives if we will stay in our truth and authenticity and not abandon ourselves, which is the lesson of the Moon; and things will be successful in our lives if we communicate effectively, and bring content and timing together in our communications, which is the lesson of Mercury; and things will be successful in our lives if we put consistent energy into our relationships or career, rather than relying on marathon energy or resisting and holding back our energy, which is the lesson of Mars.

6) **The Eight of Disks** is *prudence*. Fear of failing and worry can also be alleviated by utilizing prudence. This symbol is the Harvest Tree which reminds us that we can all have harvest if we utilize prudence and wisdom. Harvest follows order, it does not follow chaos; and harvest follows trust, it does not follow control. The astrological aspect is Sun in Virgo, which reminds us that if we don't overextend ourselves to make things happen, nor resist and hold back, the results of wisdom or prudence will bring the Harvest Tree. Virgo reminds us to attend to details, to organize things, and to handle things as they come up. The true meaning of prudence or wisdom is revealed by balanced action which generates and maintains the Harvest Tree.

7) **The Nine of Disks** is *gain*. Things become gainful in our lives when worry and fear are alleviated. If we will follow what has heart and meaning, and if we will attend to details, the result is gain. This is reflected by the astrological aspect of Venus in Virgo – having heart in what we are doing is Venus; attending to details, or bringing beauty, balance, and harmony into our lives is Virgo. The combination of heart and discipline allows us to experience a gainful life or the experience of hitting the bulls-eye.

8) **The Ten of Disks** is *wealth*. This is internal and external wealth that is created by utilizing our communication gifts (Mercury), and our healing gifts, which is pictured by the caduceus. Inner and outer abundance inspires and

motivates ourselves and others, which is symbolized by the stars on the coins. Communication, healing, and inspiration are three keys that can generate abundance. The Ten of Disks reminds us that organized and inspirational communication can sustain our health and well-being. Communication that is healing generates and mirrors to us the internal riches and wealth that can be manifested externally.

This concludes a look at the portals for growth and the portals for initiation. We've reviewed the thirteen Bardo states and the twenty-seven gifts, talents and resources in which we can transform those internal and external tests and challenges that we face in life. The Minor Arcana as a whole is a portraiture that dynamically reveals the truth of Emerson's quote: "What lies before us and what lies behind us is but a small matter compared to that which lies within us."

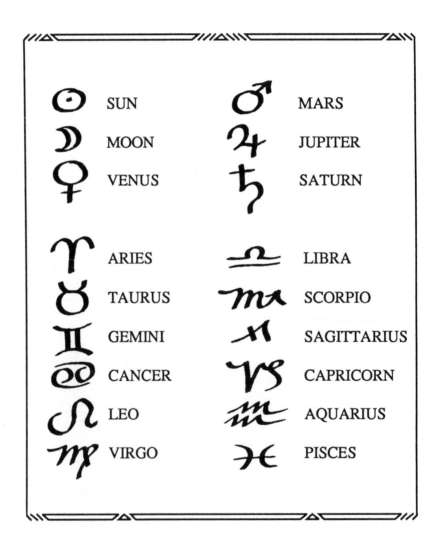

☉	SUN	♂	MARS
☽	MOON	♃	JUPITER
♀	VENUS	♄	SATURN
♈	ARIES	♎	LIBRA
♉	TAURUS	♏	SCORPIO
♊	GEMINI	♐	SAGITTARIUS
♋	CANCER	♑	CAPRICORN
♌	LEO	♒	AQUARIUS
♍	VIRGO	♓	PISCES

13 TESTS & CHALLENGES IN CONSCIOUSNESS

(These are problematic states in consciousness which are referred to by Jungian psychologists as the *shadow aspects* of who we are; by the Egyptians as the *Bardo States*; and by shamanic cultures as the *Journey into the Underworld* as a journey of reowning personal power)

SWORDS Mental Challenges (Beliefs, Attitudes, Thoughts)

3 of Swords	5 of Swords	7 of Swords	8 of Swords	9 of Swords	10 of Swords
Sorrow	Fear of Defeat	Futility	Interference Doubt/ Confusion	Self-Cruelty	Fear of Ruin

CUPS Emotional Challenges (Responses, Reactions, Difficult Feelings)

5 of Cups	7 of Cups	8 of Cups
Disappoint-ment	Debauch Indulgences	Indolence Over-Extension

WANDS Energetic, Intuitive, Spiritual Challenges

5 of Wands	10 of Wands
Anxiety Strife	Oppression

DISKS Physical External Challenges, Health, Finances, Work, Creativity, Relationships.

5 of Disks	7 of Disks
Worry	Fear of Failure

There is no such thing as the dark night of the spirit, there is only the dark night of the ego
– Frances Vaughan

SECTION VI

A REVIEW

NINE ARCHETYPAL CONSTELLATIONS FOUND WITHIN THE

TAROT

INTRODUCTION

The following section explores how all the cards or symbols are related to each other. The symbols that naturally cluster together are referred to as *constellations*; and the shape that forms the constellation is called the *archetypal matrix* or form that holds the constellation together.

In the Tarot, there are nine natural constellations with a specific ruler or Major Arcana symbol that is the center of each constellation. Each constellation has a universal shape or outline, the archetypal matrix, that holds the constellation or cluster of symbols together.

Definition of Terms:

Constellation: 1) a number of fixed stars arbitrarily considered as a group, usually named after some object, animal, or mythological being that they supposedly suggest in outline; 2) any brilliant cluster, gathering, or collection.

Archetype: From Greek *archetypon* (*archos* = first + type) 1) the original pattern, or model, from which all other things of the same kind are made; 2) a perfect example of a type or group.

Matrix: 1) the womb; uterus 2) that within which, or within and from which something originates, takes form; 3) a die or mold for casting or shaping; 4) an impression duplicated; 5) the formative cells.

These nine constellations can also be used as spreads for gathering further information about the self.

(Constellation material was edited by Lynne Novy)

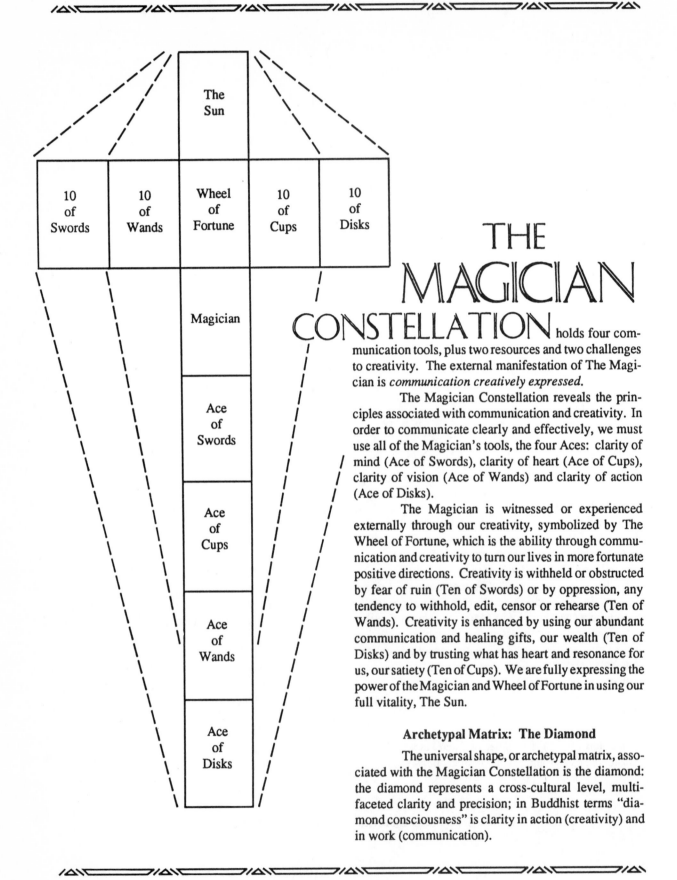

| 10 of Swords | 10 of Wands | Wheel of Fortune | 10 of Cups | 10 of Disks |

The Sun

Magician

Ace of Swords

Ace of Cups

Ace of Wands

Ace of Disks

THE MAGICIAN CONSTELLATION

holds four communication tools, plus two resources and two challenges to creativity. The external manifestation of The Magician is *communication creatively expressed*.

The Magician Constellation reveals the principles associated with communication and creativity. In order to communicate clearly and effectively, we must use all of the Magician's tools, the four Aces: clarity of mind (Ace of Swords), clarity of heart (Ace of Cups), clarity of vision (Ace of Wands) and clarity of action (Ace of Disks).

The Magician is witnessed or experienced externally through our creativity, symbolized by The Wheel of Fortune, which is the ability through communication and creativity to turn our lives in more fortunate positive directions. Creativity is withheld or obstructed by fear of ruin (Ten of Swords) or by oppression, any tendency to withhold, edit, censor or rehearse (Ten of Wands). Creativity is enhanced by using our abundant communication and healing gifts, our wealth (Ten of Disks) and by trusting what has heart and resonance for us, our satiety (Ten of Cups). We are fully expressing the power of the Magician and Wheel of Fortune in using our full vitality, The Sun.

Archetypal Matrix: The Diamond

The universal shape, or archetypal matrix, associated with the Magician Constellation is the diamond: the diamond represents a cross-cultural level, multifaceted clarity and precision; in Buddhist terms "diamond consciousness" is clarity in action (creativity) and in work (communication).

THE HIGH PRIESTESS

CONSTELLATION contains four intuitive re-

sources, and the external manifestation of this archetype is modeling one's self-trust, self-resourcefulness, independence, and intuition.

Supporting the principle of intuition, this constellation holds our capacity for increasing and sustaining self-sufficiency and self-resourcefulness. The High Priestess reminds us that the intuitive process is present and accessible mentally when the mind is in a state of peace (Two of Swords) and emotionally when in states of empathy and love (Two of Cups). As a source of energy that seeks to harmonize and unify, intuition is ever present for us to use to create states of balance or dominion (Two of Wands). Since the intuitive process is never static or fixated, it is always fluid and open to change, which is the only constant (Two of Disks). Operating from the states of peace, love, balance and flexibility, we become more self-trusting, intuitive and resourceful like The High Priestess.

We know that we are functioning with The High Priestess archetype externally when we operate from our passion and strength (Lust/Strength), our awareness that our beauty has tamed the beast within. It is from this place of strength that we are able to view personal and professional issues from a holistic perspective (The Aeon). The Aeon reminds us that the High Priestess externalizes intuition through the use of good judgment as we give birth to new forms in relationships and in career. Good judgment means assessing where to be or not to be without interpretation or critical value judgment.

Trusting and following intuition allows us to manifest our strength and to look at situations in life from a broader perspective. Our intuition propels the arrow; our intention sets the direction.

Archetypal Matrix:

The Arrow

The universal shape, or archetypal matrix, associated with the High Priestess constellation is the arrow: *sense of direction known; intention of hitting the mark.*

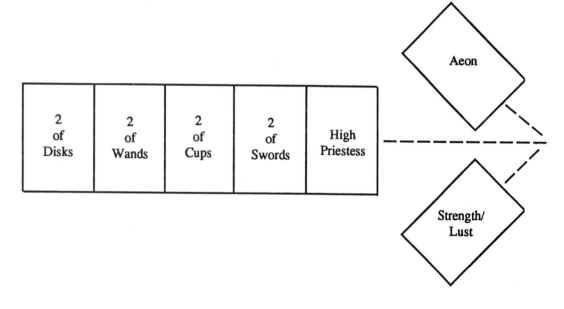

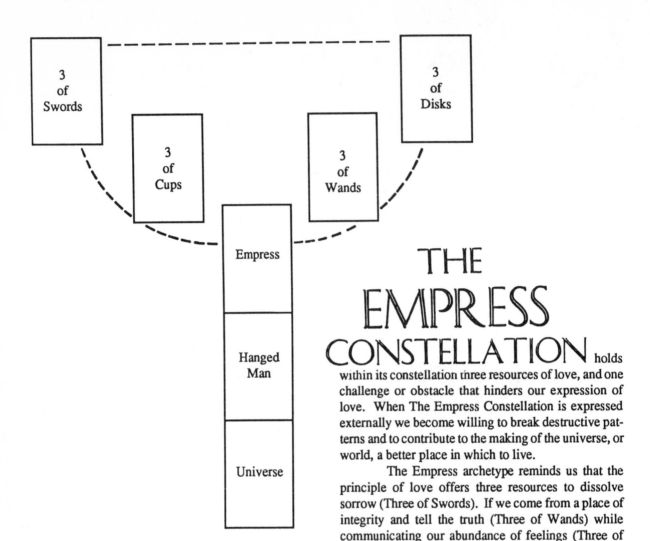

Archetypal Matrix:

The Cup

The universal shape, or archetypal matrix, associated with The Empress Constellation is the cup: the capacity to fill our emotional nature; the ability to nurture, love, comfort and heal ourselves in equal proportion to nurturing, loving, comforting and healing others.

THE EMPRESS CONSTELLATION holds

within its constellation three resources of love, and one challenge or obstacle that hinders our expression of love. When The Empress Constellation is expressed externally we become willing to break destructive patterns and to contribute to the making of the universe, or world, a better place in which to live.

The Empress archetype reminds us that the principle of love offers three resources to dissolve sorrow (Three of Swords). If we come from a place of integrity and tell the truth (Three of Wands) while communicating our abundance of feelings (Three of Cups), knowing what our intention, focus, priorities and commitments are so that we can give everything "the works" (Three of Disks), we can heal sorrow (Three of Swords).

When we no longer want to bind ourselves with limiting or unproductive patterns and when we are willing to turn ourselves up-side-down to get new perspectives on old issues, obstacles and fixations (The Hanged Man), we can transform control to trust. We know we are externalizing the principle of love when we are willing to trust, surrender and move beyond ego, which is the essence of The Hanged Man. Once old patterns are faced and released, we discover new worlds within and without our nature (The Universe). Representing the quality of love extended into the community, culture and world, The Universe symbolizes universal love: the capacity to heal sorrows of the earth and each other.

THE EMPEROR CONSTELLATION

reveals the principle of personal power and leadership, and asks us to assess and demonstrate the qualities of leadership that maintain our own power and empower others. By solving problems through negotiation, or truce (Four of Swords), while coming from a place of emotional fulfillment, or luxury (Four of Cups), and communicating a sense of wholeness, or completion (Four of Wands), we empower ourselves and others (Four of Disks).

Externally, The Emperor archetype manifests in leadership that which is strong and fearless, yet unattached to outcome. To let go and move forward freely (Death/Release), we need peace of mind or resolution (Four of Swords) and a sense that everything is complete or finished (Four of Wands). To initiate something new from a place of courage and no fear (The Fool), we need to own and demonstrate our power (Four of Disks) and to follow what has emotional resonance (Four of Cups).

When we wear The Emperor's crown, particularly in times of endings and beginnings, we act with the freedom of unattachment and the anticipatory wonder of no fear through the four resources of leadership; we empower ourselves and others.

Archetypal Matrix:
The Crown

The universal shape, or archetypal matrix, associated with The Emperor constellation is the crown: the universal symbol of expanded consciousness; recognition of an individual's personal power and leadership. All cultures have headdresses and crowns which demonstrates an archetypal awareness of leadership and honoring the head or crown of consciousness. The Emperor Constellation holds four resources for accessing personal power and leadership.

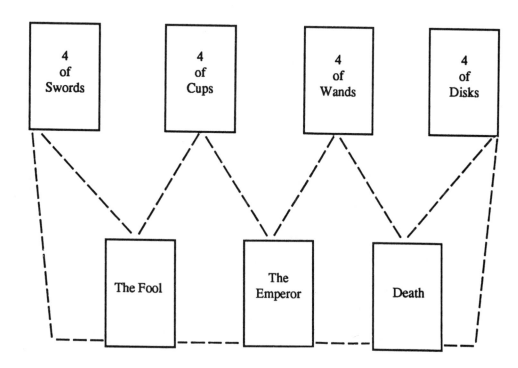

Art
5 of Disks
5 of Wands
5 of Cups
5 of Swords
Hierophant

THE HIEROPHANT

CONSTELLATION holds the four

challenges which obstruct our accessing the wisdom of the inner teacher. The Hierophant archetype represents the qualities of the inner teacher who is able to confront, face and incorporate the wisdom gained from major tests and challenges in life. Internally, the four major teachings of wisdom that all humankind encounter are to move through thoughts or fears of defeat (Five of Swords); to deal with the emotionality of our disappointments (Five of Cups); to access and trust our intuition in order to relieve anxiety, frustration or strife (Five of Wands); and to stay clearly in present time, rather that flitting to past or future, which releases worry (Five of Disks).

Wisdom is the process of tempering conflict within and without. We know that the teaching/learning challenges are being met internally and The Hierophant archetype is being expressed externally when we see the principle of integration, synergy and alchemy (Temperance/Art) at work. Art is the union of opposition, paradox and polarity, out of which a greater whole is created. This synergistic principle forms the basis of our greatest art form for true creative power is to resolve conflict. This is the work of the entire Hierophant Constellation.

Archetypal Matrix: The Staff or The Rod

The universal shape, or archetypal matrix, associated with The Hierophant constellation is the rod or the staff: transmitting teachings or wisdom. (The rod or staff is a Western symbol; its equivalent in the Orient is the "singing reed"; and in Native American Indian traditions, it is the "talking stick")

THE LOVERS CONSTELLATION holds

the four keys to maintaining a successful relationship of any kind, and when this constellation is fully expressed externally, one is able to see the quality of humor and joyousness expressed in balanced relationships.

Supporting the principle of relatedness, The Lovers Constellation balances the duality of complementary opposites. It is this union, mythically referred to as the *journey of the twins*, that integrates polarities, bringing together two people or ideas or visions or parts of oneself to create a greater whole.

The Lovers archetype holds the keys to manifesting successful, fulfilling relationships: by seeing things as they are and being objective (Six of Swords) and spicing our relationships with play and pleasure (Six of Cups), we can achieve a win/win victory situation (Six of Wands) with our partner, which gives both of us the sense of manifesting success (Six of Disks) within the relationship.

Externally, we know we are uniting polarities and resolving conflicts in our relationships with others, as well as within ourselves, when we are able to manifest humor like The Devil or Pan. When we don't take things so seriously that we lose our center, we can stand with the perfect balance of the pillars, independent yet related.

Archetypal Matrix: The Pillars

The universal shape, or archetypal matrix, associated with The Lovers Constellation is the pillars: cross-cultural symbol of balance; independence vs. relatedness; space vs. boundaries; separation vs. unity; the structure that provides an opening or gateway between two possibilities.

6 of Wands	6 of Disks
6 of Cups	6 of Swords
"Pan"/ Devil	Lovers

Archetypal Matrix:
The Spiral

The universal shape, or archetypal matrix, associated with The Chariot is the spiral: symbol of growth and evolution; the experience of changing or evolving to new levels. This shape holds the three challenges and the one resource for facing and sustaining growth and evolution. Outwardly expressed, this is the process of rennovation and restoration.

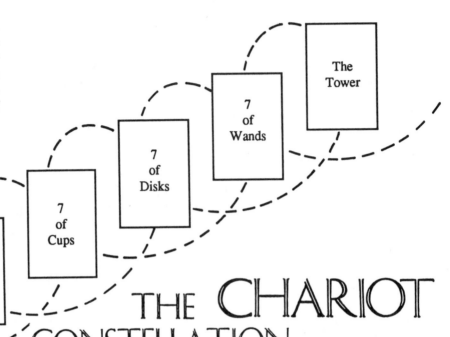

THE CHARIOT
CONSTELLATION carrying the principle of

movement and change, shows us the three internal challenges that we encounter in the process of growth and evolution and the one internal gift that can maintain or sustain movement. We resist change through debauch, or indulgence patterns that are detours to change (Seven of Cups); through fear of failure or fear of success, which restrains movement or change (Seven of Disks); and through futility (Seven of Swords), the tendency in the mind to sabotage what we want, which retards growth and halts our intentions to change. Once we face and move through these internal blocks, we are able to go for what we want without settling for less or compromising ourselves, which is valour, the willingness to stay by what we value (Seven of Wands).

We know we've changed internally, when we are willing externally to dismantle old, artificial, and conditioned forms and parts of ourselves that are superficial and no longer workable. This is the process of restoration, renovation and reclamation of what is actual in our natures. Internal change witnessed externally in action and behavior is symbolized by The Tower, the process of awakening to that which is actual and true within the nature that goes beyond conditioning, family, ego and culture.

Like the spiral, we grow and evolve into expressing even more of who we are through change (The Chariot), which requires that we renovate and restore who we are at deep levels (The Tower).

Archetypal Matrix:

The Star

The universal shape, or archetypal matrix, associated with Adjustment/Justice is the star: universal symbol of awakening, of internal and external radiance, of self confidence. This matrix holds the two challenges and two resources that can be accessed to realign and balance that which is out of balance or in states of confusion or chaos.

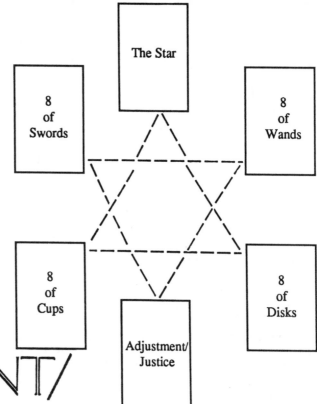

ADJUSTMENT/ JUSTICE

CONSTELLATION addresses the principle of alignment and balance in all areas of our lives, challenging the veils of delusion, illusion and self-deception. The basic issue underlying this archetype is the expression of self-esteen, for when we are balanced within, our radiance shines clearly without. When we express ourselves without effort or holding back, we know we are in balance or alignment.

Two qualities that throw us out of balance are over-analyzing situations to create doubt, confusion and interference (Eight of Swords), and indolence, which is depletion and inertia which comes from over-extending ourselves and not setting limits (Eight of Cups). Two gifts that restore our balance are prudence, the wisdom to act from a centered place (Eight of Disks) and swiftness, the willingness to drop procrastination and combine immediate action with direct communication (Eight of Wands).

Self-esteem expressed in the world manifests as the bright light of radiant confidence that is neither inflated nor deflated, like The Star. Internal confidence, the ability to confide in oneself, comes from moment-to-moment realignment within and attracts external recognition and validation without triggering arrogance or conceit. When our sense of self-worth is authentic, we illuminate and beautify the world; we serve as reminders that we are all walking stars on a giant star.

THE HERMIT CONSTELLATION

contains the principle of introspection and completion, and shows us the way that completion opens the space to initiate or expand something new. The archetype of the way-shower within points to one major challenge that we meet during times of introspection, completion and transition: it is cruelty (Nine of Swords), the beast of self-criticalness and self-doubt born of perfectionism, that stops us. Yet, The Hermit reminds us that we have three internal gifts that counter self-judgment: deep inner spirit is always strong, and if we trust ourselves we tap our strength (Nine of Wands); when our heart is involved in what we do, we complete things happily (Nine of Cups); when we trust our inner guidance, we are aligned with our purpose and always stand to gain (Nine of Disks).

Manifesting internal wisdom externally is bringing light into darkness like The Moon. While The Hermit expresses the internal choice-making process that allows us to take action externally, The Moon reminds us of the universal moment-by-moment choice of falling back into the old dutiful false persona or of stepping forward into expanded expression of our authentic self. The Moon is the inner light of The Hermit shining forth into the darkness without. The result of internal wisdom's unwillingness to abandon truth or authenticity is the capacity to bring more light and awareness to every transition or crossing, bridging within ourselves the familiar with the unknown.

Archetypal Matrix:

The Bridge

The universal shape, or archetypal matrix, associated with The Hermit is the bridge: cross-cultural symbol of transition – endings and beginnings; the process of crossing. This matrix holds one challenge and three resources for completing the old and opening the new.

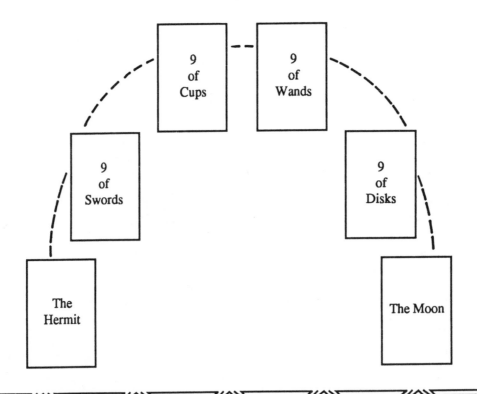

SECTION VII
METHODOLOGY
THE TAROT PROFILE

SYMBOLS THAT APPLY TO YOUR LIFE

*"Symbols are the instrumentalities whereby people
codify experience, or create a 'map' of the
territory of experience"*
–Hugh Dalziel Duncan
Symbols in Society

This section shares the methodology of how to
find out your Life-Time Symbols and your current
Growth Symbol and current Growth Cycle.

YOUR TAROT PROFILE

(After you find out your symbols by computing your birthday as shown in the Tarot Profile Methodology, (p. 231 - 232), then fill in the following Profile from the Major Arcana Chart on p. 234.)

Life time symbols are symbols that come from your birthday. Life-time symbols are both your Personality Symbol and your Soul Symbol. They both represent your inherent potential and purpose in this life time.

Personality Symbol:

(Write in the Major Arcana Symbol that represents your personality expression. The **Personality Symbol** represents your expression in the outer world, your talents, gifts, resources; and how others see you.)

Soul/Spiritual Symbol:

(Write in the Major Arcana Symbol that represents your soul/spiritual essence. The **Soul/Spiritual Symbol** represents the deepest core of who you are. This symbol provides an internal base of energy and natural resource for you to draw upon for your personality expression. This spiritual resource is what inspires you at the core of who you are.

Growth Symbol for current year:

Your **Growth Symbol** (This symbol changes every year. It is based on your birthday plus the current year. See Annual Growth Symbols Methodology, p. 242-243, plus the Major Arcana Chart on p. 234 to determine your current growth symbol.)

(The growth year is from birthday to birthday, not the calendar year.) This symbol reveals all the possibilities for growth, opportunities, expansion, and challenge during the current year from birthday to birthday.

Zodiac Symbol Attributed to Tarot:

(See Major Arcana Chart on p. 234. Read the meaning of the **Zodiac Symbol** at bottom of Major Arcana Chart.)

Sensory Ability:

Your Sensory Ability attributed either by Life-time Symbol or Zodiac Symbol: (See Major Arcana Chart on p. 234. Read the meaning of the **Sensory Ability Symbols** and how they apply to you at the bottom of Major Arcana Chart.) If you don't have a specific sensory symbol, it means that you are wanting to use all the senses.

Major Path Placements:

Major Path Placements: (See Life Path Pyramid Chart on p. 240. This shows the Path of your Life-time Symbols. Write in the path or paths that correspond with your Life-time numbers.)

The symbol is an object of the known world hinting at something unknown; it is the known expressing the life and sense of the inexpressible.

Symbolism in the Visual Arts , by Aniela Jaffe

TAROT PROFILE METHODOLOGY

(Methodology material edited by Cintra Harbach)

To find your personality and soul symbols as represented in the Tarot, add the day and month of your birthday together; to this total add the year of your birth. Add the final total horizontally and reduce to a single digit.

How to Find Your Life-Time Personality and Soul Symbols

Example: if the birthday is September 9, 1956

month	9
day	+ 9
	18
year	1956
	1974 = 21 = 3 (1 + 9 + 7 + 4 = 21); (2 + 1 = 3)

If your final total equals a double digit number, 21 or less, reduce to a single digit. The double digit number is your personality number, the single digit number is your soul number. **Refer to the Major Arcana Chart** (p. 234) to discover your soul and personality symbols.

Example:

month	9
day	+ 9
	18
year	1956
	1974 = 21 = 3

In this case, the number 21, The Universe, is the personality symbol; number 3, The Empress, is the soul symbol.

If your final total equals a single digit number you have one number for both your personality and soul. **Refer to the Major Arcana Chart** (p. 234) to discover your soul and personality symbol.

Example:

month	3
day	+ 21
	24
year	1983
	2007 = 9

Number 9, The Hermit, is both the personality symbol and the soul symbol

If your final total equals 19 it will reduce to 10 and then 1. This is the only combination of three numbers.

Example:

```
month      7
day      + 11
          18
year     1954
         1972  = 19 = 10 = 1
```

Here, 19, The Sun, is the personality symbol; 1, The Magician, is the soul symbol and 10, The Wheel of Fortune, is the creativity symbol.

If your final total equals 22, it reduces to 4 and also become 0. In numerology 22 is the number for 4 (2 + 2 = 4) and also the number for 0 (2 – 2 = 0).

Example:

```
month      10
day      +  4
          14
year     1952
         1966  = 22 = 4
```

In this case, 0, The Fool, is the personality symbol, and 4, The Emperor, is the soul symbol.

If your final total equals a double digit number higher than 22, reduce to a single digit. You will have one number for both your personality and soul symbols. **Refer to the Major Arcana Chart (p. 234)** to discover your soul and personality symbol.

Example:

```
month      12
day      + 24
          36
year     1940
         1976  = 23 = 5
```

5 – The Hierophant is the personality symbol and the soul symbol.

> **Special Note: The Range of Life-Time Combinations is located on p. 235. See Range of Life-Time Combinations Chart, especially the last three lines.**

Major Arcana Descriptions

After you have found out your Lifetime Personality and Soul symbols, refer to Section III, Section VI for in-depth information of your symbols. Additional brief synopsis of each symbol is found in Index B; and synthesized chart is found on p. 236-239.

TAROT PROFILE
MAJOR ARCANA CHART

(Reference chart to use once you have computed your Life-time Symbol and Growth Symbol)

Major Arcana Number	Major Arcana Symbol	Corresponding Zodiac Sign	Specifically Associated Sensory Ability
0	The Fool		
1	The Magician		
2	The High Priestess		
3	The Empress		
4	The Emperor	Aries	Sight
5	The Hierophant	Taurus	Sound
6	The Lovers	Gemini	Smell
7	The Chariot	Cancer	
8	Adjustment/Justice	Libra	
9	The Hermit	Virgo	Touch
10	Wheel of Fortune		
11	Lust/Strength	Leo	Taste
12	The Hanged Man		
13	Death/Rebirth	Scorpio	
14	Art/Temperance	Sagittarius	
15	Devil/Pan	Capricorn	
16	The Tower		
17	The Star	Aquarius	
18	The Moon	Pisces	
19	The Sun		
20	The Aeon	Leo	
21	The Universe		

Sometimes your Life-time Symbol and Zodiac Sign are the same. When they are, you are making sure that you use the potential of the Major Arcana Symbol involved. If your Life-time Symbol and Zodiac symbol are different, the Tarot symbol assigned to your Zodiac sign is an inherent or natural gift that is assisting you with your life-time purpose.

The Sensory abilities are associated either with your Zodiac Sign or your Life-time Symbol. If you do not have any specific sensory ability assigned to you, it indicates that all of the senses are important for you to use and explore in this life-time. If one or two are assigned, either by Zodiac Sign or Life-time Symbol, then these particular senses are heightened and want to be used or learned in this life-time.

RANGE OF LIFE TIME COMBINATIONS CHART

Combining Numerology and Tarot Symbols: Indicators of Personality Expressions and Potential

	Personality	Creativity	Soul
19 - 10 - 1	The Sun	Wheel of Fortune	The Magician (Mercury)
* 10 - 1	Wheel of Fortune	Wheel of Fortune	The Magician (Mercury)
20 - 2	The Aeon/Judgment (Leo)		The High Priestess
+11 - 2	Lust/Strength		The High Priestess
* 2	The High Priestess		The High Priestess
21 - 3	The Universe/World		The Empress (Venus)
+12 - 3	The Hanged Man		The Empress (Venus)
* 3	The Empress (Venus)		The Empress (Venus)
0 - 4	The Fool (Dionysus)		The Emperor (Aries)
+13 - 4	Death/Rebirth (Scorpio)		The Emperor (Aries)
* 4	The Emperor (Aries)		The Emperor (Aries)
+ 14 - 5	Art/Temperance (Sagittarius)		The Hierophant (Taurus)
5	The Hierophant (Taurus)		The Hierophant (Taurus)
# 15 - 6	The Devil/"Pan" (Capricorn)		The Lovers (Gemini)
6	The Lovers (Gemini)		The Lovers (Gemini)
16 - 7	The Tower		The Chariot (Cancer)
7	The Chariot (Cancer)		The Chariot (Cancer)
17 - 8	The Star (Aquarius)		Adjustment/Justice (Libra)
8	Adjustment/Justice (Libra)		Adjustment/Justice (Libra)
18 - 9	The Moon (Pisces)		The Hermit (Virgo)
9	The Hermit (Virgo)		The Hermit (Virgo)

* New for the first time for persons born in the 1970's.

+ Found in persons who are currently 50 years old or older; or in new babies born in the1970's.

Persons who are 38 years of age and older; or in new babies born in the 1970's.

Double numbered people (Example: 21–3) are the integraters/synthesizers.

Single numbered people (Example: 6) are the specializers.

People numbered 19, 10, or 1, need to express creativity in an original and innovative way.

FIND YOUR LIFE-TIME PERSONALITY AND SOUL SYMBOLS ON THIS CHART AND DISCOVER HOW THEY ARE RELATED TO ANCIENT AND MODERN SYMBOLS. See the affirmations that you can work with to support your natural talents and resources.

SYMBOL	GENERAL QUALITIES	SAMPLE AFFIRMATIONS	EXAMPLES OF ANCIENT/MODERN MANIFESTATION
The Fool	Radiance, Courage Transcendance	*I am a radiant being* *I am a living treasure*	Great Spirit; Trickster; Clown; Mime; Jester; Genii
The Magician	Expression; Communication Timing; Flexibility	*I communicate effectively* *I create magic when I use my inherent gifts and talents*	Wizards; Merlin; Mercury; T.V. /Media; Satellites; Shaman; Sorcerer; Computers
The High Priest/Priestess	Intuition; Independence; Clarity	*I trust myself* *I value my sense of integrity* *I am an intuitive, perceptive person*	Isis; Virgin Mary; Delphi Oracles; Goddess; Psi; Parapsychology; Altered States; Psychics; Nuns/Priests
The Empress	Nurturance Support Care; Beauty	*I am a nurturing and supportive person* *I enjoy beauty, harmony, and order* *I give wisely and receive wisely*	Earth Mother; Venus; the Queen; Moon; Yin; Anima; Siren; Mother Nature; Cooks; Nurses; Models; Mothers; Designers
The Emperor	Leadership Builder; Doer Pioneer/Futurist	*I am a good facilitiator* *I value my leadership ability* *I enjoy starting and initiating things*	Kings; Leaders; Warriors; Father; Sun; Yang; Animus; Authority; Arthur and the Grail; Presidents; Directors
The Hierophant	Teacher; Counselor Consultant; Resource; Manager; Inspiration	*I am inspired by learning/ teaching situations* *I honor what is sacred within me*	High Priest of the Eleusinian Mysteries; Advisors; Buddha; Jesus; theologians; Zeus; Kronos; Rabbi; Pope; Inner Teacher
The Lovers	Love; Unification; Relationships Duality; Oppositions	*I am a loving and caring individual* *I relate well with others* *I make choices easily*	Anthony and Cleopatra; Adam and Eve; unified anima and animus; yin/yang; sun/moon; Cupid; dove and serpent

SYMBOL	GENERAL QUALITIES	SAMPLE AFFIRMATIONS	EXAMPLES OF ANCIENT/MODERN MANIFESTATION
The Chariot	Motivation; To Cause Intention Victory/Triumph	*I stimulate and motivate others positively* *I am responsible for what I cause* *I accomplish things effortlessly and well*	Alexander the Great; Knights; Gladiators; Conquerors; Crusades; Apollo the Charioteer; automobiles; boats; airplanes; Space Shuttles; explorers
Adjustment/ Justice	Balance; Truth; Arbitration To Measure; Legality	*I am balanced and centered* *I value being truthful in difficult situations* *I honor my word and commitments*	Scales; Measuring devices; Trials; Juries; Dharma; Karmic adjustment; writing; publishing; Equalization; Themis; Maat; Titaness
The Hermit	Illumination; Seeker; Completion; Revelation Introspection	*I enjoy the feeling of completion and resolution* *I enjoy exploring my inner worlds in meditation and times alone* *I value that which is meaningful and significant*	Pilgrim; Monk; Sage; Philospher; lamps; lanterns; electricity; illuminators; Way-showers; Rogue; guides; ushers; detective; spy; journey-man
Wheel of Fortune	Prosperity; Abundance Cycles; Evolution and Involution; Probability; Breakthrough; Chance	*I am a prosperous individual* *I enjoy manifesting internal abundance externally* *I am flexible during periods of change*	Mandala; Circle; Prayer Wheels; Rosaries; Worrybeads; Roulet; Concepts of Destiny and Fate; Smuts's term – 'holism'; Chakras; Merry-go-rounds; FerrisWheels; compass; clocks; Medicine Wheels
Strength/Lust	Courage; Power; Fortitude; Vitality; Passion; Will	*I enjoy expressing my energy, vitality, and enthusiasm in all that I experience* *I am an individual of character and strength*	Hercules; Samson; Mars; Basht; Sekhet; Fortuna; Nureyev; Lion-trainers; Pavlova; Olympics; Survivors; exorcists

SYMBOL	GENERAL QUALITIES	SAMPLE AFFIRMATIONS	EXAMPLES OF ANCIENT/MODERN MANIFESTATION
The Hanged Man	New Perspective; Surrender; Faith; Sacrifice; Duty; Initiation	*I enjoy looking at the same situation from as many different perspectives as possible* *I value breaking ineffective old patterns* *I accept and receive well from others*	Odin; Thoth; Yggdrasil, the World Tree; Head-stands; back-bends; Neptune; Poseidon; diving ; `a hang-up'; Crucifixion/Resurrection Combined
Death/ Rebirth	Transformation Change; Emergence Release	*I am excited about growing and becoming even more of who I am* *I let go of people and situations with ease and dignity*	Skeleton; Snake shedding skin; Phoenix; Lotus (mud to blossom); Swan (ugly duckling to swan); Butterfly; the Reaper
Art/ Temperance	Synergy; Alchemy; Combination; Integration; Assimilation	*I am a creative, well-integrated individual* *I am as strong in my magnetic nature as I am in my dynamic nature*	Creation myths; Philosopher's Stone; Artemis; Centaur; Sphinx; Consumation; artists; writers; musicians; miners; mythologists and symbolists
The Devil/ Pan	Temptation; Desire; Mirth, Humor, Vitality Endurance; Sensation Stability	*I retain my sense of humor in areas of experience which be-devil me* *I enjoy my sensuality* *I am a vital, joyful and grounded person*	Goat; Satyr; Bacchus; Dionysus; Dragon; Dweller of the Threshold; Vesta; Eye of Siva; Lingam and Yoni; Pan; Ra; Tantra
Tower	Purification; Restoration; Self-Realization; De-structuring Re-structuring	*I am able to restore my energy easily* *I have a commitment to actualize who I really am* *My body is a temple for my spirit*	Tower of Babel; Coit Tower; Leaning Tower of Pisa; citadel; Faust; Houses; Real Estate; Anatomy; diets; exercise; furnaces; fire-places; fevers; no masks

SYMBOL	GENERAL QUALITIES	SAMPLE AFFIRMATIONS	EXAMPLES OF ANCIENT/MODERN MANIFESTATION
The Star	Confidence; Hope Vision; Light; Recognition Self-Esteem	*I am a walking star* *I value who I am* *I see what can be of benefit to people in the future*	Orion; Pleiades; Siris; Star of Bethlehem; Star of David; Star of Wonder; Hollywood; All-Stars; Stars for each state in US flag; stars for grade school children (symbol of recognition/achievement)
The Moon	Passage; Choice; Truth; Illusion; Romance	*I enjoy making important decisions* *I value honesty and integrity in relationships* *I like what is mysterious in me and in others*	Magic Mirror; Masks; Anubis; Scarab; Tzaddi; Moonflower; moon-shot; rainbow; collective unconscious; portals; gates; Luna; Soma; Hathor; Selene; moon-cycles
The Sun	Synergy; Collaboration Co-operation; Co-creation Team-work	*I work well in teamwork situations* *I enjoy making contributions to group efforts* *I am a co-operative individual*	Networking; solar energy; Eye of Ra; Osiris; Siva; Helios; Sunflower; Club of Rome; United Nations; The Curies; Masters and Johnson; Shields and Yarnell
The Aeon/ Judgment	Understanding; Good Judgment; Observations; Origins/Actualization	*I observe people and situations objectively and fairly* *I value the composite of my qualities and characteristics*	Last Judgment; Agni; Vulcan; Pluto; Goddess Nuit; Diplomats; Mediators; Judges; 'bringing light into darkness'; Prometheus; Mazda
The Universe	Manifestation Self-Actualization Expansion; Liberation Attainment	*I love exploring the unknown* *I am excited about bringing my ideas into tangible form* *I love to travel*	Planet Earth; Ecology; the Cosmic Egg; The New World; Galaxies; Discovery; The Womb; The Void; Nirvana; Dancing Sky; Kundalini; Globes; other planets; world community; global consciousness

LIFE PATH PYRAMID CHART

Placement or Points of Emphasis for Individual Expression Within Life Time

This applies to Section VII on Your Tarot Profile p. 230. The following paths are the paths which have particular emphasis for you during this life-time based on your life-time personality and soul symbols. Circle your life-time numbers.

0–4 (The Fool - Emperor) people have the Path of Balance since The Fool (0) is the state of *no fear* **which is a pathless state; Symbols 19, 10, and 1 have three paths; if your Personality and Soul numbers are the same, then you are exploring one path in-depth; if your Personality and Soul symbols are different you are exploring two paths for development.** Record your path or paths on YOUR TAROT PROFILE (Section VII) p. 230 (Your Path Placement)

0 equals THE FOOL – that state of consciousness
before birth and after death, which can be experienced
during lifetime as transcendent experiences, peak experiences,
mystical experiences; and meditative states.

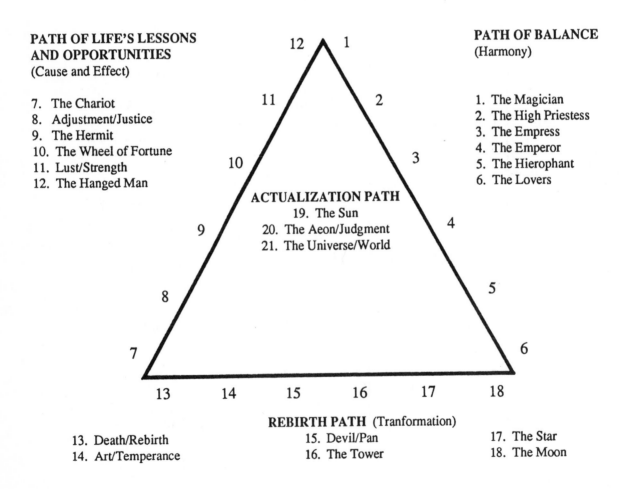

**PATH OF LIFE'S LESSONS
AND OPPORTUNITIES**
(Cause and Effect)

7. The Chariot
8. Adjustment/Justice
9. The Hermit
10. The Wheel of Fortune
11. Lust/Strength
12. The Hanged Man

PATH OF BALANCE
(Harmony)

1. The Magician
2. The High Priestess
3. The Empress
4. The Emperor
5. The Hierophant
6. The Lovers

ACTUALIZATION PATH
19. The Sun
20. The Aeon/Judgment
21. The Universe/World

REBIRTH PATH (Tranformation)

13. Death/Rebirth
14. Art/Temperance
15. Devil/Pan
16. The Tower
17. The Star
18. The Moon

ANNUAL GROWTH SYMBOLS

AND

GROWTH CYCLES

*Divine things are revealed unto each
created spirit in proportion to its powers*
– Dionysus

**Growth Symbols:
Rules for Finding
Your Current
Growth Symbol and
Growth Cycle**

To find your growth symbol for this year as presented in the Tarot, add the day and month of your birthday together; to this total add the year of your current birthday (which is not always the same as the calendar year). Add the final total horizontally.

Example:

```
month     9
day      + 9
          18
year     1982
         2000  = 2   (2 + 0 + 0 + 0 = 2)
```

NOTE: **Since we use the birthday to determine the growth year, your growth year goes from birthday to birthday rather than from calendar year to calendar year.**

If your final total equals a double digit number, 21 or less, do not reduce to a single digit. **Refer to the Major Arcana Chart** (p. 234) to discover your growth symbol for this year.

Example:

```
month     12
day      + 24
          36
year     1982
         2018  = 11
```

Number 11, Strength/Lust, is the growth symbol for this year.

If your final total equals a single digit number **refer to the Major Arcana Chart** (p. 234) to discover your growth symbol for this year.

Example:

```
month      7
day      + 11
          18
year     1983
         2001  = 3
```

Number 3, The Empress, is the growth symbol for this year.

If your final total equals a double digit number, 22 or higher, reduce to a single digit. **Refer to the Major Arcana Chart** (p. 234) to discover your growth symbol for this year.

Example:

```
month     10
day      + 4
          14
year     1979
         1993  = 22 = 4
```

Number 4, The Emperor, is the growth symbol for this year.

If your final total equals 28, it will reduce to 10; do not reduce to a single digit.

Example:

```
month     10
day      + 4
          14
year     1985
         1999  = 28 = 10
```

Number 10, The Wheel of Fortune, is the growth symbol for this year.

Before going any further, go to p. 230, YOUR TAROT PROFILE, and fill in your Growth Symbol for the current year. Information about your growth symbol can be found on p. 252-255.

GROWTH CYCLES

To compute your growth cycles, repeat the growth symbol procedure for each year of your life. After you have followed this procedure, fill in the charts on p. 247-249.

See p. 252-255 for Growth Cycle material and information.

GROWTH YEAR AND GROWTH CYCLES:

Directions

Follow the procedures for finding your Growth Year on p. 242 and 243 (rules for finding your Growth Symbol for each year of your existence).

Read a brief description of all the options or possibilities that might occur in your current Growth Year on pp. 252-255.

After you have followed the procedure for finding your Growth Symbol, go back to the time you were born and find out the Growth Cycle for each year of your life until you are one hundred years old. (See Rules on pp. 242-243). Then fill out the sample charts on pp. 247-249.

Basics to Remember:

The Fool and The Magician are never Personality Growth Symbols because every human being has courage (The Fool) and the ability to learn language for communication (The Magician). In the Growth Cycle, the number 22 is always factored to 4 (The Emperor). Whenever you have the number 28, your Growth Symbol is 10 (The Wheel of Fortune). You do not factor 10 down to 1 in computing your Growth Cycle; 10 remains 10 (The Wheel of Fortune).

You will find that your numbers will go in a consecutive sequence for awhile and then there will be a jump or a break in the consecutive sequence. **When there is a jump in numbers, this marks the end of one Growth Cycle and the beginning of a new Growth Cycle.** This often is a transition year where there are definite endings and new beginnings. **This marks a turning point time.**

Growth Cycles:

Any cycle beginning with the number 2 (The High Priestess) is your Creative/Self-Sufficiency Cycle or Individuation Cycle. It is a cycle of nine to ten years where you are required to become self-trusting, self-sufficient, and independent.

Any cycle beginning with the number 3 (The Empress) is your Creative/Venus Cycle or your Path of Heart Cycle. This cycle requires that you follow what has heart and meaning. It is a cycle to resolve motherhood issues or issues surrounding maternal figures in your life. It is the cycle where you deeply connect with important people in your life and can find an important companion. This cycle has you discover work or creativity that becomes a passion for you.

Any cycle beginning with the number 4 (The Emperor) is your Creative/Leadership Cycle. These cycles are good times for building solid foundations; they also require that you own your own leadership skills especially in any new ventures. Often these cycles reveal to you patterns that you repeat over and over again so that you will consciously become aware of the pattern and choose to break those patterns that bind, limit, or restrict your leadership capacities. It is a good cycle to resolve fatherhood issues or paternal issues. It is time to own one's own authority rather than have issues with authority figures.

Any Cycle beginning with 18 or 19 is a four or three year cycle only. It is the shortest cycle anyone can have, and not everyone gets this cycle in their growth pattern. This is a Reposturing/Repositioning/ Realignment cycle. The individual is taking three or four years to reassess what he or she needs and wants in life as far as relationships are concerned and what is his or her professional direction or placement in the world. If you have this cycle in your Growth Cycle, the last time that you have it is an integration of the Sun, Aeon, and Universe in your life. You become clear on your direction and placement in personal and professional aspects of your life.

Cycles beginning with 5, 6, 7 and 8 are cycles which appear later in life for most people, or with the new generations, these cycles may appear earlier in life. Basically, you take the meaning of the number or Major Arcana card and apply it to the entire cycle.

5 – The Hierophant: Cycle of family and community and
                       spiritual development
6 – The Lovers: Cycle of practicing the art and craft of relating
7 – The Chariot: Cycle of incorporating both quietude and activity
8 – Adjustment: Cycle of simplification, balance, and clarity
9 – Hermit: Cycle of introspection, completion and order

(Growth Cycles and their applications to Tarot
were first discovered by Twainhart Hill)

There is a great variation in the ultimate symbols of religion, art, science, but such symbols share one thing; they cast a halo of eternity about the temporal
        Hugh Dalziel Duncan
        Symbols in Society

GROWTH CYCLE CHECK SHEET

This sheet is a check list to see if you have computed your growth numbers correctly. The numbers listed here **are not your birth years.** The numbers listed here are the final totals from adding the month, date, and year you were born. Example: Birthday is December 24, 1940. Add 12 + 24 = 36 + 1940 = **1976.** I look for **1976** and next to it I will find one of my life-time symbols. Going down the chart vertically and into the next columns I find my life-time growth pattern. Do the same thing for your birthdate. The crossbars indicate the end of one cycle and the beginning of another.

1880	17	1916	17	1952	17	1988	8	2024	8
1881	18	1917	18	1953	18	1989	9	2025	9
1882	19	1918	19	1954	19	1990	19	2026	10
1883	20	1919	20	1955	20	1991	20	2027	11
1884	21	1920	12	1956	21	1992	21	2028	12
1885	4	1921	13	1957	4	1993	4	2029	13
1886	5	1922	14	1958	5	1994	5	2030	5
1887	6	1923	15	1959	6	1995	6	2021	6
1888	7	1924	16	1960	16	1996	7	2032	7
1889	8	1925	17	1961	17	1997	8	2033	8
1890	18	1926	18	1962	18	1998	9	2034	9
1891	19	1927	19	1963	19	1999	10	2035	10
1892	20	1928	20	1964	20	2000	2	2036	11
1893	21	1929	21	1965	21	2001	3	2037	12
1894	4	1930	13	1966	4	2002	4	2038	13
1895	5	1931	14	1967	5	2003	5	2039	14
1896	6	1932	15	1968	6	2004	6	2040	6
1897	7	1933	16	1969	7	2005	7	2041	7
1898	8	1934	17	1970	17	2006	8	2042	8
1899	9	1935	18	1971	18	2007	9	2043	9
1900	10	1936	19	1972	19	2008	10	2044	10
1901	11	1937	20	1973	20	2009	11	2045	11
1902	12	1938	21	1974	21	2010	3	2046	12
1903	13	1939	4	1975	4	2011	4	2047	13
1904	14	1940	14	1976	5	2012	5	2048	14
1905	15	1941	15	1977	6	2013	6	2049	15
1906	16	1942	16	1978	7	2014	7	2050	7
1907	17	1943	17	1979	8	2015	8	2051	8
1908	18	1944	18	1980	18	2016	9	2052	9
1909	19	1945	19	1981	19	2017	10	2053	10
1910	11	1946	20	1982	20	2018	11	2054	11
1911	12	1947	21	1983	21	2019	12	2055	12
1912	13	1948	4	1984	4	2020	4	2056	13
1913	14	1949	5	1985	5	2021	5	2057	14
1914	15	1950	15	1986	6	2022	6	2058	15
1915	16	1951	16	1987	7	2023	7	2059	16

GROWTH CARDS

After you have computed your Growth Cycle and used the Growth Cycle Check Sheet for mathematical verification, fill in the following chart. You may want to photocopy these four pages before filling them in to use for other people's Growth Cycles.

In the Year column, place the year you were born beside the age 0 and proceed with each year until your current age. In the Personality column, place your Life-time Personality or Soul number and card in this column. The numbers change each year as shown on the Growth Cycle Sheet. The Spirit column is a universal pattern which is shared by all humankind. It is the internal symbol that supports our outer personality growth patterns. After you have filled in your Personality Growth column, you may want to write brief memories or experiences that you had in those years to see how the Major Arcana symbols work for you.

YEAR	AGE	PERSONALITY Fill in with your growth symbols.	SPIRIT Universal pattern that supports each of us	NOTES Your Memories of these years
	0		0 Fool	
	1		1 Magician	
	2		2 High Priestess	
	3		3 Empress	
	4		4 Emperor	
	5		5 Hierophant	
	6		6 Lovers	
	7		7 Chariot	
	8		8 Adjustment/Justice	
	9		9 Hermit	
	10		10 Wheel of Fortune	
	11		11 Strength/Lust	
	12		12 Hanged Man	
	13		13 Death/Rebirth	
	14		14 Art/Temperance	
	15		15 Devil/Pan	
	16		16 Tower	
	17		17 Star	
	18		18 Moon	

Permission is granted to photocopy this page.

YEAR	AGE	PERSONALITY Fill in with your growth symbols.	SPIRIT Universal pattern that supports each of us	NOTES Your Memories of these years
	19		19 Sun	
	20		20 Aeon/Judgment	
	21		21 Universe	
	22		0 Fool	
	23		1 Magician	
	24		2 High Priestess	
	25		3 Empress	
	26		4 Emperor	
	27		5 Hierophant	
	28		6 Lovers	
	29		7 Chariot	
	30		8 Adjustment/Justice	
	31		9 Hermit	
	32		10 Wheel of Fortune	
	33		11 Strength/Lust	
	34		12 Hanged Man	
	35		13 Death/Rebirth	
	36		14 Art/Temperance	
	37		15 Devil/Pan	
	38		16 Tower	
	39		17 Star	
	40		18 Moon	
	41		19 Sun	
	42		20 Aeon/Judgment	
	43		21 Universe	
	44		0 Fool	
	45		1 Magician	

Permission is granted to photocopy this page.

YEAR	AGE	PERSONALITY Fill in with your growth symbols.	SPIRIT Universal pattern that supports each of us		NOTES Your Memories of these years
	46		2	High Priestess	
	47		3	Empress	
	48		4	Emperor	
	49		5	Hierophant	
	50		6	Lovers	
	51		7	Chariot	
	52		8	Adjustment/Justice	
	53		9	Hermit	
	54		10	Wheel of Fortune	
	55		11	Strength/Lust	
	56		12	Hanged Man	
	57		13	Death/Rebirth	
	58		14	Art/Temperance	
	59		15	Devil/Pan	
	60		16	The Tower	
	61		17	Star	
	62		18	Moon	
	63		19	Sun	
	64		20	Aeon/Judgment	
	65		21	Universe	
	66		0	Fool	
	67		1	Magician	
	68		2	High Priestess	
	69		3	Empress	
	70		4	Emperor	
	71		5	Hierophant	
	72		6	Lovers	

Permission is granted to photocopy this page.

YEAR	AGE	PERSONALITY Fill in with your growth symbols.	SPIRIT Universal pattern that supports each of us		NOTES Your Memories of these years
	73		7	Chariot	
	74		8	Adjustment/Justice	
	75		9	Hermit	
	76		10	Wheel of Fortune	
	77		11	Strength/Lust	
	78		12	Hanged Man	
	79		13	Death/Rebirth	
	80		14	Art/Temperance	
	81		15	Devil/Pan	
	82		16	Tower	
	83		17	Star	
	84		18	Moon	
	85		19	Sun	
	86		20	Aeon/Judgment	
	87		21	Universe	
	88		0	Fool	
	89		1	Magician	
	90		2	High Priestess	
	91		3	Empress	
	92		4	Emperor	
	93		5	Hierophant	
	94		6	Lovers	
	95		7	Chariot	
	96		8	Adjustment/Justice	
	97		9	Hermit	
	98		10	Wheel of Fortune	
	99		11	Strength/Lust	
	100		12	Hanged Man	

EXAMPLE OF MARILYN MONROE'S GROWTH PATTERN
Born: 6/1/1926 – 1962
Life-Time Symbols: Personality - The Tower (16)
Soul/Spiritual Symbol - The Chariot (7)

		PERSONALITY CHOICE			SPIRIT CHOICE	
Age	Year	Tarot Card	Path		Tarot Card	Path
0	1926	16 Tower	Rebirth	0	Fool	
1	1927	17 Star	Rebirth	1	Magician	Balance
2	1928	18 Moon	Rebirth	2	Priestess	Balance
3	1929	19 Sun	Actualization	3	Empress	Balance
4	1930	20 Aeon	Actualization	4	Emperor	Balance
5	1931	21 Universe	Actualization	5	Hierophant	Balance
6	1932	4 Emperor		6	Lovers	Balance
7	1933	14 Art	Rebirth	7	Chariot	Lessons & Opport.
8	1934	15 Devil	Rebirth	8	Adjustment	Lessons & Opport.
9	1935	16 Tower	Rebirth	9	Hermit	Lessons & Opport.
10	1936	17 Star	Rebirth	10	Wheel of Fortune	Lessons & Opport.
11	1937	18 Moon	Rebirth	11	Lust	Lessons & Opport.
12	1938	19 Sun	Actualization	12	Hanged Man	Lessons & Opport.
13	1939	20 Aeon	Actualization	13	Death	Rebirth
14	1940	21 Universe	Actualization	14	Art	Rebirth
15	1941	4 Emperor		15	Devil	Rebirth
16	1942	5 Hierophant	Balance	16	Tower	Rebirth
17	1943	15 Devil	Rebirth	17	Star	Rebirth
18	1944	16 Tower	Rebirth	18	Moon	Rebirth
19	1945	17 Star	Rebirth	19	Sun	Actualization
20	1946	18 Moon	Rebirth	20	Aeon	Actualization
21	1947	19 Sun	Actualization	21	Universe	Actualization
22	1948	20 Aeon	Actualization	0	Fool	
23	1949	21 Universe	Actualization	1	Magician	Balance
24	1950	4 Emperor		2	Priestess	Balance
25	1951	5 Hierophant	Balance	3	Empress	Balance
26	1952	6 Lovers	Balance	4	Emperor	Balance
27	1953	16 Tower	Rebirth	5	Hierophant	Balance
28	1954	17 Star	Rebirth	6	Lovers	Balance
29	1955	18 Moon	Rebirth	7	Chariot	Lessons & Opport.
30	1956	19 Sun	Actualization	8	Adjustment	Lessons & Opport.
31	1957	20 Aeon	Actualization	9	Hermit	Lessons & Opport.
32	1958	21 Universe	Actualization	10	Wheel of Fortune	Lessons & Opport.
33	1959	4 Emperor		11	Lust	Lessons & Opport.
34	1960	5 Hierophant	Balance	12	Hanged Man	Lessons & Opport.
35	1961	6 Lovers	Balance	13	Death	Rebirth
36	1962	7 Chariot	Lessons & Opport.	14	Art	Rebirth

She died in her Chariot year (7) which is the first time that she had her soul/spiritual number since birth.

GROWTH CYCLE

GROWTH CYCLE INTERPRETATIONS OF MAJOR ARCANA
(Based on research analyzing growth cycles of 3,000 people – *Arrien/Study 1974 – 1980*)

(The Fool and The Magician are universal principles that all humankind have as resources at all times: The Fool is the symbol of the Great Spirit and fearlessness; The Magician is the symbol of the ability to communicate)

– II –
The High Priestess

Appears generally just once in someone's life; very rare to have it twice; marks period of independence; little tolerance for being limited, restricted or restrained; need to be on one's own or may find that circumstances force one to be on one's own; may live near water; need for balance and harmony; will withdraw or leave if situations too disharmonious; not a recommended year for marriage. Marks creative cycle.

– III –
The Empress

Year of assessing emotional needs and wants; for most women can be a year where there are issues surrounding motherhood; for both males and females it is the best year to resolve issues with their own mothers or with female authority figures or important maternal figures in their lives; also, year that most people get in touch with what they need and want in emotional relationships that will mirror both of those qualities so that clarity is achieved. Year of striving for emotional balance; not over-extending or under-extending one's emotional expression – to do either would produce disharmony.

– IV –
The Emperor

This symbol and The Chariot are the major symbols of change and new beginnings in the entire Tarot system. During Emperor years, individuals attempt to own their own leadership; may start new projects; become leaders, directors, or have important responsibilities; may take a major trip or travel; resolve issues concerning fatherhood or with their own father or male authority figures; learn about moving in new directions from an Aries person; may start a business or creative project on one's own; interest in the visual art or photography.

– V –
The Hierophant

Year of learning and teaching involving the family (father, mother, siblings) or with important Taurus people in your life; may consider going back to school or getting involved in some kind of special training; entry of important teacher in your life or someone you learn new things from; music and art could become important interests or areas that could provide nurturement; year that you could be tested on old issues or patterns; year of assimilating and integrating what was begun in Emperor year.

Major decisions concerning relationships; either the coming together and the deepening of relationships or the distancing and splitting apart of relationships – this could include friendships, co-working relationships, family, and deep emotional relationships; learning from Gemini people; most common year for marriages, commitments, separations, or divorces. Best year to work with groups of people or people of all ages.

**– VI –
The Lovers**

Whatever was set into motion during the Emperor year is accelerated during the Chariot year; also, whatever relationship decisions were made in the Lover's year are experienced or action is definitely taken in the Chariot Year; people move or find themselves experiencing a definite change tied with family and home; they may travel more extensively; career changes are most often experienced during this year or major thoughts of moving in new directions with career are entertained during this year; if you don't move, generally there will be remodeling or redecoration or movement of furniture to create the feeling of change; financial and health changes could occur; whatever directions one takes during this year are more fortunate, positive ones for the individual (you hold the wheel of fortune in your hands); could be entry of Cancer person in your life; or directions with Cancer individual changes.

**– VII–
The Chariot**

Best year to handle legal issues; finances begin to come into balance; best year to publish or synthesize new ideas or projects; year of wanting things to be simple, direct and clear; little tolerance for anything complex, covert, or non-direct. Attention to health, exercise, nutrition; attempt to balance and re-align health and care for the body; a year of adjustment – wanting to assimilate and adjust all the changes which occurred during Chariot year. Balance could be mirrored to you by an important Libra person in your life.

**– VIII–
Adjustment**

Best year to complete any unresolved issues from the past; symbol of transition; things definitely ending or being resolved and definite movement in new directions; opportunities presented by older people in your life, either Virgo people or significant older men, someone a few years older or significantly older. A year that one cannot compromise values; a need to have things meaningful or significant or would rather spend time alone. A strong need for the feeling of space and time alone to assimilate the major completions and new beginnings.

**– IX –
The Hermit**

Whatever was initiated during your Emperor or Chariot years comes to fruition or harvest during this year. This is a year of major breakthroughs, self-realizations, and deep commitment to turn one's life in more fortunate, positive direction. It is a year of unexpected creative opportunities, unexpected monies or inheritances, and attainment of abundance through past efforts. It is a year of seeking opportunity and pulling unexpected rewards or harvest toward you. Reward comes from past effort!

**– X –
The Wheel of Fortune**

– XI –
Strength/Lust

Return of wonder, awe, passion, vitality, excitement! Demonstration of creative and physical strength. Attraction to creative, passionate people. The capacity to utilize all of one's multi-faceted talents into one area. Passion for some form of creativity. Strong internal center is developed. Important Leo people in one's life. Symbol for theatre; one who is gifted in playing many different parts/roles well. Overcoming 'the beasts' within; strong trust in self or possessing a strong faith.

– XII–
The Hanged Man

Committed to breaking through all repeated patterns; a desire to see old issues from a fresh perspective; year to accept and surrender – to no longer resist; year that if one did not complete things during their Hermit year (things associated with the past) that one is forced by events to complete unresolved issues or patterns from the past. If issues were completed during Hermit year, then individual is rewarded during Hanged Man year. Major Rite of Passage Symbol – tired of old patterns and willing to break old patterns or not repeat them. Karmic issues resolved.

– XIII –
Death/Rebirth

Least likely year for physical death; more associated with ego death; ends of relationships or restructuring processes in relationships; the release of a new quality, attitude, belief system; the death of an old identity, attitude, behavior or belief system. Major letting go; the symbol for emergence of *even more* of who the individual is. Entry of important Scorpio people in your life.

– XIV–
Art/Temperance

Highly creative year; year of assimilation, integration, and stability; a year of desiring balance, beauty, and harmony. Important Sagittarius people in your life. Year where one is actively involved in some major creative project or idea.

– XV –
The Devil/Pan

Year where one could experience a strong physical relationship; or year where one explores more of one's own sensuality and sexuality; the ability to view one's sexuality from a place of mirth and humor – not take it so seriously; year of working hard and playing hard like a Capricorn; year of having the willingness to view one's own 'be-devilments' from a place of humor and sure-footedness. A year where one is not easily thrown by external situations.

– XVI –
The Tower

Year of rennovating self, ideas, houses, life-style; de-structuring old forms and restoring what is actual and true for self; health, exercise becomes an emphasis. Interests in healing, design work, photography might surface.

The year of increased self-confidence, sense of worth, and self-esteem. Best year for external recognition to come toward you. Year that most people manifest important ideas, projects, or work. Year that one could learn from an Aquarian individual.

– XVII –
The Star

Determined to turn difficult situations around into positive directions; year of choice – between two issues, two opportunities, two people, two situations; year of facing what is realistic rather than illusionary in relationships; year of exploring deeper aspects of the self; year of applying internal realizations into the external reality where they can be seen. Recognition of the light and dark sides of self. Year of definite decision. Important Pisces people in your life.

– XVIII –
The Moon

Year of entering or leaving a teamwork effort or project; best year to collaborate or move into co-creative projects; couples could find themselves working with each other; formulation of important partnerships or dissolution of partnership. Need to experience sense of community or co-operation. Year where friends become lovers or lovers become friends.

– XIX –
The Sun

Best year to resolve or integrate career and family issues; desire to break through patterns of self-judgment projected upon others; the ability to handle judgment from others in new ways; best year to integrate the past into present experience...a desire to look at all things from a holistic view rather than segmented or fixed frame of reference. Abundant creativity in both familiy concerns and career issues.

– XX –
The Aeon

This symbol and The Hermit are the two major transition symbols in the Tarot map. The Universe year is one where a major block, obstacle, obstruction has been overcome; it is a time of new directions and beginnings as a result of major endings, resolutions, or completions. It is a year where the individual is inspired to expand his/her universe of experience – especially during the months of Aquarius, Taurus, Leo and Scorpio. It is bringing applied creativity into institutional structures from a place of futurist vision and deep emotional commitment. It is the desire to change some aspect of the universe (internally or externally) for the better. It is being community-minded; service-oriented; and globally aware. Strong need to travel, explore, experience something new.

– XXI –
The Universe

SECTION VIII

WAYS OF WORKING WITH TAROT

INTRODUCTION

Working
with Tarot affords the opportunity
of using symbols as a visual self-help tool. The symbols
in Tarot provide a means of looking at what synchronistically is in
resonance with our inner and outer processes and can offer guidance in showing us
what's in balance or out of balance. Tarot can offer us daily guidance in looking at our daily
experience and relationships and give us a creative opportunity to manifest more of our gifts,
talents, and resources; it can also apprise us of certain tests and challenges that might arise during
the day for us to face and transform. As a tool that can assist us in our creative expression, it reflects
back to us what we are aware of consciously or unconsciously. Tarot is often a picture of our
current self-esteem and of how well it is functioning, or not functioning, in different aspects of
our lives. In this section, there are five different basic spreads, or layouts that present ways of
making that which is unconscious more conscious.

PATH OF BALANCE SPREAD

The Path of Balance is an opportunity for us to see how balance is present in six areas of our nature: in our self-esteem and self-trust; in our ability to give love and extend love; in what we are learning and teaching; in use of power and leadership; and in our relationships.

This six-card spread can be used seasonally, because each season is an opportunity to see whether we are in the natural rhythm of: spring, which is rebirth; summer, which is a time for fruition; fall, which is a time of harvest and letting go; and winter which is the time of incubation and gestation. The Path of Balance can be utilized once a season as a way to view the current balances and imbalances. The positions of the spread reflect the components that are necessary for total balance to be sustained; communication, self-esteem, love, leadership, learning/teaching, and relationships are areas of our lives where balance or imbalances are experienced. The Path of Balance Spread, designed by this author, is a way by which we can view the arenas of our life wherein we are experiencing balance or imbalance.

Path of Balance Shuffle Procedure:

1. Shuffle all 78 symbols focusing on one's current state of consciousness and well being.

2. Divide the stack into two separate piles. Determine which stack is your Sun/Yang Stack and which one is your Moon/Yin Stack.

3. Take the Sun/Yang Stack and shuffle it focusing on your energy, personal power, ability to start, initiate, set things into motion. Focus on the quality of your out-put.

   After shuffling, take the *top card of this stack and put it POSITION 5 as shown on the next page.*

   Take the bottom card of this stack and put it into POSITION 4.

4. Take the Yin/Moon Stack and shuffle it focusing on your capacity to receive, complete things, pull opportunity toward you, and trust self. Focus on the quality of your in-put.

   After shuffling, *take the top card of this stack and put it into POSITION 2 as shown on the next page.*

   Take the bottom card of this stack and put it into POSITION 3.

5. Shuffle the Sun/Yang stack and the Moon/Yin stack together and make a large fan. Decide which end of the fan is your head and which end of the fan is your feet.

   Select one card from the head region of the fan and put it into POSITION 1 as shown on the next page.

   Select one card from the feet region of the fan and put it into POSITION 6.

Positive symbols indicate inherent qualities that are manifesting at this time. Problematic symbols indicate challenges that one has the opportunity to move through and handle differently.

Turn the symbols over in the order listed on page 261.

PATH of BALANCE

Beyond ideas of wrong-doing and right-doing, there's a field. I'll meet you there.
– Jalal al-Din Rumi, 13th Century Persian Poet and Mystic

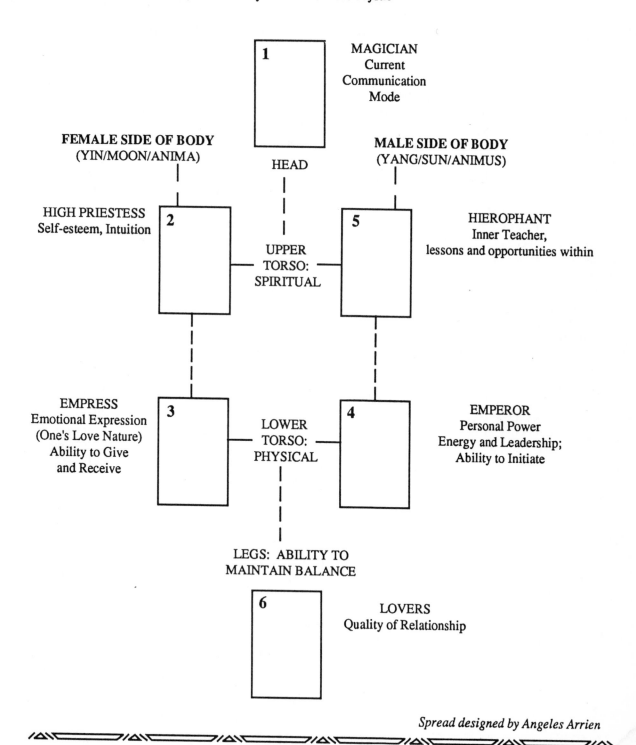

1

MAGICIAN
Current
Communication
Mode

HEAD

FEMALE SIDE OF BODY
(YIN/MOON/ANIMA)

MALE SIDE OF BODY
(YANG/SUN/ANIMUS)

HIGH PRIESTESS
Self-esteem, Intuition

2

5

HIEROPHANT
Inner Teacher,
lessons and opportunities within

UPPER
TORSO:
SPIRITUAL

EMPRESS
Emotional Expression
(One's Love Nature)
Ability to Give
and Receive

3

4

EMPEROR
Personal Power
Energy and Leadership;
Ability to Initiate

LOWER
TORSO:
PHYSICAL

LEGS: ABILITY TO
MAINTAIN BALANCE

6

LOVERS
Quality of Relationship

Spread designed by Angeles Arrien

DAILY SPREAD

Shuffle Procedure for Daily Spread:

The Daily Spread can be used in the morning or in the evening. In the morning it can be used as an indicator of the day's creative probabilities for actualizing the gifts, talents and resources that are strongly indicated by the symbols represented; or this spread can indicate the probable challenges or tests that might arise during the day. Through conscious choice, we can manifest that which is positively presented and consciously face and transform the challenges represented. It is important to remember in any of the spreads that positive symbols indicate gifts that want to be manifested and any problematic or challenge cards indicate that which we are ready to confront and handle, otherwise they wouldn't appear. It is an opportunity during the day to face, embrace, and transform the problematic areas of our life.

(Daily spread information was synthesized and edited by Judith Rozhon)

The shuffle procedure for the Daily Spread is to take the cards and shuffle them, focusing on asking for inner guidance and how you can best use this day; or if you do this Daily Spread in the evening, it's asking for guidance in what it is that you learned and benefited by during the day.

Whether it is done in the morning or the evening, the shuffle procedure is as follows:

1. Take all 78 cards, and shuffle the cards while focusing on the quality of day that you would like to have, or the quality of day that you have just experienced if you are doing this in the evening.

2. Make a very large fan, face-down, and decide which end of the fan is your head and which end is your feet.

3. Ask yourself these three questions:

(1) **Where do I feel the strongest sense of who I am between my head and my feet at this point in time?** Pick out a card in the general area of the fan that corresponds with where you are experiencing the strongest sense of self, between your head and your feet. Put the selected card in position Number 1 as shown on the next page.

(2) **Where do I trust my decision-making ability?** Select a card from the fan and put that in position Number 2, face-down.

(3) **Between my head and feet, where do I feel the healthiest in my body, or the least tension?** Select a card from the fan and put it in position Number 3.

In this spread, position Number 1 shows how you are being spiritually supported in manifesting either a talent or in moving through a challenge or stuck place; it is your spiritual guidance and inner-resource. Position Number 2 reflects your current thinking, your attitudes and beliefs; position Number 3 is a picture of the quality of action or behavior you may manifest in regards to health, finances, work, creativity, relationships during that day.

Turn the cards over, beginning with position Number 1, which is the spiritual support that you will have during the day. If a problematic card appears in this position, it indicates that you have spiritual resources and assistance available to move through that challenge today. Position Number 1 is the best position in which to have a problematic card. It tells you that you are ready to handle the challenge from the core of who you are. Position Number 2 reflects your current quality of thinking; and position Number 3 reflects how you will manifest what you want in the external world.

If you do this spread in the morning, it reveals general guidelines and direction for the day, the attitude and quality of thinking for the day, and the probable action for the day. If you do the Daily Spread in the evening, it indicates how you were assisted internally during the day, which is position Number 1, the spiritual position. Position Number 2 indicates a review of your attitude and beliefs during the day; and position Number 3 reflects the quality of action, behavior, and creativity implemented and exhibited during the day.

DAILY SPREAD

My boat struck something deep. Nothing happened. Sound, silence, waves. Nothing happened, or perhaps everything has happened, and I'm sitting in the middle of my new life.
   – Juan Ramon Jimeniz
       Nobel Prize Winner in Literature

This spread is a quick mirror of where you are presently, and where you are going; it indicates the direction in which your soul is presently taking you; how it is your body and external world is supporting that movement; and how your mind is keeping you on or off the track (free choice).

This spread can be used for feed-back about a major decision; it can indicate the direction of the soul.

Heart connects all three

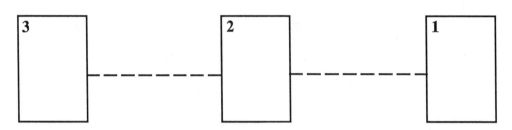

SUN 19 - Body
(External Reality)

How magnetic you are
right now

Co-worker issues

How you deal with a great
number of people

The physical environment

Is the body in motion to
handle what the soul is
doing?

AEON 20 - Mind
(Attitude, Beliefs,
Quality of Thinking)

Represents the choice factor

How you are judging yourself,
others, and your creativity

The state of your mind

Competitive factors

(The goal is to handle the
creativity of self and others
without being competitive)

UNIVERSE 21 - Soul
(Quality of Energy or
Internal Guidance, and
Direction)

Direction the soul is moving

What the soul wants you to
look at and is supporting –
either you moving through
a challenge or manifesting
a talent

The next three sheets will enable you to keep a log for your Daily Spreads. Enter your Daily Spread in the columns and sheets provided.

Designed and created by Angeles Arrien

DAILY SPREAD RECORD

Purpose of Record Keeping: By keeping a daily record and filling in this grid, at the end of the year you are able to see readily which symbols have repeatedly appeared to be used, or are representative of your focus of learning this year. The cards or symbols that rarely or never appear during the year indicate qualities that you have either incorporated and are modeling or are qualities or experiences that do not apply to your growth this year.

This grid will record one year's worth of daily readings. You might want to photo-copy extra copies of the chart before you begin to fill in the dates.

Instructions: For each card you pull, log the date of the Daily Spread in which it appeared. Do not move to the next column of any card until you pull that same card again.

DAILY SPREAD RECORD

0 FOOL																	
I MAGICIAN																	
II HIGH PRIESTESS																	
III EMPRESS																	
IV EMPEROR																	
V HIEROPHANT																	
VI LOVERS																	
VII CHARIOT																	
VIII ADJUSTMENT																	
IX HERMIT																	
X WHEEL OF FORTUNE																	
XI LUST																	
XII HANGED MAN																	
XIII DEATH																	
XIV ART																	
XV DEVIL																	
XVI TOWER																	
XVII STAR																	
XVIII MOON																	
XIX SUN																	
XX AEON																	
XXI UNIVERSE																	
Knight of Wands																	
Queen of Wands																	
Prince of Wands																	
Princess of Wands																	
Ace of Wands																	
2 Dominion																	
3 Virtue																	
4 Completion																	
5 Strife																	
6 Victory																	
7 Valour																	
8 Swiftness																	
9 Strength																	
10 Oppression																	
Knight of Swords																	
Queen of Swords																	
Prince of Swords																	
Princess of Swords																	
Ace of Swords																	
2 Peace																	
3 Sorrow																	
4 Truce																	
5 Defeat																	
6 Science																	
7 Futility																	
8 Interference																	
9 Cruelty																	
10 Ruin																	
Knight of Cups																	
Queen of Cups																	
Prince of Cups																	
Princess of Cups																	
Ace of Cups																	
2 Love																	
3 Abundance																	
4 Luxury																	
5 Disappointment																	
6 Pleasure																	
7 Debauch																	
8 Indolence																	
9 Happiness																	
10 Satiety																	
Knight of Disks																	
Queen of Disks																	
Prince of Disks																	
Princess of Disks																	
Ace of Disks																	
2 Change																	
3 Works																	
4 Power																	
5 Worry																	
6 Success																	
7 Failure																	
8 Prudence																	
9 Gain																	
10 Wealth																	

DAILY LOG

Each symbol reflects a possible potential or a possible obstacle or obstruction to overcome or resolve. Beside each card, log in your experience of how this symbol worked for you during the day. You may want to photocopy extras of this log for additional use.

DATE	SYMBOL/CARD	EXPERIENCE – EVENT, PEOPLE, SITUATION

Permission is granted to photocopy this page.

WHOLE PERSON SPREAD
(Celtic Cross Spread)

SHUFFLE PROCEDURE FOR WHOLE PERSON SPREAD;

1. Shuffle entire deck focusing on the important issues one is handling in the present. The individual should think only of him or herself, and attempt to get as much energy into the cards as possible.
2. Divide all of the deck into three different stacks utilizing all of the cards. Determine which stack represents the Body, which stack represents the Mind, and which stack represents the Spirit. Pick up the **Body stack,** shuffling it thoroughly, thinking of the outer appearance of the body as well as the blood, bones, organs, cells within the body. Then, pick up the **Mind Stack,** shuffle and think about all the issues, considerations, creative projects, or relationshiips that have been 'gentle' on the mind. Finally, pick up and shuffle the **Spirit stack,** thinking of the unique qualities, feelings, and energy that makes you the special individual that you are.
3. After all three stacks have been individually shuffled, shuffle together just once the two stacks that are the closest together in size; then, shuffle the remaining stack into the combined stack.
4. Take the first ten cards off the top of what is now a single stack and put them into the numbered positions of the Whole Person Spread. The top card goes into position one, the next card on top goes into position two, and so on.

GENERAL GUIDELINES FOR INTERPRETATION:

1. Find the individual's Personality and Soul Cards and Growth Card for the current year.
2. Look at the meaning of the **position;** then, observe which **suit** may be in that position (Swords: mental gifts or considerations; Cups: emotional gifts or considerstions; Wands: internal or intuitive gifts or considerations; and Disks: physical or financial gifts or considerations); and then, check to see if this is a card which has **astrological significance** because there may be important information here that applies to the person involved; then, review the **general meanings** attached to this specific card in this position.
3. **Any cards which are reversed** indicate only that the person is in the process of CHANGE or committed to CHANGING and is using the reversed card as a tool or a guide to facilitiate that change.
4. **Royalty cards** can indicate significant "others" within the person's life who are mirroring to the individual certain gifts or qualities that they are currently mastering mentally, emotionally, perceptually, or physically.
5. **Trump cards or Major Arcana** indicate unusual ability and potential that can be manifested at this time; especially if one's own Soul or Personality card comes up, an indication that the person is receiving extra help to apply whatever is necessary or revealed by the position the card is placed.

The Whole Person Spread or the Celtic Cross Spread is the oldest spread in all of Tarot history. It is the spread that has survived since the Middle Ages, and is the spread that most people use whenever they are introduced to Tarot spreads. It is often referred to as the Celtic Cross Spread, and has undergone many permutations; however, it remains one that is consistently used by all people who work with Tarot. This spread is referred to as the Whole Person Spread primarily because it is a spread that takes a look at every issue that could possibly be presented for an individual. It is the best spread to do, once a year, as an overview for the quality of work that you want to manifest in all arenas of your life, personally, professionally, and spiritually.

WHOLE PERSON SPREAD

If I really see you, I will laugh out loud, or fall silent, or explode into a thousand pieces.
And if I don't, I will be caught in the cement and stone of my own prison.

– Jalal al-Din Rumi
13th Century Persian Poet and Mystic

WHOLE PERSON SPREAD: A general survey of your present state of consciousness: Important emotional, mental, physical and spiritual considerations; an indicator of unusual creative opportunities and talents; and possible tests or obstructions for lesson learning. This spread is used once a season or once a year or as an over-view of the many different aspects of your life.

```
                                          ┌──────┐
                 ┌──────┐                 │ 10   │
                 │ 3    │                 │      │
                 │      │                 │      │
                 │      │                 └──────┘
                 │      │                 ┌──────┐
                 └──────┘                 │ 9    │
                                          │      │
                                          │      │
 ┌──────┐   ┌──────┐    ┌──────┐          └──────┘
 │ 5    │   │ 1  ┌─┴────┐│ 6    │
 │      │   │    │ 2    ││      │
 │      │   └────┤      │└──────┘          ┌──────┐
 │      │        │      │                  │ 8    │
 └──────┘        │      │                  │      │
                 └──────┘                  └──────┘
                 ┌──────┐
                 │ 4    │                  ┌──────┐
                 │      │                  │ 7    │
                 │      │                  │      │
                 └──────┘                  └──────┘
```

Date _____

Birthdate _____

Life-Time Archetypal Symbols

    A. Personality Symbol _____

    B. Spiritual Symbol _____

Current Growth Symbol _____

Current Growth Cycle _____

KEY TO CARDS

1. Heart in the past; emotional concerns of the past

2. Heart in the present; emotional opportunities or concerns in the present

3. Conscious mind: areas of concern; hope; issues; desires; conscious awareness

4. Subconscious mind: areas of concern; hope/desires; issues not in awareness

5. Work/creativity: opportunity/obstacles; ability to pull situations toward you

6. Decision-making ability; courage to act or assume responsibility

7. Possible effects one might manifest or break through as far as work and creativity is concerned

8. Relationships: friends/family; co-working relationships; deep emotional relationships

9. Hopes and fears

10. Natural expression or what one wants to release from one's natural expression

The psychological mechanism for transforming energy is the symbol
– C.G. Jung

SUMMARY OF WHOLE PERSON SPREAD

After you do the Whole Person Spread, it's wonderful to take a look at what I call the Summary Spread. The Summary Spread is created by rearranging the same ten cards that you use in the Whole Person Spread, and to rearrange them, suit by suit. Wands will indicate what is happening to you at the spiritual or intuitive level. Swords will show you what is happening as far as to your mental attitudes, beliefs and thoughts. All the Cups in your Whole Person Spread will show you the quality of feeling, your emotional responses and reactions. Disks will reflect to you your relationship to the external reality and the areas of health, finances, work, creativity, and relationships. The Major Arcana cards will show you the inherent gifts, talents and resources that are already working in your collective unconscious. Trumps come from the root word *to triumph*. These are your ways to triumph. The Major Arcana are the archetypal energies working deep within that can help you manifest what you want, which is shown by Disks. Cups show you the emotional support that you have in order to manifest what it is that you want. Swords reveal your attitudes, thoughts, beliefs about your ability to manifest what you want; and Wands indicate the quality of energy, vision, insight, spiritual faith and trust that you have in manifesting what it is that you want.

SUMMARY OF WHOLE PERSON SPREAD

Take the same cards from the Whole-Person Spread and arrange them suit by suit for an over-view summary. List the cards in their appropriate columns.

WANDS
Fire
Intuition
Perception
Spirituality

SWORDS
Air
Mental
Beliefs
Attitudes
Thoughts

CUPS
Water
Feelings
Emotional
Responses
Reactions

DISKS
Earth
Physical
External Reality
Health
Finances
Creativity
Relationships

MAJOR ARCANA
Archetype
Trump – "Way to Triumph"
Gifts, Talents,
Resources to be utilized
at this point in time

Once the problematic areas of your current consciousness are removed or released (X-ed out), the pattern of consciousness can realign to form a new pattern. List the symbols without the problematic cards present and see the quality of consciousness you can experience without these problematic symbols present.

Choose meditation symbols from the positive cards in your spread that can facilitate change in consciousness or help release problematic states and list them here:

SELF ESTEEM SPREAD

The Self-Esteem Spread, designed by the author, can be done as often as one likes. The basic recommendation for doing this spread is when self-esteem is at low ebb, or doing it as a self-esteem check, thus using the spread to sustain and maintain levels of self-esteem.

Self-esteem has three components: self-love, self-trust, and self-respect. To the level that one is not in self-love, one will be confronted with fear; to the level that one is not in self-trust, one will be confronted with the need to control; and to the level that one doesn't have self-respect, one will find oneself stuck or fixated on what is *not* working in one's life and will be unwilling to take a look at what *is* working.

The Self-Esteem Spread is one that can assist you in knowing what is the quality of self-esteem that is present within your nature. The six steps that support and sustain self-esteem are represented by the six cards that are arranged in a vertical line, and correspond with the six steps to success. The six steps to success which are determined by one's self-esteem are: 1) being able to follow things step-by-step, which is a discipline that can sustain self-esteem; 2) being open, flexible, and resilient maintains self-esteem; 3) following what has heart and passion and meaning sustains self-esteem; 4) staying in one's truth and authenticity, and not abandoning oneself, supports self-esteem; 5) communication that is delivered where content and timing are in sync sustains self-esteem – blunt communication is an announcement of great content, but poor timing – confused communication is an announcement of possible good timing but poor content – both sabotage self-esteem; and 6) consistent, sustained energy put into creative endeavors and relationships, rather that erratic energy put into what we do, will maintain self-esteem.

Shuffle Procedure for the Self-Esteem Spread:

Shuffle the cards focusing on your current self-esteem. Then place the cards face down and make a large fan in front of you. Carefully select a card focusing on the meaning of each position before you select the card.

Example: For position number 1, focus on your current ability to set limits and boundaries and to honor your own limits and boundaries, then select a card from the fan and place it in postion number 1.

SELF ESTEEM SPREAD

1

Ability to set limits and boundaries

2

Flexibility and openness

**Self-Esteem has
three major components:**
1) Self-love
2) Self-trust
3) Self-respect

3

Ability to give and receive love; follow heart

Self-Esteem Sabotagers:
1) Fear
2) Control
3) Fixation or
   Stubborness

4

Capacity for staying in one's truth or integrity

5

Communication skills

Affirmation: *"I am enough."*

6

Sense of honor and respect about oneself

Spread designed by Angeles Arrien

RELATIONSHIP SPREAD

This Relationship Spread, designed by the author, can be used any time you want to assess the quality of relationship that you have either with important friends, family members, colleagues, or with deep emotional relationships. It's also a spread that can be used to assess the relationship that you have with yourself or the relationship that you might have with a creative project or with your own work or career. It's a spread that is very thorough in that it can show you your mental, emotional, spiritual, and physical relationship to another person, or to a concept or to a project. It is recommended that this spread not be over-used, but used as a guide-line, and for guidance to check the quality of relationship that is being experienced.

This spread can be used with two people using one or two decks. When possible, it is more effective to use two decks because a card can be pulled by either or by both persons.

Shuffle Procedure for The Relationship Spread:

As the cards are shuffled, each person focuses on the relationship, thinking about the first time they met and reviews all that they have experienced together to the present time. Each person makes four stacks and designates which stack represents his or her 1) mental beliefs, 2) emotional beliefs, 3) spiritual beliefs, and 4) physical expression. Each shuffles his or her mental stack, focusing on the positive and negative thoughts or beliefs about this relationship. Each makes a fan from the mental stack and selects one card and places it in positions 1 and 2. Then each person shuffles the emotional stack, focusing on the positive and negative feelings about the relationship. They each make a fan out of their emotional stacks and select a card and put it in positions 3 and 4. Each person then shuffles the spiritual stack, focusing on the spiritual tests and challenges that the relationship has revealed. From a fan of the spiritual stack, each person selects a card and puts it in positions 5 and 6. The same procedure of shuffling and making a fan is followed for the physical stack, this time focusing on the quality of physical expression that they extend to each other creatively and sexually in their actions and behaviors with each other. The selected cards are put in positions 7 and 8. Finally, the cards are turned over in their numerical order.

RELATIONSHIP SPREAD

Art is the invisible painting that two people or things create between each other.
— Anonymous

	PERSON A	PERSON B
Mental Beliefs and Thoughts about Relationship	1	2
Emotional Feelings and Reactions about Relationship	3	4
Spiritual Growth and Opportunities in this Relationship	5	6
Physical Expression; Quality of Actions and Behavior in this Relationship	7	8

Spread designed by Angeles Arrien

Tarot as Visual Affirmation

Carl Jung indicated that "the psychological mechanism of transforming energy is the symbol." By working with each of the Tarot symbols, looking at them visually, we can evoke a non-verbal affirmation of certain qualities that we would like to manifest, enhance or support within our natures. In the methodology section of this book, there is a chart that corresponds with each one of the Major Arcana cards. Listed next to the Major Arcana cards are sample affirmations that go with each one of these symbols. Developing affirmations – personal affirmations – to correspond with each one of these cards can be an opportunity to further one's growth and development. (See pages 236-238).

Tarot symbols can be used as book marks to give visual affirmation of a quality that you want to support internally and externally. The cards can be placed by your bedside in the morning or the evening as a visual affirmation of what it is that you would like to enhance, deepen or support within your nature. They can be placed upon a mirror or on the back of a closet door, where they can be seen easily. Two reference books that are very good in supporting your work with affirmations and using symbols as affirmative tools are: Shakti Gawain's book, *Creative Visualization*, and Robert Johnson's book, *Inner Work*.

Tarot as a Meditation Tool

Meditation is the process of going inward for guidance. Universally, there are four meditation postures: sitting meditation, which accesses wisdom; lying meditation, which accesses healing and love; standing meditation, which accesses presence, and cultivates our ability to honor our limites and boundaries; and walking or moving meditation, which accesses inner creativity.

In working with the Tarot as a meditative tool, take the cards within the deck that inspire and motivate you, place one, and no more than three, of these in front of you before beginning your meditation process. Have the cards in front of you, or carry them with you in a pocket or book if you are involved in walking meditation. Look at the cards before you begin the meditative process, and then go inward and ask for guidance in how these visual affirmations can assist you in your spiritual growth and development. The best definition or distinction between prayer and meditation was given by a 9-year-old boy, who said that "prayer is when you talk to God, and meditation is when you listen to what God has to say."

It is important to remember that Tarot is a visual portraiture or bridging language. The universal language is symbols which function as a bridging language that connects invisible and visible experiences. Meditation is the opportunity to access the invisible worlds and through symbols, make those internal experiences visible.

APPENDICES

APPENDIX A

GLOSSARY

The following symbols glossary contains specifically the astrological signs and short descriptions and meanings of each; the meanings of the planets, with short descriptions and meanings of each of the planets; and descriptions and meanings of the colors and the universal meanings attributed to colors. All other symbols appear listed in the index, and are thoroughly described with each card in the deck.

Earth Signs

The three Earth Signs represent three different ways in which you can manifest or make things tangible in areas of health, finances, work, creativity and relationships.

Capricorn (December 21st - January 21st) The sign of the Goat. This is the Earth Sign which is most associated with tenacity, the ability to go after a goal step-by-step. It is the ability to cultivate, apply, implement and produce.

Virgo (August 21st - September 21st) The symbol is the Virgin. It's the ability to organize and systematize; to create order and balance is a primary function of Virgo energy.

Taurus (April 21st - May 21st) is an earth sign ruled by Venus, the planet of love, beauty and creative power. It is the form maker, the builder, wanting to bring ideas tangibly into form in a beautiful aesthetic way.

Water Signs

The three Water Signs are associated with the different qualities of feeling. They reflect three types of water found in nature. Cancer is associated with the lakes; Pisces is associated with the rivers, and Scorpio is associated with oceanic depths.

Cancer (June 21st - July 21st) is associated with the heart that knows how to nurture, comfort, support, and heal others. It is associated with family and the home.

Pisces (February 21st - March 21st) is the sign most associated with spiritual growth and evolution; or feelings that are fluid, expansive, exploratory, especially in the realms of unconditional love and service.

Scorpio (October 21st - November 21st) is passionate feeling, a deep commitment to exploring the depths of feeling, and a commitment to change and transformation. It's a deep feeling for the mystery of love and a high regard for privacy. It is associated with three signs: the scorpion, the snake and the eagle. All are symbols of Scorpio's intention to transform.

The three Fire Signs, representing the qualities of energy and vitality, spirituality and vision are the explorers of those attributes.

Fire Signs

Aries (March 21st - April 21st) is a fire sign that represents pioneering work. It's the ram, the adventurer, the explorer, the builder, the traveler.

Sagittarius (November 21st - December 21st) is the visionary, the dreamer. It's associated with direct communication.

Leo (July 21st - August 21st) is the fire sign most associated with unlimited creativity, or creative power that is multi-faceted.

The Air Signs are associated with different qualities of thinking.

Air Signs

Gemini (May 21st - June 21st) is associated with the ability to integrate, synthesize, mediate, look at both sides of things.

Aquarius (January 21st - February 21st) is the pioneering, innovative, futuristic, creative mind.

Libra (September 21st - October 21st) is the quality of thinking that is balanced, clear, simple, direct and to the point. It's represented by the scales.

Planets

♄

Saturn is the planet that is most associated as the Teacher. It's the planet of discipline and of honoring ones limits and boundaries, and of setting limits and boundaries. It is also committed to bringing what is out of balance back into balance in ones nature and of following things step-by-step.

♃

Jupiter is the planet of flexibility, expansion, growth, opportunity, and luck.

♀

Venus is the planet of love, beauty and creative power.

☽

The **Moon** is the planet that most represents truth, authenticity, the feminine, the magnetic energy and *yin* energy.

☉

The **Sun** represents dynamic energy; it's the principle of being able to generate, motivate, stimulate; it's *yang* energy, or often what is referred to as masculine energy.

☿

Mercury is the planet of communication, particularly communication that honors the synthesis of content, context and timing.

♂

Mars is the planet most associated with energy, vitality and assertion.

♆

Neptune is the planet of inspiration as well as delusions, illusions and deceptions.

♇

Pluto is the planet most associated with dismantling that which is outgrown and false-to-fact, and renovating or restoring that which is actual and true.

♅

Uranus is the planet that produces sudden, unexpected changes.

The following are the colors that are found on the cards, or the meaning of colors from a universal point of view, or cross-cultural perspective.

Colors

Blue, cross-culturally, is seen as the color that represents wisdom and clarity. It also represents emotionality, because it is associated in alchemy with the emotional nature, or the waters.

Green is associated with creativity, regeneration, fertility and productivity.

White is associated, cross-culturally, with purification, integration and synthesis.

Red is associated with love, desire, and trusting one's feelings.

Orange is associated with energy, vitality, spontaneity, and life-force.

Purple is associated with leadership and owning one's personal power, the color of royalty.

Brown is the color most associated with the earth, or grounding; the ability to apply, implement and produce.

Black, cross-culturally, is seen as the color of letting-go. It represents the unknown and often is referred to as a color depicting strength.

Grey symbolizes balance, it is the integration of white and black.

Yellow is cross-culturally seen as humankind's representation of light, sunlight, moon-light, star-light. It represents spirituality.

APPENDIX B
Major Arcana Summary
(Summary compiled by Mary Culberson from class notes taken for each card)

0 – THE FOOL

"**One Who Walks Without Fear**" –The state of courage; operating with the power and enthusiasm of Dionysus, the Spring-time God (Aries – March 21–April 21); basically represents transpersonal or transcendent states of consciousness; symbolizes that state of awareness before birth and after death that can be utilized in present life (i.e., peak experiences, mystical and ecstatic experiences). Commitment toward attaining wholeness. High creative power, evolution and unfoldment. Holds fire and water; alchemical process of combining mental creativity and emotional richness. The hero's journey of moving through life; balancing, expanding, developing equal relationships; biting into one's own creativity; releasing abundance and fruitfulness; developing both the feminine and the masculine.

When persons are drawn toward this card, they are attempting to manifest their creativity, move toward wholeness and re-own their courage. There is attention to the "spiritual journey."

I – THE MAGICIAN

"**The Communicator**" – One who has an artful sense of timing and flexibility in all aspects of communication; gifted in the visual and auditory arts (musically inclined), and in written and oral communication. Gifted in areas of mediation, diplomacy, and mass media/public relations. This is Mercury, the "winged messenger," surrounded by seven symbols: 1) coin – sense of body and health, physical and financial space and well-being; 2) floating kerub is the Aladdin's lamp, the geni, the magic of communication is available; 3) the Phoenix head – an understanding of abstract thinking; 4) floating scroll – the media, the ability to transfer knowledge; 5) flying egg – rebirth symbol, commitment to changing communication patterns; 6) cup – sense of emotional space; 7) sword – mental space being available. All this is a gift along with humor and joyous communication. Great ability to see people"s communication patterns. There is desire for honest communication.

When a person is drawn toward this card it indicates communication is of high priority.

II – THE HIGH PRIESTESS

"**The Independent Self-Knower**" – Balance, intuition/insight, independence, and self-knowledge. One who has the ability to nourish the self from deep inner sources, unwilling to limit or restrict the self or others; strong independent expression that is both receptive and assertive; deep love for harmony, beauty and balance. This is the goddess, Isis; she sits on a throne in water, with an oasis of abundance before her. She is balancing the masculine (straight lines) and feminine (curved lines). When she is balanced, feeling her independence and using her intuition (crystals), she then experiences high self-esteem.

When a person is drawn toward this card, it is an indication of the beginning of a creative cycle, a time to assert independence, to need balance, to increase self-esteem and to become aware of intuition as a gift. There may be a desire to be totally on one's own, perhaps alone. Being near water will feel healing. A time for discovering the oasis within oneself.

III – THE EMPRESS

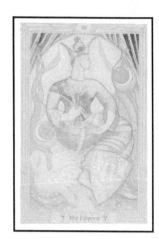

"**The Nurturer, Comforter, Beautifier**" – One who has a strong love for nature; a natural "mother"; strongly service oriented; perfect unity between mental and emotional expression – cannot be easily categorized as "intellectual or emotional"; strong leadership ability; can insprire and motivate other women. The Empress is the great earth mother, Venus, the yin, receptive, feminine balancer of emotions, the lover of beauty. She is coming from water to earth, bringing what is inside out to the external, she has a magnetic quality which has the ability to draw people toward herself and make them feel safe with her, she has the ability to give to others and to be open to receive as much as is given. There is a great desire to explore the unconscious and travel through the psychic world.

When a person is drawn toward this card, it is a movement toward balancing of emotions, time to nurture self, deal with issues of motherhood or with mother and maternal figures; highly creative time; time to own one's leadership ability.

IV – THE EMPEROR

"**The Pioneer, Builder, Doer, Visionary**" – One who establishes strong foundations and creates what is needed for future generations; a natural "father" or strongly paternal figure; a deep love for travel, adventure, and change. Strong leadership ability; gifted in starting or initiating creative projects/careers of one's own. Aries the ram is the earth father. There is a need to be in leadership positions or working with others who are clear leaders. There is special emphasis on sight, visionary perception, gifted in anything using sight – film, photography – analytical ability to show how one sees things; an eye for what is and is not working. Gifted critics, writers, and artists. There is abundance, compassion, dignity and refinement. The fire is vitality and changeable, warmth and nurturing. There is a deep love for the creative process, setting something new in motion, need to change both internally and externally.

When a person is drawn toward this card it indicates high movement forward; career changes; issues to resolve with father, authority figures; time to demonstrate leadership ability, deal with issues of fatherhood.

V – THE HIEROPHANT

"**The Teacher, Counselor, Consultant**" – One who is gifted in imparting information or inspiring others; committed to the concept of community, family, cooperation; grows by experiencing learning/teaching situations; attracted to sound/ music – equal abilities in listening and speaking; wants to make ideas tangible, usable, applicable. The Hierophant is the inner spiritual teacher; Taurus, the bull, encircles him indicating the desire to bring the inner spriitual teaching out in a tangible, useful way. The Hierophant is the Egyptian god Osiris (leadership); the woman is Isis, goddess of intuition, the High Priestess; the child is the god Horus, god of perception. Spiritual marriage, major family card, commitment and loyalty. There is deep desire to share creativity, to have it seen, to experience being stretched with new experiences.

When a person is drawn toward this card it is an indication of a desire for self teaching and learning. A time for making things tangible and practical; issues may revolve around family; could get into counseling, teaching, consulting, managerial work. There is desire for a major breakthrough, to apply creativity and feel stretched.

VI – THE LOVERS

"The Synthesizer of Dualities, Polarities, and Oppositions" – One who has extraordinary gifts working with people of all ages; deep understanding, application and synthesis of the concept of paradox, polarity, and opposition; relationships are an important focal point for personal growth and development; committed to the process of unification; desire to balance the giving and receiving aspects of self. There is the ability to do multi-level thinking and can bring seemingly different things together and see something new. Good with team work, learn and grow the most when working with people. This is the Gemini twins, the marriage of polar opposites. There is great insight and perception of what is going on with people (good therapists). There is a need to feel things changing in a relationship.

When a person is drawn toward this card, it indicates relationships are an issue, it is a time for expanding and deepening some, others will be strained and split. It is a time of triangle relationships, a time for marriage or divorce. This is the highest card of balance in the whole deck. There are gifts for working with people.

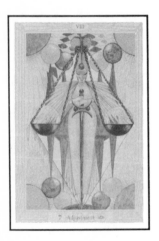

VII – THE CHARIOT

"The Generator, Motivator, Traveler" – One who is gifted in setting ideas, projects, and life experiences into motion; ability to "move" people, situations, and projects; can accomplish a wide variety of things simultaneously – usually three or four projects, ideas, and interests in motion at the same time; needs change, variety, and stimulation; little regard for anything dull, boring, or routine; wants strong home base from which to create. Gifted at many different jobs, there is resistance to specialization. The Charioter holds the Wheel of Fortune, has the ability to turn in any direction with fortunate results. Sitting in the lotus position indicates a strong introspective nature, and taking a long time to make a decision. There is an ease with moving into high states of consciousness and awareness. Cancer the crab is the symbol of the outer shell protecting what is on the inside, there is a strong need to move in the true inner direction of the spirit.

When a person is drawn toward this card, it is an indication of change, a time of movement, making career changes, putting some creative idea or project into motion.

VIII – ADJUSTMENT/JUSTICE

"The Mediator, Adjuster, Arbitrator" – One who has a deep love for simplicity, clarity, fairness, and balance; capacity for handling legal situations fairly; talents for three professions: writing/publishing; law/finances; and health/healing arts or medical profession; ability to edit, synthesize, and research ideas. This is Libra the balancer, her task is to bring anything that is out of balance back into balance and harmony. She stands within a diamond which is her high creativity, her eyes are masked to indicate her sight is turned inward as she stretches to receive the perfectly formed ideas above her head. The downward pointing sword is the means she can use (mental/writing) to bring these ideas to earth. The Alpha and Omega are symbols of her need to complete anything that she begins. The webbing in the background indicates very little tolerance for complexity, there is a need to keep things simple and clear.

When a person is drawn toward this card it is an indication that balance is needed, a good time to write, start a diet, balance the check book.

IX – THE HERMIT

"**The Meditator, Philosopher, Sage, Wise Man**" – One who will not/can not compromise one's values; needs significant relationships or prefers to be alone rather than indulge in anything mundane or superficial; a natural sage, way-shower, seeker; gifted working with the hands or nurtured by touch; desire to complete things from the past before moving forward; strong organizational abilities. This is Virgo – completion, perfection and introspection. Nine is the number of completion. The Hermit has the ability to motivate and inspire others; as an earth sign, there is deep appreciation for the body and the wisdom of the earth and natural process. There is a deep love for beauty, order and harmony.

When a person is drawn toward this card, one is needing to complete any unfinished business from the past; this is a time to get into the body, to beautify the home, to be introspective and contemplative. One may seek an outer mentor to mirror one's own wise sage or to become more the mentor for others, to inspire and motivate them.

X – THE WHEEL OF FORTUNE

"**Abundance, Prosperity, Fortune**" – One who is committed to turning life experience into a more fortunate, positive direction; unusual opportunities concerning finances or creativity; the capacity to look at situations, projects, people from a holistic perspective; desire for major break-throughs and greater self-realization; creates abundance on all levels of awareness; the wheel is a symbol of wholeness; on the wheel are the Sphinx (objectivity holding the sword of wisdom), the monkey (flexibility) and the crocodile (creativity). As things change and the wheel turns, it is important to stay objective, flexible and creative.

When a person is drawn toward this card it indicates there is a determination to turn life in a more positive, abundant direction; there may be unexpected opportunities, inheritance, etc. There is a major break-through with creative process and more flexibility and insight.

XI – LUST/STRENGTH

"**Passion, Awareness, Aliveness**" – One who exhibits an excitement and enthusiasm about life. Multi-faceted creativity (Leo the lion) and passion for all of life's experiences; a desire to demonstrate one's full creative expression; ability to express oneself openly without defenses, roles, masks, or justifications (nude); gifts in acting, the theatre, and psycho-drama; strength to overcome and tame the beasts/demons within the personality structures. There is the gift of perception, extended vision, strength of insight, intuition. The woman has a tight reign on the lion, overcoming fear with creativity; she offers the urn up in trust of the Holy Spirit. Into the urn come snakes and flowers (masculine and feminine) to give birth to new creativity.

When a person is drawn toward this card it is an indication of desiring more creativity and passion for life, owning one's own strengths. This is a time for taming the beast within, overcoming fear connected with creativity, being open, naked, undefended with the Holy Spirit, willing to receive the creative life-giving force.

XII – THE HANGED MAN

"**The Transformer**" – One who is committed to breaking through stuck, fixed perspectives, attitudes, and beliefs; a willingness to turn oneself upside down to get new perspectives on repetitive patterns, situations and "hang-ups"; the ability to surrender, receive, and open-up to unknown perspectives; deep desire for change.

When persons are drawn toward this card it is an indication that they are determined to break through a fixed, stuck place. It is a time when any repetitive patterns or behaviors will come up to be resolved, anything that has been kept hidden will be exposed.

XIII – DEATH/REBIRTH

"**The Releaser, Eliminator, Expander**" – One who is committed to change, metamorphosis, transformation; gifts in cutting through limitations, restrictions, and obstacles; desires to become "even more" of oneself; desires to "let go" of anyone or anything that is constrictive, and move toward expansion and growth. This is Scorpio, who, like the butterfly going from the caterpillar to the cocoon to emerge changed, tranforms from the scorpian to the snake, sheds old skin and becomes the eagle or phoenix bird. This is shedding old beliefs and attitudes, cutting through the old structures to release something new. This is the movement from the age of Pisces to the age of Aquarius.

When a person is drawn toward this card it is a time of major transformation, setting something new into motion and at the same time letting something go, cutting through the very bones, the core, the form and structure of the old in order to release the new in a rebirth.

XIV – ART/TEMPERANCE

"**The Creator, the Alchemist**" – One who achieves balance and integration through the creative process or by working with the hands; there is a deep love for one's creative expression which is inspired from perception and emotional insights; powerful and direct communication of one's creative gifts. This is the ability to balance and blend the masculine and feminine, yin/yang, to be equally receptive and assertive. This is the alchemical process of merging fire (spiritual) and water (emotion) which makes a new element, steam (mental and spiritual creativity with passion). This is Sagittarius (the upward arrow at the heart) which is the love of truth and beauty for its own sake. The six disks at the heart is the number of The Lovers; the highest art form is that of artful relationships.

When a person is drawn toward this card it is an indication of the desire to manifest artful creativity, artful handling of duality, polarity and relationships and the desire to create something new in the blending process, the balancing of the masculine and feminine.

XV – THE DEVIL/PAN

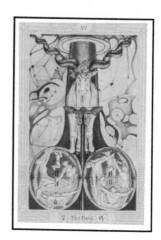

"**The Joker, Worker, Stabilizer**" – One who is determined to see things clearly in the external environment and take appropriate action; gifted in protecting oneself from judgments or viewpoints projected by others; unusual appeal and sensuality; the quality of mirth – the ability to laugh at oneself; capacity for working hard and playing hard. This is the merry goat, Capricorn, not thrown easily by external reality; the ability to stand steady while working on what "bedevils" us. This is the card of humor and sexuality (only card with genital symbols). The third eye is the willingness to look solidly at issues internally and externally. The grapes are a symbol of fruitfulness; spiral horn, commitment to growth and change; circular rainbow, commitment to wholeness. Devil spelled backwards is "lived," living with humor and having a stable foothold on life.

When a person is drawn toward this card it is a sign of handling life from a place of humor; a desire for more stability and grounding, more ability to work hard, play hard and be more sensual and sexual. Learning to protect oneself from the projections and opinions/judgments of others.

XVI – THE TOWER

"**The Restorer, Healer, Renovator**" – One who possesses strong healing gifts and unusual capacities for regeneration and restoration; gifts in areas of health – mental, emotional, perceptual/diagnostic, and physical; deep need to constantly eliminate what is unnatural, conditioned, false to fact, and not of the self; talents with structures of ideas, buildings, personality traits, or projects – can readily see what is working effectively and what is not working effectively; strong analytical ability. This is the place of major internal change, the spirit (fire) moving through the body burning out anything artificial, anything that is crystalized will crumble and fall; the eye of Horus is the god of perception, the ability to see things clearly, as they really are. The dove represents a compassionate nature, "Be gentle with yourself as you are changing." When a person is drawn toward this card it is an indication of major internal change, restructuring, burning out what is false and rigid, a time for telling the truth, focusing on health, exercise, diet.

XVII – THE STAR

"**Self-Confident, Self-Esteem**" – One who possesses the feeling and sense of self-worth; able to give recognition to others, and as a result, pulls strong recognition toward oneself; the symbol of fame for personal achievement or demonstration of unusual creativity in two varied areas. Gifted in intuition/perception and with the emotions; has the ability to transform the emotions into perception; has high gifts in precognition. This is Aquarius; the spinning stars are the two interests in which there is a deep desire and commitment to bring to earth. The head of the figure looks to the inner star for guidance and support.

When a person is drawn toward this card it is an indication that self-confidence and self-esteem are issues; it is a time of increasing both on a deep level within and in having that new confidence and esteem to be mirrored externally; there is a deep desire to bring in something new (Aquarian), to do something well at this time.

XVIII – THE MOON

"**The Chooser, the Romantic**" – One who is gifted in turning difficult situations into positive events; committed to working through difficult situations and relationships (the scarab); a "romantic" who desires not to be deceived or deluded by others – little tolerance for self-deception or illusion; possesses unusual magnetism; often placed in positions of making choices between two issues, situations, opportunities, or directions. This is the tester of old patterns, Pisces. It is a relationship card, the honey-moon is over, reality has set in, the time when difficulties arise in the relationship, the hard working-it-through time. There is a deep love for harmony and a longing to regain lost harmony. This is continually being put into places of hard choices: the two towers, two kings, two keys (Mercury – communication, and Pluto – deep unconscious). The jackels represent the inability to tolerate delusion, illusion, deception in self or others; gifted in spotting dishonesty.

When a person is drawn toward this card it is a sign of being determined to face any self-delusion, face difficult decisions and resolve difficult relationships.

XIX – THE SUN

"**The Originator, Co-Creator, Co-operator**" – One who possesses an unusual ability to work with others in co-working or community situations for the purpose of manifesting creative talents and projects; radiates extraordinary energy, vitality, and power like the sun; "the cosmic dance of two on the green mountain of creativity"; gifted working with groups of people or in teamwork efforts – especially interested in what is new, original and innovative. This is the place where relationships become an art form, the highest card on co-relationships, allowing the other to be who they are. All signs of the zodiac indicates the ability to effect many people. There is movement toward wholeness (the rainbow) through team work.

When a person is drawn toward this card it is an indication that issues of co-relationships and teamwork are in the foreground; going into a partnership, involved in a creative project with others; a time of restructuring a long-standing relationship, lovers become friends; time to work with groups of people.

XX – THE AEON/JUDGMENT

"**The Analyst, Evaluator, Seer**" – One who has acute perception with the ability to see what can be perfected or made "whole" and more effective; gifts in motivating or inspiring people; works with common sense and good judgment; determined to break through judgmentalism, evaluation, and criticism received from or directed towards others; can easily combine career and family responsibilities. Gifted critics, great ability to speak from intuition and what has been directly experienced first hand. High fertility card, womb and three babies – a family card, great ability to combine family and career. Give birth to three children, projects, careers. This is Leo, creativity – a fire card (energetic, vital, dynamic).

When a person is drawn toward this card it is an indication that there is determniation to break through judgment, criticism and evaluation associated with three aspects of self, associated with work and creativity, and toward important family members and relationships. It's a time when one might be considering having a family. Desire to learn how to handle judgments coming from others or within self; balancing career and family – can do both well.

XXI – THE UNIVERSE

"The Completion, the Initiator" – One who is gifted in simultaneously "completing the old" and "initiating the new"; able to bring change into institutions or strongly structured environments; committed to growth and evolution; ecologically minded; deep desire to experience as much of the universe and varied peoples as possible; love for travel; and capacity to cut through any limitations and restrictions. Card of transition, the sickle is being returned to the eye of Horus, the task is finished, now something new can begin. Before age 21, there was a block to be cut through (a sexual block), there is a willingness to turn oneself inside out to overcome the block. The four figures have steam coming out of mouth and nose, they have come alive (creativity is alive, fully developed). On its side, this card is a human eye (the whole universe within an eye, looking at things holisitically). Health and health issues are important.

When a person is drawn toward this card it is an indication that something is ending and beginning at the same time; may take a trip or travel; could consider going back to school; desire to influence change within an institution; liberate a sexual block.

Minor Arcana Summary

ACE OF SWORDS

"Mental Clarity, Inventiveness, and Originality" – Inspired intellect; decisiveness – a gift to utilize for a year's time, particularly in the air sign months of Aquarius, Gemini, and Libra.

When a person is drawn toward this card it is an indication of the gift of mental clarity, inventiveness and originality; inspired intellect to utilize and manifest for the next twelve months.

2 OF SWORDS – Peace

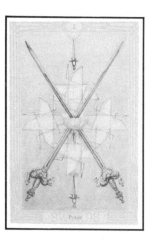

"Peace of Mind" – This is resolution about two issues, situations, choices, relationships or directions. Resolving two issues and bringing them together in harmony within the blue lotus blossom of wisdom is important in the process of mental integration. It is the unification of dualities, polarities and oppositions on the mental level. Astrological symbolism: *Moon in Libra* – peace of mind on a deep subconscious level (sword at the top of the card is holding a crescent moon) and on that level, things are being balanced out (sword at the bottom of the card is holding the sign of Libra).

When a person is drawn toward this card it is an indication that two issues, situations, choices, or relationships have already integrated at a subconscious level, the mind is now at *peace* concerning two polarities and soon the person will experience outward signs, evidence of that mental integration.

3 OF SWORDS – Sorrow

"Thoughts of Sorrow" – This card reflects past patterns that one mentally recognizes. It indicates that the individual has not released patterns or events from the past that are currently producing *sorrow*. It is also a symbol of triangular relationships. This is shown by the two swords at the top being bent by the entry of a third sword. This symbol often reflects that there is something to be resolved between three people. The central sword can also be an event that bent and pierced the receptive and dynamic sides of the person's nature. This is *Saturn in Libra*: shows that balance (Libra) will be gained by a step-by-step process (Saturn).

When a person is drawn toward this card it is an indication that some past sorrow is affecting his or her current thinking, that there is a desire to release an old pattern which is producing the current sorrow, and that it can be released in the next three weeks to three months in a step-by-step balancing process. The Empress can be drawn upon for support in that process.

4 OF SWORDS – Truce

"Mental Expansion, Resolution" – This card is mental understanding of an issue, relationship, or of some thing that needed resolution and that has now come to full resolution on all four levels of awareness – the mental, emotional, spiritual and physical (the four swords piercing the lotus blossom). This is *Jupiter in Libra*: mental expansion (Jupiter) from a place of resolution and balance (Libra); mental regeneration (light green color) from the deep spiritual core (light yellow) on four levels of consciousness (white/clarity pinwheels).

When a person is drawn toward this card it is an indication that there is expansion in one's thinking that is taking place, this expansion and regeneration is coming from a resolution (truce) on all four levels of consciousness. The individual may find that he or she is having new thoughts, expanded thoughts which want expression.

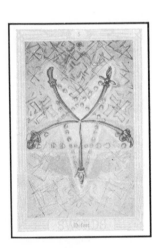

5 OF SWORDS – Defeat

"Fear of Defeat, Memory of Defeat" – This card shows that the heart nature is turned upside-down by fears and thoughts of defeat. The swords make an upside-down star. One's self-confidence and self-esteem has suffered a blow, the individual fears trying again for fear of being defeated again. There is a tendency to over-analyze and bring up past patterns and overlay them on the present situation. This is *Venus in Aquarius*: fears of defeat concerning a new (Aquarius) relationship (Venus); or fears of defeat concerning a new idea (Aquarius) that one has an emotional attachment to (Venus).

When a person is drawn toward this card it is an indication that some fear of defeat is weighing on his or her mind; there may be some memory from the past (five years before) which has damaged the self-confidence and self-esteem and making the individual afraid to try again now in a new relationship or with some new idea he or she feels strongly about. There is a desire to break through this fear and there is the possibility to do so in the next five weeks to five months. The Hierophant can be drawn upon for support at this time.

6 OF SWORDS – Science

"Objective, Logical, Rational Thinking" – This is strong analytical ability, logical scientific thinking that is felt internally and externally, symbolized by the cross. This is *Mercury in Aquarius*: communication (Mercury) about something which is completely new (Aquarius) in such a logical, objective way that it is easily understood and well received by others.

When a person is drawn toward this card it is an indication that the individual has the gift of logical, rational, scientific thinking to use in communicating about a subject that is new and needs to be put forth in a clear, objective way that will be understood and well received.

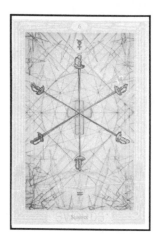

7 OF SWORDS – Futility

"Thoughts of Futility" – This is the sense of "what's the use...it won't happen because...I can't do it because... " Futility is wanting something and believing one can't have it. The central sword is what is desired, the other six swords are all the reasons one tells oneself, and believes, it can't be had, which creates the feeling of futility. This is the *Moon in Aquarius*: at a deep subconscious level (Moon) there is a desire and love to set a new idea into motion (Aquarius).

When a person is drawn toward this card it is an indication that some new idea is being stopped from development and being expressed by thoughts and beliefs that one can't do it; there is a sense of resignation, of giving up, of futility. Some event seven years before, some previous failure or frustration, may have produced this feeling. There is a desire to break through this feeling of futility and there is the possibility to do so in the next seven weeks or seven months. The Chariot can be drawn upon to aid in setting this new idea into motion.

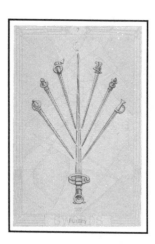

8 OF SWORDS – Interference

"Mental Interference" – This is the tendency to over-analyze situations; doubt; confusion; going over and over two issues, situations, choices, directions, etc. This is *Jupiter in Gemini:* the desire for expansion (Jupiter) concerning any duality, opposition or paradox (Gemini). Desire not to get into a fixed mental perspective; therefore, the tendency for non-decision (Gemini).

When a person is drawn toward this card it is an indication that one is over-analyzing, in doubt or confusion about a choice needing to be made. One might look back at eight years before to see if there was a similar experience of doubt and confusion. There is a desire to resolve the current situation by making a decision and there is the possiblity for resolution within the next eight weeks to eight months. The Adjustment archetype is available to be drawn upon for support in balancing and weighing the two choices and in making a decision.

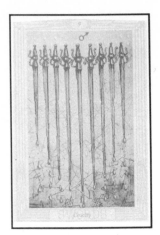

9 OF SWORDS – Self–Cruelty

"Mental Self-Cruelty" – This is the tendency, mentally, to put oneself down. This is opening old wounds from the past which reinforces feelings of defeat, or of the personality actively putting itself down. A card warning one not to make financial decisions in the month of Gemini, or warning that negative thought patterns could be mirrored to the person by a male Gemini. This is *Mars in Gemini:* dynamic energy and power in negative thinking (Mars) and the mental degradation felt both dynamically and receptively within the nature of the personality (Gemini). The spirit of the individual weeps in the background while the personality is actively putting itself down.

When a person is drawn toward this card it is an indication that there are many thoughts that put oneself down, that constitute mental cruelty to oneself. The person might look back to nine years before to see if a similar situation was going on, to see if this is a general pattern that needs to be broken. There is a desire to make this break within the next nine weeks to nine months and the individual can draw upon the Hermit for guidance and support.

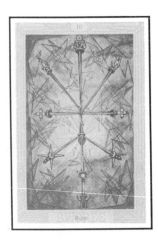

10 OF SWORDS – Ruin

"Fear of Ruin" – This is mental despair, helplessness, hopelessness about an emotional relationship (the pierced heart) or about finances (the scales at the top of the card). This is the *Sun in Gemini:* mentally gifted in synthesizing polarities, oppositions, and paradoxes (Gemini); some fear of things being ruined – especially issues concerning the emotions or finances.

When a person is drawn toward this card it is an indication that there is fear of financial ruin or of being badly hurt in the ruin or falling apart of a relationship. The person might take a look back ten years before to see if there was a similar situation concerning either money or love, or both mixed up together, which ended in ruin. There is a desire to release this fear of ruin and the possibility of doing so within the next ten weeks to ten months, and the person can draw upon the Wheel of Fortune for support in turning this situation into the direction of a more positive abundance.

KNIGHT OF SWORDS

"Passionate Thinking" – Mental drive, ambition, determination from a place of emotional reinforcement. The Knight is in the air going over water. The three birds are a symbol of the body, mind and spirit all moving forward toward some goal in unison. The long sword is the Yang (masculine), the short dagger is the Yin (feminine), both moving and being used in harmony. This is the mastery of passionate thinking, determination to succeed or accomplish one's goal.

When a person is drawn toward this card it is an indication that there are passionate thoughts concerning the accomplishment of some goal the whole being is desiring at a deep level, and on all levels (particularly the mental) to move forward and succeed at a particular task.

QUEEN OF SWORDS

"**Intellectual Thinking**" –"The Mask Cutter." This is determination to cut through roles, masks, defenses or anything unnatural. This is *air on air*, the Queen sits on a cloud, she has the gift of pure intellectual thinking and can use that sword to cut through false façade. Gifted with mental clarity (the crystal crown on her head), she also retains childlike innocence and curiosity (the child over her head). She holds the mask which has been cut away. This is the counselor in the deck, determined to cut away the superficial in self and others in order to expose the true nature.

When a person is drawn toward this card it is an indication of a desire to discard any roles, masks or defenses that hide the true person underneath childlike qualities, and to develop intellectual thinking ability. It may be a need to see a counselor at this time or to develop one's own counseling ability.

PRINCE OF SWORDS

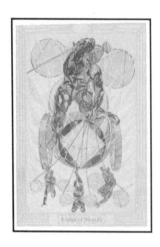

"**The Creative Intuitive Thinker**" – One who is committed to cutting through restrictions or limitations that prevent mental creativity. This is *fire and air* (creative, intuitive, spiritual thinking). The green is creative; orange/yellow is intuitive. This is Aquarius, so it's *new* thinking. The figure has his sword held high, ready to cut through anything fixed or rigid/restrictive. The three small figures in the foreground represent three relationships, fixed concepts or emotional responses which are restricting one's creative thinking.

When a person is drawn toward this card it is an indication of a need to release one's creative, intuitive thinking ability, to cut through anything that is limiting one's ability to develop some *new* Aquarian thinking which is trying to break through.

PRINCESS OF SWORDS

"**The Mood-Fighter**" – One with brilliant ability to keep moods out of the mental level of consciousness. This is *air and earth*, practical, common-sense thinking, being down to earth. The Princess fights moods that would cloud mental clarity. She has the ability to transform moods by willingness to fight them. One hand holds the sword, her common-sense mental clarity, the other hand is in touch with the earth, a pillar with disks; in this way she can stay grounded and not be thrown off balance by moody emotions.

When a person is drawn toward this card it is an indication that one's moods are out of bounds and clouding one's mental clarity. There is a need to be a *mood-fighter*, to be willing to transform moods by using one's common-sense and practical thinking, by staying grounded. This could also be an indication that one has the gift of being a *mood-fighter* and can help others learn how to strengthen their practical, common-sense thinking to control moodiness.

ACE OF CUPS

"**Emotional Balance**" – Not over-extending the emotional nature or under-extending it; reflecting accurately what is going on within the nature and expressing it without roles, masks or defenses. There is no dichotomy. *Self love*: the ability to nurture the self from deep within, symbolized by the ray of light going into the cup. There is a deep love for the spirit and a feeling that the spirit appreciates the personality systems.

When a person is drawn toward this card it is an indication that this gift of emotional balance is available to be used and drawn upon for the next year's time.

2 OF CUPS – Love

"**Deep Love Relationship**" – There is a deep, significant relationship or strong family tie that the person is experiencing. There could also be an interest or hobby or some form of creativity that one has passion for that balances out the emotional nature. *Venus in Cancer*: deep love of nature and regard for beauty and balance (Venus), especially for deep emotional relationships and family (Cancer).

When a person is drawn toward this card it is an indication that there is some deep, very significant love in that person's life, either a relationship with another or toward some form of creativity. There is a desire to fully experience and open oneself to this love at this point in time.

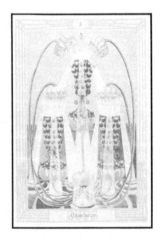

3 OF CUPS – Abundance

"**Emotional Abundance**" – This is an overflowing abundance of positive feelings that one desires to communicate to three very important people in one's life (three pomegranate cups overflowing). Abundance of feelings coming out in the rays of light that want to be communicated, which is Mercury (the communicator, messenger), to someone emotionally important, possibly a family member (Cancer). This is *Mercury in Cancer*.

When a person is drawn toward this card it is an indication that there is an outpouring of love and positive feeling toward three very significant people in his or her life; the feelings should be honored and the individual should tell each of the three people of those love, appreciation and positive feelings – communicate.

4 OF CUPS – Luxury

"**Emotional Luxury**" – This is the capacity for being able to make people feel emotionally secure, happy, satisfied and comfortable; for knowing how to entertain and make others feel the center of attention. It indicates a deep appreciation for beauty and an appreciation of the exquisite. It is a time where things are working for a person, where things are running smoothly; and one knows consciously and subconsciously why one is feeling good. This is the *Moon in Cancer*: deep love for beauty.

When persons are drawn toward this card it is an indication that it is a time in their lives when they are feeling happy, satisfied, secure and comfortable. They, therefore, have the ability to make others feel good, to feel the center of attention; out of their own good feelings, they can give to others.

5 OF CUPS – Disappointment

"**Emotional Disappointment**" – This is *Mars in Scorpio*: the person is in a place of disappointment that still has a charge to it (Mars) that is felt deeply (Scorpio). The cups are made of glass, a symbol of fragility, indicating one has been hurt or disappointed. The contents of the cups have been spilled out, lost. Although the flowers of the lily pad have been uprooted – disappointment can be uprooting – the knots of the roots form a butterfly, symbolizing that through disappointment we have the capacity for transformation. When a disappointment is faced and consciously experienced, it can be transformed into something positive and beautiful like the butterfly.

When a person is drawn toward this card it is an indication that there is some disappointment, either currently being experienced or that has been experienced in the past (possibly five years in the past) that still has a charge and is being felt deeply. There is a determination to release this disappointment within the next five weeks to five months, and the Hierophant can be drawn upon for support with this disappointment.

6 OF CUPS – Pleasure

"**Emotional Pleasure**" – This is the experiencing of pleasure and the giving of pleasure to others. This could be the experiencing of emotional pleasure from or with a Scorpio person. This is the *Sun in Scorpio*. Inside the cups are coiled snakes which symbolize that the emotional nature is being renewed, or regenerated, or emotionally healed; the cups are brass, which is the healing metal. This is the reward for letting go of disappointment.

When a person is drawn toward this card it is a sign that the emotional nature is going through a healing process, that it is being renewed and regenerated, that some disappointment has been released, giving way to a feeling of pleasure. Out of this experience of pleasure, one can give pleasure to others.

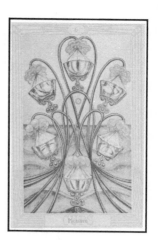

7 OF CUPS – Debauch

"**Emotional Overextension**" – This is the overindulgence of self through habits or patterns which deplete one's energies. This is overdoing, overeating, overworking, overdrinking, smoking, drug usage, or indiscriminate sex. This is depression on a very deep level. This is *Venus in Scorpio*: depression on a deep level (Scorpio) with (Venus) wanting to make things better or more comfortable. There is a tendency to feel sorry for oneself. There is also an awareness that something is depressing, as well as the awareness of the negative compensation pattern, trying to make the self feel better by doing something that will temporarily please, but won't make for happiness in the long run.

When a person is drawn toward this card it is an indication that the individual is experiencing some depression and attempting to ease the pain by overindulging. This may be a habitual pattern; the person might look back at seven years before to see if this same pattern was operating at that time. There is a desire to release this overindulgence within the next seven weeks to seven months; the Chariot can be drawn upon for assistance with this pattern.

8 OF CUPS – Indolence

"**Emotional Stagnation**" – This is the feeling of being overly tired, drained, depleted, exhausted. There is a tendency to over-give, or randomly over-extend one's self. This is *Saturn in Pisces*: a need for structure, discipline (Saturn), especially in areas where one is emotionally involved (Pisces). A warning card: not to over-extend one's energy to the point of emotional exhaustion; depletion in the month of Pisces; or the need to set limits with a Pisces person.

When a person is drawn toward this card it is an indication that the individual may be emotionally tired, drained, depleted or over-extended. There is a need for some structure or discipline to help the individual set some limits on this over-extension. The Adjustment archetype can be drawn upon to aid in regaining balance during the next eight weeks to eight months during which time the person is determined to release this pattern of over-extension.

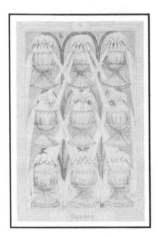

9 OF CUPS – Happiness

"**Emotional Fulfillment and Happiness**" – This is fulfillment in all aspects of one's life, both internally and externally; a sense of emotional completion. This is *Jupiter in Pisces*: emotional expansion (Jupiter) and the ability to go into one's emotional depths for the purpose of integration and harmonizing feelings (Pisces).

When a person is drawn toward this card it is an indication that one is in a time of emotional expansion evolving from a feeling of fulfillment and completion. There is an ability to go into one's emotional depths to integrate and balance feelings.

10 OF CUPS – Satiety

"**Emotional Contentment**" – This is the feeling of satisfaction that swells up from deep inside and radiates out, this is the feeling of peace inside that is not externally based. This is *Mars in Pisces*: there is energy, vitality, charge, emotional passion and enthusiasm (Mars) with excitement being experienced at very deep levels inside (Pisces).

When a person is drawn toward this card it is an indication that there is a great deal of emotional passion and vitality being experienced internally and radiating out to others. There is a feeling of peace and contentment.

KNIGHT OF CUPS

"**The Optimist**" – one who is gifted in uplifting; giving totally; openly loving. This is *Cancer the crab*: deep emotional relationships are very important; one who is loyal to family and to deep emotional relationships. There is an ability to go beyond one's own ego or emotional pride (the winged horse, Pegasus, has moved past the peacock – a symbol of pride). There is then the emotional reward of happiness. This is *air and water*, the ability to blend emotions with the intellect.

When a person is drawn toward this card it is an indication that issues of loyalty to family and deep relationships are of concern, that "ego pride" has been mastered, or is needing to be dealt with. There is at this point the gift of giving totally and openly to others.

THE QUEEN OF CUPS

"**The Emotional Reflector**" – This represents commitment to be true to the Self. The Queen is so radiant you can hardly see her. She represents emotional balance; whatever is being experienced and felt internally is also reflected externally, "as within, so without." She has the ability to reflect feelings accurately, is gifted working with children (her hand is on the stork). The crayfish shell she holds is a symbol of her career having to do with the gift to inspire and motivate others emotionally. The two water lilies are evenly balanced in the water. The stork is also a symbol of emotional rebirth from a place of balance. This is *earth and water*, which indicates the ability to stay grounded when dealing with the emotions.

When a person is drawn toward this card it is an indication that there is a need to gain emotional balance and to accurately reflect to the external world what is going on internally. The individual is able to draw upon this ability and is gifted at this point in working with children or with career issues from a balanced emotional place.

PRINCE OF CUPS

"**The Lover**" – This is emotional passion, desire; feelings are expressed fervently. The Prince has a strong passionate nature, he holds the lotus blossom pointing downward, willing to let go at any moment. This is *Scorpio* (the snake, eagle, eagle helmet). The eagle is the highest form of Scorpio and represents new perspectives on one's emotional nature. The eagle carries one across the emotional waters without the danger of drowning in the emotions. This is *water*, and water which is passionately emotional.

When a person is drawn toward this card it is an indication that there is a great deal of passion and the desire to express one's feeling fervently.

PRINCESS OF CUPS

"**Emotional Detachment, Free of Jealousy**" – the Princess loves deeply, but has worked through jealousy and possessiveness. She has the ability to offer emotional longevity, loyalty and commitment (the turtle) in a relationship, but from a place of detachment. She has already let go (the lotus blossom is floating free in space). She is able to achieve this detachment in a step-by-step way with determination (like the turtle), with fine clear communication (like the dolphin), and with a sense of emotional security (the swan, a symbol of emotional transformation). The crystals on her gown represent clear perception, the ability to see her feelings clearly. The swirls are sea-snakes, representing emotional renewal. This is *water and fire*, the ability to move to a place of spiritual love – loving in a detached way.

When a person is drawn toward this card it is an indication that the individual has mastered some possessiveness and feelings of jealousy and there is now an ability to love deeply in a loyal, committed way, but with detachment.

ACE OF WANDS

"**The Torch of Fire**" – A symbol for self-discovery; self-revelation; self-realization at a core level of one's being. This is seeing aspects of the self so clearly that there is a commitment to burn out any negativity, blocks, obstacles or obstructions that prevent one from fully actualizing one's full potential.

When a person is drawn toward this card it is an indication that there is a deep spirirtual desire for self-discovery and self-realization and that the individual has this gift to draw upon for a year's time.

2 OF WANDS – Dominion

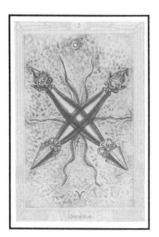

"Spiritual Sovereignty, Power" – This is a state of integration and optimum balance. This is *Mars in Aries:* Mars shows dynamic forcefulness, energy, charge and a passionate nature. Aries is the pioneer, doer, adventurer who moves forward in a new direction, but only from a place of full power, dominion and balance (the two wands that are unified).

When a person is drawn toward this card it is an indication of powerful spiritual force and drive to begin something new, to be a pioneer. There are gifts of dynamic energy and leadership ability to be expressed.

3 OF WANDS – Virtue

"Spiritual Integrity, Honesty" – This is looking at the self and external situations from a place of maximum integrity, honesty, and no compromise. This is the *Sun in Aries:* This is either in the month of Aries or with an Aries person; no compromise from the three aspects of self: body, mind, spirit (the three united lotus blossom wands).

When a person is drawn toward this card it is an indication that honesty and integrity are issues. There is a deep spiritual desire to maintain one's integrity on all levels.

4 OF WANDS – Completion

"Spiritual and Holistic Completion" – This is the ability to look at the self and external situations holistically; looking at all the aspects of the self and seeing how they make a whole, seeing how things come together. This is reflected in the symbol of the wheel. This is *Venus in Aries:* emotionally, the love nature (Venus) desires to move in new directions, or the desire to experience something emotionally that is new (Aries). Some aspect of the self is in the process of completion, while another aspect of self desires to experience something new.

When a person is drawn toward this card it is an indication that something is being completed and there is a desire to begin something new. There is also the ability to see things holistically.

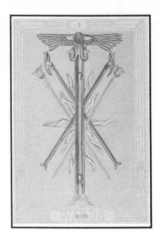

5 OF WANDS – Strife

"**Spiritual Frustration, Conflict**" – This is a sense of discord, anxiety or strife concerning a Leo person or with one's own creativity (what one is or is not doing with creativity potential). This is *Saturn in Leo:* feelings of limitation and restriction or the need to experience in a step-by-step process (Saturn) as far as one's creative expression is concerned (Leo).

When a person is drawn toward this card it is an indication that a deep sense of frustration, conflict and anxiety is being experienced in relation to one's own creative expression, or one is feeling restricted in one's creative expression by a Leo person. The individual might take a look at his or her life five years before to see if this same feeling or pattern was present. There is a deep desire and resolution to release this frustration within the next five weeks to five months, and the Hierophant can be drawn upon for assistance with this conflict.

6 OF WANDS – Victory

"**Spiritual Revitalization and Expansion**" – This is a major "win", breakthrough, or realization at a very deep level. This is *Jupiter in Leo:* expansion and good luck (Jupiter) in areas of creativity, insight and perception (Leo). Could be a major breakthrough or expansion with a Leo person, or a victory within the month of Leo.

When a person is drawn toward this card it is an indication that some major breakthrough has happened in relation to creativity, insight or perception.

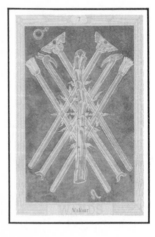

7 OF WANDS – Valour

"**Spiritual Courage, Bravery**" – This is the deepening of character from life's experience. This is *Mars in Leo:* movement forward in new directions from a place of courage and valour (Mars) that will allow one to express full creativity (Leo). Strong sense of one's values; courage to take important risks. This is associated with the Kundalini energy, having back-bone, the rise of spiritual energy.

When a person is drawn toward this card it is an indication of a rising of spiritual courage, the willingness to take risks for spiritual growth, the stirring of spiritual energy, all desiring a creative outlet.

8 OF WANDS – Swiftness

"**Spiritual Velocity, Haste, Acceleration**" – This is the capacity to handle internal processes swiftly, there is a determination to take action on something that is troublesome, or is a block, obstacle or obstruction. It is an attempt to turn a difficult situation into a positive direction through communication that is direct, articulate, and well-timed. This is *Mercury in Sagittarius:* articulate and direct communication (Mercury) that turns difficult situations into positive directions (Sagittarius). There is a spiritual bridge to wholeness (rainbow) using one's intuition and spiritual vision (the crystal).

When a person is drawn toward this card it is an indication that one is processing a high intensity of spiritual energy very rapidly. There may be a feeling of urgency and a desire to communicate clearly and directly what is being experienced.

9 OF WANDS – Strength

"**Spiritual Power, Potency, Force**" – This is internal strength; strength in communications, insight, intuition and vision. This is both the *Sun and Moon in Sagittarius:* conscious awareness (Sun) of our outer strength and also trusting our inner strength (Moon).

When a person is drawn toward this card it is an indication of a balanced (masculine and feminine) spiritual strength uniting within. There is an increase in intuition, insight and spiritual vision, and the increased ability to communicate to others this new spiritual awareness.

10 OF WANDS – Oppression

"**Spiritual Restraint, Repression**" – This is self-oppression, or withholding communications for fear of how it will be received. This is *Saturn in Sagittarius:* a person may be oppressed by two issues, choices, people, relationships or there may be two things that he or she would like to communicate (Sagittarius) but holds back for fear of how it might be received (Saturn).

When persons are drawn toward this card it is an indication that they are experiencing an internal self-repression which is stifling their expression of who they are at a spiritual level. There is fear that who they are will not be understood or accepted. This may be a long-standing pattern of self-restraint; looking back ten years before may reveal the same feelings. There is a determination to release this self-oppression within the next ten weeks to ten months and the Wheel of Fortune can be drawn upon for aid in turning this withholding into a more positive situation.

KNIGHT OF WANDS

"**The Spiritual Evolutionary**" – This is the positive revolutionary, the bringer of change. The Knight charges forward, wanting to change our point of view, our perception of the world. He holds the Ace of Wands in his hands to burn out any blocks or obstacles that stand in the way. He has the ability to turn any difficult situation around in a more positive way (the scarab on the blanket of the horse). He has the ability to shed old belief, bring rebirth and change (the reptile suit of armor) and he has extended vision, the ability to see the inside coming out (the unicorn horse). This is *fire and fire*, a double strength with spiritual insight, intuition and perception.

When a person is drawn toward this card it is an indication of evolution and change at a deep core level; old perceptions are being shed and any blocks or obstacles are being burned out in order for there to be new, extended insight and spiritual birth.

THE QUEEN OF WANDS

"**The Spiritual Self-Explorer/Discoverer**" – The Queen is the "knower of the self"; she is committed to knowing who she is. This is *fire and water*; she wears the symbol of Pisces on her chest; fire and water are alchemical when put together creating steam. There is an evolutionary, transformational quality to the Queen. The story that goes with the Queen is that originally she had black hair and sat with a panther. As she came to know herself, her hair turned to brown and the panther became a leopard. When she fully knew herself, her hair became fire-red and as the leopard began to transform into a lion, she pinched him to prevent the transformation in order to remind herself of the dark places (the black spots) from which, and through which, she had come. The pine cone she carries is a symbol of growth and evolution. She is determined to bring her self-knowledge from the inside out to earth.

When a person is drawn toward this card it is an indication that he or she is in the process of self-discovery and deeply desires more self-knowledge and understanding.

PRINCE OF WANDS

"**Spiritual Creativity**" – The Prince has the ability to see creative power and to do something with it. This is *Leo* (creativity and leadership). The lion has free reins, the creativity is being neither restricted nor restrained; there is total movement forward (the Prince's legs are in the position of the four). The green eyes of Leo and the underside of the chariot are also creative power. The Prince is determined to bring his creativity to earth; this is *earth and fire*. The fire is contained and being focused, there is more heat that way and more intense passion. The Prince has the ability to see how inner creativity can be manifested in the world. He has a deep love for creativity (lotus blossom at his heart) and the self knowledge and realization necessary to succeed at his task (halo).

When a person is drawn toward this card it is an indication that there is a deep spiritual passion to release one's creativity and express it in the world.

PRINCESS OF WANDS

"**Spiritual Self-Liberation**" – The Princess is committed to freedom, especially freedom from fear (the tiger is a symbol of fear). She has totally knocked out the tiger and has it by the tail. She has totally overcome fear. The sun wand she carries is a symbol of her ability to move in new directions with a vital new energy. The fear she has overcome is burning on the altar and being offered up as a sacrifice. She can be totally nude, defenseless, because she has nothing to fear. She has an increased self awareness after overcoming a major fear (the antenna). This is *Aries* (the rams on the altar), also, this is *air and fire*, an increased ability to overcome fears at the spiritual and intellectual levels.

When a person is drawn toward this card it is an indication that some major fear is being faced and overcome, that the individual will experience a vital new energy once the fear has been released. It has already been released internally, and there will be a new self-awareness.

ACE OF DISKS

"**Grounded, Practical, Organized**" – This is high success based on being grounded or centered, being practical, organized, not "spacey" (the large coin in the center is the symbol for this quality). This is success on all levels of experience: mentally, emotionally, spiritually, and physically (the four wings). This is the union between the spiritual and physical aspects of self. This is radiating the higher aspect of oneself and bringing it into physical manifestation.

When a person is drawn toward this card it is an indication that this gift of grounded, practical organization is available to be used and drawn upon for the next year's time.

2 OF DISKS – Change

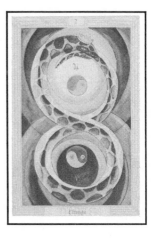

"**Physical Transition, Transformation**" – This is a period of change needed to bring balance back into one's life. The Uroborus snake is an Oriental symbol of wholeness – the Yin/Yang, symbolism of black and white, is balance which is achieved through change, "the only constant there is." This is *Jupiter in Capricorn*: expansive, positive change (Jupiter) that takes place externally in order to make things more secure, stable and solid (Capricorn). Turned on its side is a symbol of infinity, endless or unlimited space, time, distance, quantity, an indication of the never-ending universe, the ultimate in expansion (Jupiter), the on-goingness of change unending.

When persons are drawn toward this card it is an indication that they are in the middle of a major transition which will bring new expansion and balance into their external life, their physical experience. This is advice to flow with the change, not to fight it, as change will happen whether one likes it or not.

3 OF DISKS – Works

"Physical Persistence, Tenacity, Endurance" – This is strong determination to give any external situation the "works"; full commitment to a situation regardless of any difficulties, blocks or negativity (waves of mud); operating at a high level of energy and commitment (pyramid) with clarity (blue light) from body, mind, and spirit (three red wheels). This is *Mars in Capricorn:* dynamic energy (Mars) to make things more secure and tangible (Capricorn).

When persons are drawn toward this card it is an indication that there is some external situation that they are determined to stick with and to see through, no matter how difficult or frustrating the task may be. They have a great deal of dynamic energy to draw upon to aid them in this task.

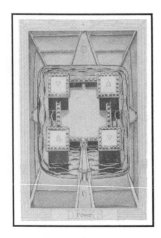

4 OF DISKS – Power

"Physical Potency, Vitality, Forcefulness" – This is owning one's own personal energy, power and vitality. This is the feeling of self-assuredness; there is a lack of self doubt. This is the *Sun in Capricorn:* the need, ambition and desire to demonstrate one's personal vitality and creativity in the external world. The four towers symbolize the tapping of full power on all four levels: mentally, emotionally, physically and spiritually. The towers form a structure, that of a well-balanced, defended fortress; this is a solid foundation (Capricorn).

When a person is drawn toward this card it is an indication that personal power and potency is the issue at hand. There is a desire to feel more self-assurance and express one's vitality and creativity in the external world. This capacity is there to be tapped and used on all levels.

5 OF DISKS – Worry

"Physical Concern, Anxiety, Rumination" – This is worry about finances, health, or external situations or relationships. It is the state of *being/consciousness* that always takes one back to the *past* or into the *future*, but never has one handling the *present.* This is *Mercury in Taurus:* worry about communication patterns (Mercury) and how one is coming across while communicating (Taurus). This (like the 5 of Swords) is the upside-down star; one's self-confidence and self-esteem has suffered a blow, and worry and doubts are only keeping one in a state of anxiety.

When a person is drawn toward this card it is an indication that the individual is worrying a lot about money or health or some other external situation in his or her life. There are doubts about one's own ability to handle the situation, particularly about one's communication skills and how one comes across to others. The individual might take a look at his or her life five years before to see if a similar situation existed at that time. There is a determination to release this negative "worry" pattern, and the Hierophant can be drawn upon in the next five weeks to five months to help.

6 OF DISKS – Success

"**Physical Attainment, Accomplishment**" – This is the *Moon in Taurus:* a deep desire at the subconscious level (Moon) to make some tangible results; to see results of one's efforts or productivity (Taurus). This is success, achievement in all aspects of one's life by the willingness to work in a step-by-step manner (Saturn); the willingness to take risks and to expand when there is the opportunity (Jupiter); the willingness to be emotionally committed to what one is involved with (Venus); to trust one's intuition (Moon); the ability to communicate effectively (Mercury) with energy, vitality and commitment to one's endeavors (Mars).

When a person is drawn toward this card it is an indication that there is a deep desire to be successful at some external venture. This card offers some good advice about how to achieve the desired success: by being willing to risk, being committed, trusting one's own intuition, using clear communication and really throwing one's energy into the task.

7 OF DISKS – Failure

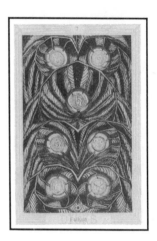

"**Physical Failure, Nonsuccess**" – This is the fear of failure or the feeling of having failed; the fear of failure could be associated with finances, health, relationships or any external situation (Disks). This is *Saturn in Taurus*: step-by-step process in making something tangible or productive for the self; failure is a result of not handling things one step at a time. This is a warning card not to make any financial decisions in the month of Taurus; or that fears of failure could arise during the month of Taurus. This could also be the feeling of failure in relationship to a Taurus person.

When a person is drawn toward this card it is an indication that there are fears of failure eating away at the individual, failure relating to finances, health or relationships. The individual might look back at seven years ago to see if there was a situation like the current one operating. There is a determination to release these fears of failure within the next seven weeks to seven months, and the Chariot can be drawn upon for assistance.

8 OF DISKS – Prudence

"**Physical Caution, Carefulness, Prudence**" – This is wisdom operating from a place of balance and integration; making sure all bases are covered or protected while experiencing change. This is *Sun in Virgo*: attention to beauty, order, balance, structure, and details. This is the state of consciousness of not overextending the self externally, or underextending the self, either; it is operating from a near the center, and integration.

When persons are drawn toward this card it is an indication that they are needing to proceed forward in their growth and life experience with care and caution. There is a need to move slowly, and thoroughly, attending to the details of their external life, not over-looking the importance of order and structure in their lives.

9 OF DISKS – Gain

"**Physical Profit, Benefit, Gain**" – This is gain on every level – mentally, emotionally, physically, financially, and spiritually. This is *Venus in Virgo*: physical gain in external reality from projects, relationships, or situations (Venus). There is concern about weight, or money gain or loss, and taking action on either situation.

When a person is drawn toward this card it is an indication that weight, or money gain or loss, is the issue at hand. There also might be an important relationship from which one stands to gain.

10 OF DISKS – Wealth

"**Physical Prosperity, Abundance, Wealth**" – This is *Mercury in Virgo*: the ability to communicate with an abundance of varied ideas or resource materials (Mercury). An abundance of communication and information (Mercury) that is delivered in an organized, beautiful, balanced fashion (Virgo). This is a state of wealth and prosperity on all levels of consciousness that is manifesting in the external world.

When a person is drawn toward this card it is an indication that the external world holds wealth for the individual, there could be an inheritance, some unexpected prosperity. This is also the gift of prosperous communication, delivered in a beautiful, organized fashion.

KNIGHT OF DISKS

"**The Physical Doctor, the Healer**" – This is the diagnostician; he has a deep commitment to health. This is *earth and earth*; he is concerned with the care of the body. He carries the threshing tool and wants to bring a harvest into the world. His sun disk is a symbol of health and financial well-being. This is *Leo;* the lion is on the sun disk. He is a leader, a guide (indicated by Leo and the horned animal on his helmet). This is a high natural health card.

When a person is drawn toward this card it is an indication that there is a concern for the body and good health; there is an interest in health care and there is the ability to be a leader and guide to others concerning health care issues.

THE QUEEN OF DISKS

"**The Physical Nutritionist**" – This is concern for good exercise, health foods and the natural environment. The Queen sits on a giant pineapple, she is taking action to beautify the body, to restore the body to natural health. There is the ability to shed off unhealthy dietary habits (she wears reptile clothing). There are gifts concerned with making the physical form beautiful. The Queen looks back to the barren desert of the past, left behind as she goes into abundance. She holds the world in her hands with great care; this is *Aries, fire and earth* (the ram and horn head piece); this is giftedness in body work and the desire to experience something new in relationship to the body. She holds the crystal wand, a symbol of clear seeing; she is clear about her needs and wants; she sees that the body is the temple of the spirit.

When a person is drawn toward this card it is an indication that the beautifying of the body and healthy nutrition is an issue. This might be a time of shedding off old unhealthy eating habits, beginning a new diet or buying new clothes.

PRINCE OF DISKS

"**The Physical Architect**" – This is physical activity; the doer; builder; sportsperson. The body is totally exposed, there is good muscle tone. This is *Taurus*, the determination to apply gifts of building in the world. There is an eye for beauty, determination to move forward with steel-like determination (steel chariot) in building a new world for the self that will be more fruitful and abundant with less obstruction (the many little boulders on the back of the chariot). This is *air and earth*. There is a winged bull on the Prince's helmet, indicating the Taurus earth energy is very influential in one's thinking – concrete, practical thinking.

When a person is drawn toward this card it is an indication that there are issues concerning physical activity, building, sports, good muscle tone. There is a steel-like determination to move forward with less blocks or obstacles. There is also the gift of practical thinking.

PRINCESS OF DISKS

"**The Pregnant One**" – This is being pregnant with either concept, project or child. The Princess has unusual gifts in creativity (both Scorpio and Aries). The Princess is the bearer of new life, she has come on a long journey over mountains and through briars to bring her gift. She holds the balance of masculine and feminine (the Yin/Yang) and has the gift of intuitive sight and perception (the crystal spear). Her snake robe (Scorpio) is a symbol of regeneration and rebirth. Her inner light is coming to earth. This is *water and earth* (Scorpio), physical creation with emotional passion. She has fertility and the harvest (the pedestal upon which she leans).

When a person is drawn toward this card it is an indication that issues of motherhood and pregnancy may be present. There may also be a birth happening with ideas, projects, identity and aspects of oneself.

APPENDIX C

Tracings of Cards in Europe

(Research compiled by Alfred Douglas)

1275	Games are mentioned in the Townbook of Augsburg, Germany, but cards are not referred to.
1289–99	The Code of Nuremberg, Germany, does not include cards amongst its list of prohibited games.
1328–41	A French manuscript, *Renard le Contrefait*, written between these dates, contains a passage that might refer to cards.
1377	Cards and card games are described by a monk at the monastery of Brefeld, Switzerland.
1378	Cards are banned in Regensburg, Germany.
1379	Purchase of cards is recorded in the accounts of the Dukedom of Brabant (Belgium).
1380–84	Cards are permitted by the Code of Nuremberg.
1381	Cards are condemned in the records of a notary of Marseilles, France.
1392	A decree in Paris includes cards; also, the Treasurer's accounts of Charles VI of France includes a payment for three packs of handmade cards. (A painter by the name of Jacquemin Gringoneur designed them especially for the amusement of the King.)
1393	Cards are listed amongst the permitted games in Florence.
1397	A decree in Paris includes cards amongst a list of games forbidden to commononers on working days.
1415	Tarot cards are painted for the Duke of Milan, later known as the Visconti deck.
1423	Cards are condemned in a speech made at Bologna by St. Bernardin of Siena. He does not refer to the Tarot major trumps.
1423–77	Townbooks of Nuremberg name several women as card-painters.
1427	Two Master Card-makers are named in the Guild registers of Brabant.
1440	The date from which are found the earliest surviving cards printed from wood-blocks – French court cards.
1440	Playing cards are printed at Stuttgart.
1441	The importation of foreign playing cards is prohibited by the authorities of Venice.
1450–70	A Franciscan Friar preaches a sermon in Northern Italy condemning dice and cards. He made a clear distinction between the four suits and the 22 major trumps.
1463	The importation of foreign cards into England is forbidden in a statute of Edward IV, to protect home manufacturers.

BIBLIOGRAPHY

TAROT: IMPORTANT REFERENCES and RELATED MATERIALS

Best Sources tracing historical origin of Tarot:

Chatto, W.A. *Speculations on the Origin and History of Playing Cards.* London: John Russell Smith, 1848.
Douglas, Alfred. *The Tarot: The Origins, Meaning & Uses of the Cards.* New York: Penguin Press, 1972.
Huson, Paul. *The Devil's Picturebook.* London: Abacus/Sphere Books, Ltd., 1971.
    (Includes a description of the origin of tarot cards)
Mackenzie, D.A. *The Migration of Symbols.* London: Kegan, Paul Trench, Trubner, 1926.
Willshire, W.H. *A Descriptive Catalogue of Playing and other Cards* in the British Museum, printed by order of the Trustees, 1876.

Books related to the Egyptian beliefs and usage of Tarot cards:

Budge, E.A. Wallis. *The Gods of the Egyptians.* New York: Dover Books, 1969
Doresse, Jean. *The Secret Books of Egyptian Gnostics.* London: Hollis & Carter, 1960.
Elie, Alta. *Le Tarot Egyptian.* Vichy: Bouchet, Dreyfus, 1922.
Kingsland, W. *The Great Pyramid in Fact & Theory.* 2 vols. London: Rider & Co., 1969.
Ouspensky, P.D. *The Symbolism of the Tarot: Philosophy of occultism in pictures and numbers.*
    New York: Dover, 1976. (Originally published by Trood Ptq & Pubg. Co., 1913).
Stewart, T.M. *The Symbolism of the Gods of the Egyptians.* London: Baskerville Press, 1929.

Related Books on the Tarot and general symbolism:
(See **Additional Bibliography** for more complete references.)

Baring-Gould, Sabine. *Curious Myths of the Middle Ages.* London: Rivingtons, 1873.
Cooper, Louise. *The Book of Paradox.* New York: Dell Publishing Co., Inc., 1973.
Frazer, J.G. *The Golden Bough: The roots of religion and folklore.* New York: Avenel Books/Crown Publishers, Inc. 1981. (Originally published, 1890).

Haich, Elizabeth. *Wisdom of the Tarot.* New York: ASI Publishers, Inc, 1975. (also Egyptian emphasis).
Harding, Ester. *Women's Mysteries.* New York: Harper & Row, 1980.
Jung, C.G. *Memories, Dreams and Reflections.* New York: Vintage Books, 1961.
Khan, Yitzhac. *Tarot & The Game of Fate.* San Francisco: Sebaac, 1971.
Kopp, Sheldon. *The Hanged Man: Psychotherapy and the Forces of Darkness.* Palo Alto, Ca: Science & Behavior Bk, Inc., 1974.
Steiner, Rudolf. *Ancient Myths: Their Meaning and Connection with Evolution.* Toronto: Asiner, London & Steiner Book Centre, 1971.
Willeford, William. *The Fool and His Scepter.* Evanston, IL: Northwestern University Press, 1969.

OTHER BOOKS ON THE TAROT

(The majority of annotative descriptions listed below are provided by Mary K. Greer)

Balin, Peter. *The Flight of the Feathered Serpent*. Venice, Ca.: Wisdom Garden Books, 1978.

Bennett, Sidney. *Tarot for the Millions*. California, 1967. 157 pages.
> Presents various card spreads and sample tarot readings along with description and meanings for each of the Major and Lesser Arcana.

Buess, Lynn M. *The Tarot and Transformation*. Marina Del Rey, CA: DeVorss & Co., Publishers, 1973.

Butler, Bill. *Dictionary of the Tarot*. New York: Schocken Books, 1975.

Case, Paul Foster. *The Book of Tokens: Tarot Meditations*. Los Angeles, Ca.: Builders of the Adytum, 1968.
> Comprises meditations on the occult meaning of the twenty-two Hebrew letters.

Case, Paul Foster. *Highlights of Tarot*. Los Angeles, CA.: Builders of the Adytum, 1970. 64 pages.
> Occult meanings of the Tarot, instructions for coloring the B.O.T.A. deck of cards, correspondences of tarot to various mystical systems.

Cavendish, Richard. *The Black Arts*. New York: Capricorn Books, 1968.
> Section on the tarot called "The Paths and the Tarot", pp. 99–115.

Cooke, John and Rosalind Sharpe. *G – The Royal Maze: Guide to the Game of Destiny*. Cleveland, Ohio: Western Star Press, 1969. 60 pages.
> Game of psychological awareness and sense of purposeness to be played with the new tarot designed by tbe authors. Contains a short bibliography.

Cooke, John and Rosalind Sharpe. *The New Tarot: Tarot for the Aquarian Age*. Kentfield, Ca.: Western Star Press, 1969.
> New Tarot cards and meanings given in sessions with a ouija board to the authors – designed for the new Aquarian Age Man. Humanistic and Jungian psychology approaches.

Crowley, Aleister. *The Book of Thoth: A short essay on the tarot of the Egyptians*. York Beach, Maine: Samuel Weiser, Inc., 1969 (originally published in 1944).
> Crowley designed his own deck of tarot and anyone wishing to study this book should use his deck. Crowley goes very heavily into archetypes, myth, religion and astrology. The cards were illustrated by Lady Frieda Harris.

Culberson, Mary. *A Transpersonal Approach to Symbolic Therapy: Dreams and Tarot*. (Unpublished)
> A doctoral dissertation at Institute of Transpersonal Psychology, San Franscisco, 1982.

De Laurence, L.W. *The Illustrated Key to the Tarot*. Chicago: The de Laurence Company, 1918. 176 pages.
> An inferior version of Waite's book.

Doane, Doris Chase, and King Keyes. *How to read Tarot Cards*. New York: Funk and Wagnalls, 1967. 207 pages.
> Original title: *Tarot-Card Spread Reader*. Mainly a compilation of various divinatory spreads – a different kind for each different type of question. Uses the Church of Light tarot deck (Egyptian) but this deck is not necessary to the use of this book. Has unusual meanings for many of the cards.

Douglas, Alfred. *The Tarot: The Origins, Meaning and Uses of the Cards*. New York: Penguin Books, 1972.
> Has a lot of information about Tarot cards other than just the meanings of the cards. Card illustrations by David Sheridan – based on the Waite deck. Good history and good Jungian interpretations.

Fairfield, Gail. *Choice-centered Tarot*. Self-published, 1982. Available from Choice-centered Astrology and Tarot; PO Box 31816; Seattle, WA 98103.
> Excellent book on Tarot; well-organized, succinct, and is humanistic in its approach.

Gardner, Richard. *Evolution through the Tarot*. New York: Samuel Weiser, Inc., 1977.
> Reprint of the book previously published under the title ACCELERATE YOUR EVOLUTION.
> Describes the twenty-two Major Arcana cards in metaphysical terms.

Gearhart, Sally. *A Feminist Tarot: A Guide to Intrapersonal Communication.*. San Francisco: Persephone Press, 1977.

Gettings, Fred. *The Book of Tarot*. London: Triune Books, 1973. 144 pages.
> Excellent comparison of various tarot decks. Occult symbology as used in the tarot.

Gibson, Walter B. and Litzka R. Gibson. *The Complete Illustrated Book of the Psychic Sciences*. 67–91. New York: Doubleday and Co., Inc., 1966.
> Gives meanings for the Major and Minor Arcana.

Graves, F. *Windows of Tarot*. Dobbs Ferry, NY: Morgan & Morgan, 1973.
> Gives meanings for the Major and Minor Arcana and explains the symbolism used by Palladini in his Aquarian Tarot deck.

Gray, Eden. *A Complete Guide to the Tarot*. New York: Crown Publishers, Inc., 1970. 160 pages.
> Handy all-in-one reference. Gives history, divinatory methods, the relation of the tarot to the Kabala, Astrology, Numerology and the uses in meditation.

Gray, Eden. *Mastering the Tarot: Basic Lessons in an Ancient, Mystic Art*. New York: Signet Books/New American Library, 1971.
> Gives meanings of the cards and the methods of reading them. Includes many sample readings.

Greer, Mary K. *Tarot for Yourself: A Workbook for Personal Transformation*. North Hollywood, CA: A Newcastle Book, 1984.
> The best book that offers practical ways in how to use the tarot. Well-done and valuable resource.

Haich, Elizabeth. *Wisdom of the Tarot*. New York: ASI Publishers., Inc., 1975.

Harner, Michael. *Way of the Shaman*. New York: Bantam, 1982.

Heline, Corinne. *The Bible and the Tarot*. Marina del Rey, Ca.: DeVorss & Co., Publishers, 1969.
> Correlates the tarot and the bible. Also develops correspondence with the Kabala.
> Pictures are ancient Egyptian designs.

Hoeller, Stephan A. *The Royal Road: A Manual of Kabalistic Meditations on Tarot*. Wheaton, IL.: The Theosophical Publishing House, 1975.

Holy Order of Mans. *Jewels of the Wise*. San Francisco: Epiphany Press, 1979.
> Concentrates on the tarot as a spiritual tool. Excellent.

Hoy, David. *The Meaning of Tarot*. Nashville, Tenn.: Aurora Publishers, Inc., 1971. 168 pages.
> Good basic book. Covers well the preparation for giving a reading.

Huson, Paul. *The Devil's Picturebook: The Compleat Guide to Tarot Cards*. New York: Putnam, 1971.
> Describes the Major Arcana and the Minor Arcana cards and presents the methods of laying out the cards and reading the pack. Includes a description of the origin of tarot cards.

Kahn, Yitzhac. *Tarot and the Game of Fate*. San Francisco, Ca.: Sebaac Publishers, 1971.
> Very useful for interpretation. Has an interesting theory for inter-relating Tarot with Astrology.

Kaplan, Stuart R. *Tarot Cards for Fun and Fortune Telling*. New York: Wehman, 1970. 96 pages.
> Illustrated guide to the spreading and interpretation of the popular seventy-eight cards of tarot.
> Muller and Cie, Switzerland.

Kaplan, Stuart R. *Tarot Classic.* New York: Grosset and Dunlap, 1972. 240 pages.
> Excellent bibliography and description of the historical development of the cards with illustrations of the old cards. Written to go with the "Tarot Classic" set of cards but may be used with any deck.

Kasdin, Simon. *The Esoteric Tarot.* New York: Samuel Weiser, 1965. 96 pages.
> Describes the twenty-two Major Arcana using unusual symbols with specific reference to the Hebrew alphabet and the Sepher Yetzerah.

Laurence, Theodor. *How the Tarot Speaks to Modern Man.* Harrisburg, Pa.: Stackpole Books, 1972. 216 pages.
> Explores the Major Arcana of the tarot from three different planes: the Material, the Psychological, the Spiritual. Explains ways of utilizing the forces at each of these levels at their highest potential.

Lind, Frank. *How to Understand the Tarot.* London: The Aquarian Press, 1969. 63 pages.

Mathers, S.L. MacGregor. *The Tarot, Its Occult Signification, Use in Fortunetelling and Method of Play.* New York: Weiser, 1973. 60 pages.
> Nothing original.

Mayananda. *The Tarot for Today.* London: The Zeus Press, 1963. 255 pages.
> Expounds his own theories of the tarot as relates to occult symbolism and concepts. Builds system upon system for revealing the esoteric meanings of the tarot.

Metzner, Ralph. *Maps of Consciousness.* New York: Collier Books, 1971.
> Chapter: "Tarot: Signposts on the Way", pp. 54–81. Relates the tarot to concepts of Actualism, Tantra, Yoga, Astrology, Alchemy. A modern psychological and personal approach. The whole book is well worth it.

Micca, R. *Tarot: An Illustrated Guide.* New York: St. Martin, 1972.

Nichols, Sallie. *Jung and Tarot: An Archetypal Journey.* New York: Samuel Weiser, 1980.
> This book is currently the best book describing the major arcana from a Jungian perspective.

Noble, Vicki. *Motherpeace: A Way to the Goddess through Myth, Art and Tarot.* San Francisco: Harper & Row, 1983.
> Tarot from a strong feminist perspective. The beauty of the motherpeace deck is that it is the first round deck.

Nordic, Rolla. *The Tarot shows the Path.* New York: Samuel Weiser, 1960.
> Describes each of the twenty-two Major Arcana cards, methods of divination, sample readings and methods for spreading the cards.

Ouspensky, P.D. *A New Model of the Universe.* New York: Vintage Books, 1971.
> Chapter V: "The Symbolism of the Tarot," pp. 186–215.

Papus. *The Tarot of the Bohemians: The absolute key to occult science.* 3rd Ed. Hollywood, Ca.: Wilshire Book Co., 1978.
> A complete work describing tarot codices and diagrams and summarizing the personal thesis of the author. Supports the Egyptian origin of cards as the most ancient book of the world.

Pollack, Rachael. *Seventy-Eight Degrees of Wisdom: A Book of Tarot.* Part I: The Major Arcana. Part II: The Minor Arcana. Wellingborough, Northamptonshire: The Aquarian Press, 1980–83.

Raine, Kathleen. *Yeats, The Tarot and the Golden Dawn.* Dublin, Ireland: Dolmen Press, 1972. 60 pages plus illustrations.

Rakoczi, B.I. *The Painted Caravan: A Penetration into the Secrets of the Tarot Cards.* New York: Wehman Bros., 1954.
> Describes tarot history according to gypsy lore.

Roberts, Richard. *Tarot and You.* Dobbs Ferry, New York: Morgan & Morgan, 1972.
> Illustrates the tarot through sample readings. Based on the Aquarian Tarot deck designed by David Palladini.

S.M.R.D. and Others. *The Tarot Book: The Secret Writings of the Golden Dawn*. England: Helios, 1967. 149 pages.
> Describes the 78 tarot symbols toegther with their meanings. Assigns each card to the elements and zodialogical symbols.

Sadhu, Mouni. *The Tarot: A Contemporary Course of the Quintessence of Hermetic Occultism*. Hollywood, Ca.: Wilshire Book Co., 1962. 494 pages.
> Describes in a series of 101 lessons, the 22 Major Arcana from the standpoints of symbolism, hermetism, numerology, relationship to the Hebrew alphabet and astrological relationships.

Steiger, Brad and Ron Warmoth. *The Tarot*. New York: Award Books, 1969. 168 pages.
> Personal story of Ron Warmoth's psychic ability with tarot cards.

Tarot Instructions. Tarot Productions, Inc., P.O. Box 46265, Los Angeles, Ca., 1968.

Uesher, Arland. *Twenty-two Keys of the Tarot*. Chester Springs, Pa.: Dufour, 1971.

Waite, A.E. *The Pictorial Key to the Tarot*. San Francisco: Harper & Row, 1971.

Wang, Robert. *An Introduction to the Golden Dawn Tarot*. New York: Samuel Weiser, 1978.

Wang, Robert. *The Qabalistic Tarot: A Textbook of Mystical Philosophy*. York Beach, Me.: Samuel Weiser, 1983.
> One of the best books to date on tarot and cabala.

Wanless, Jim. *The New Age Tarot*. Carmel, Ca.: Merrill-West Publishing, 1986.

Williams, Charles. *The Greater Trumps*. New York: Farrar, Straus & Giroux, 1950.
> A novel describing the power and use of the tarot.

Zain, C.C. *Sacred Tarot*. Los Angeles, Ca.: Church of Light, 1969. 416 pages.
> A series of lessons with questions in the back of the book. Have their own version of the Tarot known as the Eqyptian deck. Much of it varies from standard interpretation but much to be gained out of it.

ADDITIONAL BIBLIOGRAPHY

Assagioli, R. "Jung & psychosynthesis." *Journal of Humanistic Psychology* 14(1): 35–55 (1974).

Assagioli, R. *Psychosynthesis: A manual of principles and techniques*. New York: The Viking Press, 1965.

Assagioli, R. "Symbols of transpersonal experience." *The Journal of Transpersonal Psychology* 1(1): 35–45 (1969).

Beane, Wendell and Doty Williams, eds. *Myths, Rites, Symbols, a Mircea Eliade Reader*. Vols. I & II. New York: Harper & Row, 1975.

Benavides, R. *The prophetic tarot and the great pyramid*. Luis Gonzalez Obregon, Mexico: Editores Mexicanos Unidos, S.A., 1974.

Blackmore, S. "An investigation into the Tarot." In W.G. Roll, ed. *Research in parapsychology: 1979 abstracts and papers from the twenty-second Annual Conference of the Parapsychological Association*. Metuchen, N.J.: the Scarecrow Press, Inc., 1980.

Blakeley, J.D. *The mystical tower of the Tarot*. London: Watkins Publishers & Booksellers, 1974.

Bolen, Jean Shinoda. *The Tao of Psychology: Synchronicity and the Self*. New York: Harper & Row, 1982.

Bolen, Jean Shinoda. *Goddesses in Everywoman*. San Francisco: Harper & Row, 1984.

Bucke, R.M. *Cosmic consciousness: A study in the evolution of the human mind*. New York: E.P. Dutton and Company, 1901.

Budge, E.A. Wallis. *The Book of the Dead*. New York: University Books, New Hyde Park, 1960.

Caligor, L., & May, R. *Dreams and symbols: Man's unconscious language.* New York: Basic Books, Inc., Publishers, 1968.

Campbell, J. *The Hero with a Thousand Faces.* Princeton: Bolingen Series, Princeton University Press, 1949.

Campbell, J., ed. *Myths, dreams and religion.* New York: E.P. Dutton & Co., Inc., 1970.

Campbell, J. *Myths to live by.* New York: A Bantam Book, 1972.

Campbell, J., ed. *The portable Jung.* New York: Viking Press, 1971.

Campbell, J. *Inner Reaches of Outer Space: Metaphor as Myth and as Religion.* Toronto: Alfred Vander Marck Editions, St. James Press, Ltd., 1986.

Campbell, P., & McMahon, E. "Religious type experience in the context of humanistic and transpersonal psychology." *Journal of Transpersonal Psychology* 6(1): 11–17 (1974).

Case, P.F. *The Tarot: A Key to the Wisdom of the Ages.* Richmond Va.: Macoy Publishing Co., 1947.

Chaudhuri, H. "Pschology: Humanistic and Transpersonal." *The Journal of Humanistic Psychology* 15(1): 7–15 (1975).

Cirlot, J.E. *A Dictionary of Symbols.* New York: Philosphical Library, Inc., 1962.

Clark, F.V. "Exploring Intuition: Prospects and possibilities." *Journal of Transpersonal Psychology* 5(2): 156–170 (1973).

Clark, F.V. "Transpersonal perspectives in psychotherapy." *Journal of Humanistic Psychology* 17(1): 69–81 (1977).

Cooper, J.C. *Symbolism, The Universal Language.* Wellingborough, Northamptonshire: The Aquarian Press, 1982.

Deikman, Arthur. *The Observing Self: Mysticism and Psychiatry.* Boston: Beacon Press, 1982.

de LuBicz, I.S. *HER-BAK: Egyptian Initiate.* New York: Inner Traditions International, Ltd., 1956.

de LuBicz, R.A.S. *Symbol & the Symbolic: Ancient Egypt, Science and the Evolution of Consciousness.* New York: Inner Traditions International, Ltd., 1978.

Duncan, Hugh. *Symbols in Society.* London: Oxford University Press, 1968.

Edinger, E.F. *Ego and Archetype: Individuation and the Religious Function of the Psyche.* Baltimore: Penguin Books, Inc., 1972.

Edinger, E.F. "Symbols: The Meaning of Life." *Spring*: 45–66 (1962).

English, J. *Tarot and Physics.* Unpublished manuscript, 1981. (Available from author, PO Box 7, Mt. Shasta, CA 96067)

Fadiman, J., & Frager, R. *Personality and personal growth.* New York: Harper & Row, Publishers, 1976.

Ferguson, M. *The Aquarian Conspiracy.* Los Angeles: J.P. Tarcher, 1980.

Frankl, V. "Self-transcendence as a human phenomenon." *Journal of Humanistic Psychology* 6: 97–106 (1966).

Freud, S. "Psychoanalysis & telepathy." In G. Devereux, ed. *Psychoanalysis and the Occult.* New York: International Universities Press, 1953.

Gawain, Shakti. *Creative Visualization.* Mill Valley, Ca.: Whatever Publishing, 1978.

Goble, F. *The Third Force: The Psychology of Abraham Maslow.* New York: Grossman, 1970.

Goleman, D. "Perspective on Psychology, Reality, and the Study of Consciousness." *Journal of Transpersonal Psychology* 6(1): 73–85 (1974).

Gray, E. *The Tarot Revealed: A Modern Guide to reading the Tarot Cards.* New York: Signet Books, New American Library, 1969.

Grof, Stanislav. *Realms of Human Unconscious.* New York: E.P. Dutton, 1976.

Haich, E. *Initiation.* Palo Alto, Ca.: Seed Center, 1960.

Hall, M.P. *The Secret Teachings of all Ages: An Encyclopedic Outline of Masonic, Hermetic, Qabbalistic and Rosicrucian Symbolical Philosophy.* Los Angeles, Ca.: The Philosophical Research Society, Inc., 1962.

Hall, M.P. *The Tarot: An Essay.* Los Angeles, Ca.: The Philosophical Research Society, Inc., 1978.

Hazard, B.M. "The Tarot and the Accomplishment of the Great Work: Its Interpretation Exemplified by Cards 0 and X." *Spring:* 31–42 (1942).

Husserl, E. "Phenomenological approach to consciousness." In F. Tillman, B. Berofsky, and J. O'Connor, eds., *Introducing Philosophy.* New York: Harper and Row, 1967.

Huxley, A. *The Doors of Perception.* New York: Harper & Row, 1963.

Innes, B. *The Tarot: How to use and interpret the cards.* New York: Arco Publishing Col., Inc., 1978.

Jaffe, A. *The Myth of Meaning: Jung and the expansion of Consciousness.* New York: Penguin Books, Inc., 1971.

James, W. *The Varieties of Religious Experience: A Study in Human Nature.* New York: Random House, 1902.

Johnson, Robert A. *Inner Work.* San Francisco: Harper & Row, 1986.

Joy, W.B. *Joy's Way: A Map for the Transformational Journey.* Los Angeles: J.P. Tarcher, Inc., 1979.

Jung, C.G. *Analytical Psychology: Its Theory and Practice.* New York: Vintage Books, Random House, 1968.

Jung, C.G. "Concerning synchronicity." *Spring:* 1–10 (1953).

Jung, C.G. Forward. In R. Wilhelm 3rd Ed. Translation, *The I Ching or Book of Changes.* Princeton, N.J.: Bollingen Series, Princeton University Press, 1967.

Jung, C.G. *Man and his Symbols.* Garden City, N.Y.: Doubleday, 1964.

Jung, C.G. *Mandala Symbolism.* Princeton, N.J.: Bollingen Series, Princeton University Press, 1959.

Jung, C.G. *Modern Man in search of a Soul.* New York: Harcourt, Brace, 1933.

Jung, C.G. "Parapsychology & synchronicity: A letter in response to an enquiry." *Spring:* 50-57 (1961).

Jung, C.G. *Psychology and Religion.* New Haven: Yale University Press, 1960. (Originally published, 1938.)

Jung, C.G. *Symbols of Transformation.* Princeton, N.J.: Bollingen Series, Princeton University Press, 1959.

Jung, C.G. "Synchronicity: An acausal connecting principle." *The Structure and Dynamics of the Psyche,* Collected Works, Vol. 8. Princeton: Princeton University Press, 1960.

Kaplan, S.R. *The Encyclopedia of Tarot.* New York: U.S. Games Systems, Inc., 1978.

Keen, S., ed. *Voices and Visions.* New York: Perennial Library, Harper & Row, 1976.

Kelsey, M. *The other side of silence: A guide to Christian meditation.* New York: Paulist Press, 1976.

Kerenyi, C. *Asklepios: Archetypal image of the physcian's existence.* New York: Pantheon Books, for the Bollingen Foundation, 1959.

Krippner, S., ed. *Advances in parapsychological research. 2. Extrasensory perception.* New York: Plenum Press, 1978.

Krippner, S., & Murphy, G. "Humanistic psychology & parapsychology." *Journal of Humanistic Psychology.13*(4): 3–24 (1973).

Leach and Fried, eds. *Standard Dictionary of Folklore, Mythology & Legend.* Ramsey, N.J.: Funk & Wagnall Co., Inc., 1972.

Lehner, E. *Symbols, Signs & Signets.* New York: Dover Publications, 1950.

Leonard, G. *The Silent Pulse: A search for the perfect rhythm that exists in each of us.* New York: E.P. Dutton, 1978.

Levi, E. (pseudonym of Alphonse Louis Constant). *The History of Magic* (Arthur E. Waite, trans.). London: Sphere Books, 1913.

Lewis, Joan, ed. *Symbols and Sentiments: Cross-cultural Studies in Symbolism.* London: Academic Press, 1977.

Maslow, A.H. *Religions, Values, and Peak-experiences.* Columbus: Ohio State University Press, 1964.

Maslow, A.H. *The Farther Reaches of Human Nature.* New York: The Viking Press, 1971.

Maslow, A.H. *Toward a Psychology of Being*. Princeton, N.J.: D. Van Nostrand Co., 1968. (Originally published, 1962.)

May, R. *Man's Search for Himself*. New York: W.W. Norton, 1953.

May, R., ed. *Symbolism in Religion and Literature*. New York: George Braziller, Inc., 1958.

Metzner, R. *Synchronicity, Tarot and Psi*. Unpublished manuscript, 1981. (Available from author, California Institute of Integral Studies, 765 Haight St., San Francisco, CA 94114.)

Metzner, R. *Opening to the Inner Light*. Los Angeles, Ca.: J.P. Tarcher, 1986.

Nichols, S. *Jung & Tarot: An Archetypal Journey*. New York: Samuel Weiser, 1980.

Ornstein, R.E. *The Psychology of Consciousness*. San Francisco: W.H. Freeman, 1972.

Ornstein, R., ed. *The Nature of Human Consciousness*. San Francisco: W.H. Freeman, 1973.

Ouspensky, P.D. *In Search of the Miraculous*. New York: Harcourt, Brace & World, 1949.

Pelletier, K.R. & Garfield, C. *Consciousness East and West*. New York: Harper & Row, 1976.

Paul, Robert. *The Tibetan Symbolic World Psychoanalytic Explorations*. Chicago: University of Chicago Press, 1982.

Progoff, I. *Jung, Synchronicity, and Human Destiny: Noncausal dimensions of human experience*. New York: Dell, 1973.

Progoff, I. *The Symbolic and the Real*. New York: McGraw-Hill, 1963.

Progoff, I. Waking dream and living myth. In J. Campbell, ed. *Myths, Dreams & Religion*. New York: E.P. Dutton, 1970.

Purce, Jill. *The Mystic Spiral: A Journey of the Soul*. New York: Avon, 1974.

Rhine, J.B. *Extrasensory Perception*. Somerville, Mass.: Bruce Humphries, 1964. (Originally published, 1934.)

Rhine, J.B. *The Reach of the Mind*. London: Penguin, 1948.

Roberts, R. & Campbell, J. *Tarot Revelations*. San Francisco: Self Published, 1979.

Roberts, S. *The Gypsies*. (London, 1842) quoted in M.P. Hall, *The Secret Teaching of all Ages*. Los Angeles: The Philosophical Research Society, 1962.

Roll, W.G., Morris, J.D., Morris, R.L., eds. Rubin, L. & Honorton, C. "Separating the yins from the yangs: An experiment with the I Ching." In W.G. Roll, J.D. Morris, R.L. Morris, eds., *Proceedings of the Parapsychological Association 8*: 73–75 (1971).

Ross, Ruth. *Prospering Woman*. Mill Valley, Ca.: Whatever Publishing, 1982.

Sandback, J. & Ballard, R. *The Golden Cycle: A text on the Tarot*. Chicago: Aries Press, 1981.

Sanford, J.A. *God's Forgotten Language*. New York: J.B. Lippincott, 1968.

Sibbald, L. *The One with the Water Jar: Astrology, the Aquarian Age and Jesus of Nazareth*. San Francisco: Guild for Psychological Studies, 1978.

Spiegelman, J.M. "Psychology & the Occult." *Spring*: 104–122 (1976).

Starhawk. *The Spiral Dance: A Rebirth of the Ancient Religion of the Great Goddess*. New York: Harper & Row, 1979.

Steiger, B. Medicine Power: *The American Indian's Revival of his spiritual heritage and its relevance for modern man*. Garden City: Doubleday, 1974.

Sutich, A.J. "Transpersonal therapy." *The Journal of Transpersonal Psychology 5*(1): 1–6 (1973).

Tart, C.T., ed. *Altered States of Consciousness*. New York: John Wiley & Sons, Inc., 1969.

Tart, C.T. *PSI: Scientific Studies of the Psychic Realm*. New York: E.P. Dutton, 1977.

Tart, C.T. "Scientific foundations for the study of altered states of consciousness." *Journal of Transpersonal Psychology 3*: 93–124 (1971).

Tart, C.T., ed. *Transpersonal Psychologies*. New York: Harper & Row, 1975.

Teilhard de Chardin, P. *The Phenomenon of Man*. New York: Harper & Row, 1959.

Underhill, E. *Mysticism: A Study in the Nature & Development of Man's Spiritual Consciousness*. New York: Noonday Press, 1955.

Vaughan, F.E. *Awakening Intuition*. Garden City, N.Y.: Anchor Press/Doubleday, 1979.

Vaughan, F.E. *The Inward Arc*. Boston: Shambala, 1985.

Von Franz, M.L. *Individuation in Fairy Tales*. New York: Spring Publications, the Analytical Psychology Club, 1977.

Walker, Barbara. *The Women's Encyclopedia of Myths & Symbols*. New York: Harper & Row, 1983.

Walsh, R. and Vaughan, F., eds. *Beyond Ego: Transpersonal Dimensions in Psychology*. Los Angeles: J.P. Tarcher, 1980.

Warmoth, A. "A note on the peak-experience as a personal myth." *Journal of Humanistic Psychology 1*: 18–21 (1965)

Whitmont, E. "The magic level of the unconscious." *Spring*: 58–80 (1956).

Whitmont, E.C. *The Symbolic Quest: Basic Concepts of Analytical Psychology*. New York: G.P. Putnam's Sons, 1969.

Whitney, E. "Tarok, Tarot or Taroc." *Spring*: 13–30 (1942).

Wilber, K. *No Boundary*. Los Angeles: Center Press, 1979.

Wilber, K. *The Spectrum of Consciousness*. Wheaton, Ill.: The Theosophical Publishing House, 1977.

Woudhuysen, J. *Tarot Therapy: A Guide to the Subconscious*. Los Angeles: J.P. Tarcher, Inc. 1979.

INDEX

ABOUT THE AUTHOR

Angeles Arrien is an anthropologist, educator, and corporate consultant who specializes in cross-cultural symbols, myths, and rituals. Her major work focuses on revealing the universal themes, ethics, values, and experiences shared by all humankind.

Ms. Arrien co-designed and implemented the Social and Cultural Anthropology Program at the California Institute for Integral Studies and authored the Spiritual Perspectives Module for the External Degree Program at the Institute of Transpersonal Psychology. She is a core faculty member at both of the above institutions, and also is on the faculty of Antioch University and John F. Kennedy University. In addition, she is the founder and president of the Angeles Arrien Foundation for Cross-Cultural Education and Research, and also has founded the following establishments: *The International Tarot Symposium of San Francisco,* which has been given yearly since 1979; *The Tarot Network News,* a national quarterly since 1977; and, with James Wanless, The Association of Symbolic Arts, in 1986, and its newsletter, *The Symbolist.*

Ms. Arrien has lectured widely, both nationally and internationally, and has appeared on radio and television, sharing her work on universal myths and symbols and her interest in furthering the growth and development of humankind. In 1988, she received an honorary doctorate of philosophy degree from the California Institute of Integral Studies in recognition for her meritorious contribution in the field of cross-cultural mythology and symbolism.